REAL
GARDENS
GROW
natives

# REAL
# GARDENS
# GROW
# natives

design,
plant
& enjoy
a healthy
northwest
garden

EILEEN M. STARK

SKIPSTONE

Published by Skipstone, an imprint of Mountaineers Books
Printed in China
24 23 22 21          2 3 4 5 6

Copy editor: Barry Foy
Design: Jane Jeszeck
Cover: Syrphid fly on broadleaf stonecrop (*Sedum spathulifolium*)
Back cover, top to bottom: leopard lily (*Lilium pardalinum subsp. vollmeri*); cedar waxwing on aspen (Richard P. Weber); yellow wood violet (*Viola glabella*)
Frontispiece: Madrone (*Arbutus menziesii*)
Page 3: Black-capped chickadee (Richard P. Weber)
Page 5: Wilson's warbler
Pages 6–7: Anna's hummingbird feeding on Cascara tree (*Rhamnus purshiana*)
Page 320: Syrphid fly on western bleeding heart (*Dicentra formosa*)
All photographs are by the author, except the following, used with permission: p. 31, Terry R. Glase; p. 219, Paul Slichter; p. 244, Rosemary Taylor; and pp. 19, 21, 24, 27, 34 (top and bottom), 35, 38, 41, 46, 119, 121, 133, 135, Richard P. Weber. Photos on pp. 45, 51, 66 taken at Bosky Dell Natives.

*Library of Congress Cataloging-in-Publication Data*
Stark, Eileen M.
   Real gardens grow natives : design, plant, & enjoy a healthy Northwest garden /
by Eileen M. Stark.
      pages cm
   Other title: Guide for designing and sustaining your Pacific Northwest garden
   Includes bibliographical references and index.
   ISBN 978-1-59485-866-6 (pbk) — ISBN 978-1-59485-867-3 (ebook)  1.  Native plants for cultivation—Northwest, Pacific. 2.  Gardens—Northwest, Pacific.  I. Title. II. Title: Guide for designing and sustaining your Pacific Northwest garden.
   SB439.S78 2014
   635.9'51—dc23

                                        2014002656

ISBN (paperback): 978-1-59485-866-6
ISBN (ebook): 978-1-59485-867-3

Skipstone books may be purchased for corporate, educational, or other promotional sales.
For special discounts and information, contact our sales department at 800-553-4453 or
mbooks@mountaineersbooks.org.

Skipstone
1001 SW Klickitat Way, Suite 201
Seattle, Washington 98134
206.223.6303
www.skipstonebooks.org
www.mountaineersbooks.org

**LIVE LIFE. MAKE RIPPLES.**

*for the wild ones*

# CONTENTS

# preface

**ANIMALS, NO MATTER WHAT FORM THEY TAKE—FROM** adorable frogs, charismatic owls, and little pussycats to slippery slugs and tiny spiders—have been my passion for as long as I can remember. I find the wild ones particularly fascinating, and knowing what enormous stresses and threats they face has only heightened my reverence; ironically but unsurprisingly, our appreciation for biodiversity tends to grow with an increased knowledge of habitat destruction and tragically high extinction rates. My infatuation with native plants came a bit more recently, since growing up in a Midwestern city, surrounded by mostly alien species, limited my exposure. But I did spend time exploring our yard as a child, squishing snowberries between my fingers for the popping sound they made, tasting the nectar of phlox flowers, and playing in the birdbath, much to my mother's dismay (and no doubt the birds').

Occasional visits to nearby natural areas and annual treks through northern Wisconsin to the Upper Peninsula of Michigan, where my maternal grandmother lived, provided fodder for a growing respect for wild places. In high school I devoured biology lessons and read John Muir, and in college that first ecology course felt so *right*. It would be a little while, though, before I would fully grasp the facts: That native plants are entirely inseparable from native animals, and that too many people using too much spells D-I-S-A-S-T-E-R.

Black-tailed bumblebee on seashore lupine (*Lupinus littoralis*)

Humans want the entire planet to themselves. The small percentage of land that is not developed, fragmented, or otherwise degraded—protected areas, national parks, and other conservation areas—simply cannot save the wild species that are disappearing at alarmingly fast rates. At the root of the current extinction crisis is the burgeoning human footprint. When our population was a mere five billion in the mid-1980s, it was estimated that our resource depletion was more than the planet could take; now at seven billion, we are far beyond what the earth can possibly sustain without calamitous repercussions. Studies predict that, by 2050 and at current consumption levels, ten billion people will require the equivalent of up to twenty-seven planet Earths. I firmly believe there is not one wild plant or animal that would not breathe a sigh of relief if humans were to vanish tomorrow.

We all bring pollution, pipelines, climate change, and other unnatural damage to the planet, and we—especially those of us in affluent countries—need to change nearly everything about the way we live. That task is unimaginably immense. Considering the magnitude of our global ecological problems, is it futile to try to make our local ecosystem more diverse and attractive? A drop in the bucket? Probably, but if the thought of extinction due to our actions is horrifying, or at least shameful, consider doing a bit of local conservation work at home, where you can garden more empathetically and effectively, but no less enjoyably. *Real Gardens* is about bringing life to places where it once thrived and providing vulnerable creatures what they need to survive and raise young, all while giving you the nature fix you need. It may not offer instant gratification

(although it's amazing how quickly pollinators will find flowers!); for this you will need a little time and patience, because decades of damage cannot be undone overnight. But your actions will have lasting effects—some of which you'll never witness—down the road and downstream.

This book is not about me and my garden, although I share the personal and practical experience I've gained in twelve years of turning my mundane Portland yard into a humane and sustainable one, and from my work on clients' gardens as well. As you might expect, designers do not always practice what they preach, and I'm no exception, so learning from my mistakes will hopefully prevent yours, as you learn what works best in your unique site. The goal is to help you consider the ecology of your site, and then design, implement, and sustain a garden that enhances the immediate environment and results in tangible benefits. For larger landscapes there is additional advice gleaned from the principles of restoration ecology.

But this is not a restoration manual. In many ways, it is a be-kind-to-animals book. After working in the animal protection field for many years, I can tell you that ignorance is often the root cause of mistreatment of animals (when it's not greed), whether intentional or not. Usually, the more we know about something, the more respect and compassion we will develop for it. Authors such as Richard Louv (*Last Child in the Woods*) have articulated the profound lack of nature in our lives, especially in children's lives. Besides being linked to attention disorders, depression, and obesity, "nature deficit disorder" is a real danger to the future of the natural world. Without the compassion that comes with understanding, future adults will have little respect for other species.

Young children do not have an innate fear of nature—they *learn* that wild things are scary or creepy. Negative responses to insects or spiders, or anything else, are passed down by example. I once volunteered with educators at the Denver Audubon Society who sought to teach inner-city children to respect and value wildlife. Aged approximately four to seven, they had never been to the nearby Rocky Mountains, let alone out of the city. The initial angst I felt about trying to reach kids I expected would fear or be repulsed by the neighborhood insects I would introduce them to turned out to be completely unwarranted. To my surprise and delight, they were intensely interested and seemed to be charmed by the insects, not the least bit afraid or squeamish. Clearly, teaching little ones to be kind and gentle to creatures they may meet while playing not only prevents unnecessary harm, but possibly also future cruelty to animals, which often begins in early adolescence. If fear can be learned, so can compassion, which will lead to a more protective attitude toward wildlife conservation in adulthood.

Writing this book has strengthened my relationship with the natural world and reminded me how intimately our choices affect intensely vulnerable flora and fauna that provide the essential ecological services and quality of life upon which we depend. I fought back tears while researching the disturbing extent to which biodiversity is quickly fading, trying not to imagine the world without so many wondrous life forms that have flourished for eons, only to be extinguished in an evolutionary minute. Having an awareness of the things we do wrong can help us do them right—at least in our neck of the woods. Although modern life doesn't require an understanding of and appreciation for wild things like other eras and cultures did, we are all deeply dependent on the natural world, and that cannot be ignored. Opening our eyes and hearts to the plight of wild ones reveals a whole new world.

# INTRODUCTION
## *a welcome mat for wildlife*

"We have met the enemy and he is us."
—Walt Kelly, *Pogo*

**HAVE YOU EVER WONDERED WHAT YOUR** neighborhood might have been like several hundred years ago—before ancient trees were felled and creeks were buried, before streets and houses crept in, before the organization of nature that existed then was ravaged? Judging by nearby natural areas, I imagine mine was part of a towering Douglas-fir and western hemlock forest—mixed with alder, vine maple, red-flowering currant, salal, and licorice fern—rich in species and sustenance and stable in function and capacity. Pacific bleeding heart might also have joined the plant community at ground level: I found tiny remnants of the delicate but resilient native plant tucked in shady corners of my otherwise conventional front yard when I first explored it a dozen years ago. Regardless of whether its roots survived the earthmovers a hundred years ago or it was planted later, it reminds me of what once may have been.

I've reintroduced many of the native plants that may have grown historically in my yard to try to restore a little bit of what was erased long ago, with the intention of aiding wildlife that has survived despite blatant changes to the landscape. To borrow words from Alice Walker, it's part of "the rent I pay for living on this planet."

Although our yards bear little resemblance to what existed centuries ago, we can help other species survive by reintroducing some of the local flora that may once have existed.

Amphibians, like this Pacific chorus frog, need our help and care.

## Join the Club

At a time of increased awareness of unrestrained human expansion and the earth's fragility, many of us feel helpless or hopeless over the destruction of the planet, and for good reason. Leading ecologists and conservationists agree—with varying degrees of pessimism—that unless we immediately start curbing our population growth and adapt our ways to protect ecological processes, we are doomed to witness even more environmental destruction and consequent species extinction. At the rate we're going, research shows most native plants

and animals becoming extinct, and much of that loss will be within our lifetimes.

Large percentages of birds, mammals, reptiles, invertebrates, and others that we take for granted are endangered, threatened, or in severe decline. Animals that are especially sensitive to environmental changes, disease, and toxins, such as amphibians like frogs, toads, and salamanders, are disappearing at probably the highest rate; scientists predict that half of the places they inhabit will be empty of their kind by 2033. Some are dying out even faster; one third of these ancient species that have survived through thick and thin are on the International Union for Conservation of Nature (IUCN) Red List of Threatened Species. The only wildlife expected to survive are those whose habitats are highly protected, or those that can tolerate a degraded habitat with human activity. As Alan Weisman laments in his book *The World Without Us*, "We don't have to shoot songbirds from the sky to kill them. Take away enough of their homes and sustenance and they fall dead on their own." Besides pervasive habitat loss, there are pesticides and other toxins, wildlife control programs, reflective windows, lighted buildings, introduced competitors and predators, hunting pressures, pollution, and other deadly threats that continue to devastate many wildlife species.

Over two-thirds of the earth's wild plants, the oxygen-giving basis of the food chain and the backbone of ecosystems, are threatened with extinction, according to an IUCN sampling. What little undisturbed wild habitat remains must be fiercely protected, but it is far from adequate. Where natural places have been erased, we must try to replicate them as best we can. If we don't, "the future of biodiversity in the United States is dim," writes entomologist and ecologist Douglas Tallamy in his best-seller, *Bringing Nature Home: How You Can Sustain Wildlife with Native Plants.* When ecosystems collapse, our survival is threatened too, regardless of where we live. Artificial habitats lacking biodiversity are not an option.

Though the Pacific Northwest is dominated by lush forests, high mountain ranges, weathered coastline, and fertile river valleys, much of the landscape has been drastically changed; even so-called wild lands often bear little resemblance to what existed prior to European settlement. Native flora that sustains wild fauna (and vice versa) has been replaced by roads, buildings, and nonnative plants in our residential landscapes. Once-wild grasslands and woodlands have fallen under the plow, wetlands have been destroyed, and forests have been extensively logged and altered. The land that has been preserved exists due to far-sighted planning, inaccessibility, or economics, and allows a glimpse into an earlier time when the land was relatively pristine.

There is light in the tunnel: Nature is resilient, and recovery is possible when we allow it. Surveys show that in places where people have made an effort to repair and protect habitat, some species have recovered (not to historic numbers, but to reasonably healthy populations). In an attempt to reverse or at least prevent further destruction, many people are working to maintain our region's viable ecosystems and the biodiversity within them. Within seriously degraded, formerly wild lands and drastically altered metropolitan areas, ecologists, naturalists, designers, and gardeners are looking to rural, suburban, and urban landscapes as opportunities to aid restoration of

lost habitat. Although protection of very large land reserves (and sites close to them) provides the most far-reaching effects, whatever your site's size or location, you can help positively impact crushing and seemingly irreversible problems like declining biodiversity.

It's not very hard to do, and you can do a little or a lot. Even an urban eighth of an acre can provide for other species and inspire neighbors in the process. Using nature as a guide, you can create a little piece of the world you want to live in—safe havens where habitat is shared, wildlife is welcomed, monocultures and synthetic chemicals are avoided, and maintenance and irrigation are minimized. The greatest joy from gardening may now come not just from plants' beauty and their arrangement, but from the life they provide for—the fluttering butterflies and hardworking native bees, those nests of hatchling birds awaiting their next feeding, all of which have a right to exist and an intrinsic worth apart from any usefulness to humans.

Of course, the original forest, bog, or grassland that once covered the land—long before human development brought Big Agriculture, roads, and sprawl—is long gone, and we cannot re-create exactly what once existed. What we *can* do is restore our current surroundings so that they begin to resemble and function like a real ecosystem. Nature can be resilient, but it needs a helping and protective hand.

## The Case for Natives

You may already have read or heard about the benefits of growing native plants, which have belonged for millennia to this place we call home. Adapted to the climate and soils of areas where they naturally occur, native species are

Native yellow-faced bumblebee on goldenrod
(*Solidago canadensis*)

typically very low maintenance when grown in similar conditions. Since they have developed defenses against pests and diseases they require no pesticides, and artificial fertilizers are also unnecessary. Natives are also often long-lived and usually drought tolerant, able to survive only on rainfall and other naturally occurring water in their habitat once they are established.

Growing natives also helps conserve plant species that are threatened in the wild, and adds a regional authenticity and character

to gardens like nothing else can. Needless to say, their lush beauty rivals that of exotics, and many make exquisitely textured and shaped garden plants. Some species also improve water quality or stabilize soil, and many share resources with their neighbors, underground. And, as previously mentioned, natives are absolutely crucial for supporting local and regional biodiversity. As Dr. Tallamy painstakingly describes in his book, there are specific biological reasons why wild fauna is dependent on native flora and vice versa.

It's often noted that native flora and native fauna depend on each other because the two have evolved together over millennia, but that's a bit vague. More precisely, when two (or more) species affect each other's evolution reciprocally, it is called *coevolution*. That is, a change in one species occurs in response to a change in another species with which it lives and interacts in some functional and essential way, such as by providing a specific soil nutrient, pollination services, or a meal. Coevolution usually happens between species that have close ecological ties with each other. These include *mutualistic* species (those that benefit from one another), *competitive* species (those that compete for food, shelter, or territory), and *predator-prey* species. Usually, but not always, plants and insects coevolve in mutually beneficial ways. For example, many flowering plants attract and are wholly dependent on pollinators to disperse their pollen, and many pollinators rely on those plants' nectar and/or pollen for sustenance. Plants that have evolved flower shapes, colors, and/or scents

RIGHT Who says native plants aren't dazzling?
(*Lilium pardalinum* subsp. *vollmeri*)

Nearly all North American birds feed their young high-protein insects, not seeds.

they eat. Their menu is short: They must rely on only certain types of plants, with certain chemical compositions, and cannot exist where those plants don't exist. If the plants they subsist on are removed, they are likely doomed. The less numerous, nonspecialist species are called *generalist* insect herbivores and are able to feed on more types of plants.

Studies show that native plants support about fifteen times more insect life of both types of insect herbivores than nonnative plant species support. All those mouthwatering insect herbivores are food for predators such as other insects, birds, spiders, and other hungry mouths. Those predators may then, in turn, be eaten by other animals, which may then be eaten by still others further up the food chain, and so on. When plants and animals die, they contribute to the ecosystem again by providing for an array of invertebrates and microbes that dine on dead matter.

The shelter provided by plants and the recycling of nutrients are also part of the complex web of life in which everything is thoroughly connected. Thanks to this interspecies dependence, in a healthy ecosystem it is highly unlikely that any one creature will get out of hand and become a severe pest (more on this in Chapter 5).

## The State of Our Yards
Currently, the average American yard is part of an impoverished ecosystem dominated by lawn. Nearly devoid of life, lawns are monocultures composed mostly of exotic grasses, blanketing approximately 40 million acres nationwide. Though often unused, they soak up precious water: It's been estimated that landscape irrigation accounts for about a third of all residential

that appeal to effective pollinators will bear the most seed and be the most successful reproductively.

On a molecular level, each plant species manufactures unique chemical compounds that may affect its edibility. These tasty or toxic compounds serve to attract and support or repel certain organisms that feed on plants, including herbivorous insects. Insect herbivores make up more than a third of the world's animals, and their role is indispensable: By converting plant material to protein, they are nature's only way of getting plants' energy into animals that don't eat plants directly. Renowned biologist E. O. Wilson's speculation that if insects, which make up almost 85 percent of all known animal species, were to vanish from the face of the earth, "the environment would collapse into chaos," makes sense. Not only would there be no food for animals that feed on insects, but pollination would nearly cease, the majority of plants would disappear, and so on.

Most insect herbivore species are known as *specialists*, meaning they can't choose what water use nationwide, with the typical suburban lawn consuming 10,000 gallons annually, above and beyond rainwater. Maintenance costs total around $40 billion and include the application of ten times the amount of pesticides used by conventional farmers and 3 million tons of fossil fuel–derived fertilizers, on average. To top it off, 800 million gallons of gasoline are burned and 17 million gallons are spilled nationwide trying to beautify lawns each year. The damage that synthetic chemicals and fossil fuels do to soil, water, wildlife, and air is incalculable. Pollutants released into the atmosphere from gas-powered yard equipment include carbon monoxide, nitrogen oxides, and volatile organic compounds. Leaf blowers also stir up respiratory illness–inducing "fugitive dust." Such dust has both large and fine particles (the latter remain airborne much longer), and consists of soil minerals, but also pollen, pesticides, fungal spores, and tire particles.

Particularly within newly developed rural and suburban areas, "landscaping" often refers to the removal and destruction of what once was. Endemic flora is usually replaced with a certain type of grass mown to a certain length, and garden-variety plants are grown merely as decoration. Add in components like impermeable hardscape, hot tubs, fire pits, super-sized patios and decks, and what happens? Native fauna is evicted. We can do so much better! If we put as much effort into species-rich landscaping that repairs and conserves, rather than harms, some ecological crises would diminish.

## Real Garden Connections

Merriam-Webster defines *real* as genuine, fundamental, authentic, ideal, and essential. Imagine a garden that genuinely belongs in its

Predatory insects like dragonflies are an integral part of the food web.

setting and reflects the essential natural world, where native plants welcome wildlife from bumblebees to woodpeckers. Hardly new, this rediscovered way of gardening asks us to mimic natural ecosystems so that the diversity, function, and structure of those systems are revived and protected, creating an exchange that lasts. Beauty goes beyond the aesthetic, given that there is a certain allure in natural relationships that take place in a dynamic and lively space.

"Real" gardens also require less effort: Instead of trying to force exotic plants from other continents to fit in and thrive (sometimes a laborious and frustrating task), they are alive with what will grow and survive naturally in the site's light, soil, and moisture conditions. Real gardens are also compassionate gardens, which humanely and gently provide for our needs while doing no harm to other creatures and the earth's assets. Working *with* the land, as hosts of nature, we can create vibrant spaces that allow a site to be relatively close to what it once was, but with a twist—leg and elbow room for people. Lawns are minimized or replaced with plants arranged in natural compositions, chosen when possible according to local plant communities, rather than as single specimens.

## come closer, closer

"Life on earth remains so little known that you can be a scientific explorer without leaving home," wrote Pulitzer Prize–winning biologist E. O. Wilson in his *Letters to a Young Scientist*. Indeed, focusing your eyes on life rarely noticed will put a face on biodiversity and increase your appreciation of the intricate communities just outside your door. Such new knowledge fosters awareness and cultivates compassion for the tiny and not so tiny creatures that are everywhere. A macro camera lens is the best tool for this type of investigation—enlarged images on the computer screen will reveal intricacies akin to an undiscovered wilderness—but even just a hand lens can really open up your yard's micro-world to you.

Life is everywhere, especially on or near plants. It seems like wherever I point the camera I find teeny-tiny creatures and amazingly complex structures that normally would elude me. Simply turning over a leaf or following a sunbeam can reveal a kaleidoscope of secrets. Keep a log of the species you see (and hear) and you will be amazed at the life within your yard. Consult regional guidebooks that can help identify almost anything, as well as online resources that offer everything from recorded birdcalls to photos for comparison. For those that give you trouble, e-mail your photos to experts at universities and cooperative extensions. Open your eyes wide, childlike, and you will want to enhance and protect habitat even more.

Predator-prey relationships, such as this native western blood-red ladybird beetle salivating over aphids on lupine, become more evident at close range.

Backyard visitors, like this Townsend's warbler, brighten up dreary winter days.

To be most beneficial, gardens need to connect—to each other and to the larger world—to provide continuous passage for wildlife and allow each garden to work and blend harmoniously with others nearby. A single naturalistic garden has benefits, but when in proximity to others like it, its worth multiplies. It's not difficult to imagine the transformation as lawn after conventional lawn, and border after border, is replaced or at least amended with sustainably grown native plants and other useful elements.

It often seems that an invisible thread connects us to the natural world. Yet our home ground is the part of the ecosystem where we can most easily explore a little corner of the universe. We generally spend more time at home than we do visiting wilder places; garden upkeep may be part of our routine, and many gardens are almost an extension of the house. The knowledge that we gain while planning and implementing a native garden not only helps create a beautiful space, it also sharpens our observational skills, gives us an appreciation for wilder places and natural processes, and helps us find our own sense of place. And after a short time we reap even more rewards, as wild visitors begin making an appearance.

## Introducing Invaders

A *nonnative* or *exotic* plant is one that got here with the help of humans, either intentionally or accidentally, such as when purposely

A garden escapee, herb Robert (*Geranium robertianum*), is a pretty but vigorous perennial that quickly spreads to replace native plants, even in undisturbed, pristine forests.

introduced for agricultural use or when mixed up in packing material. Not all nonnative species are problematic, and some are very beneficial, especially those that provide us with food. However, the spread of some nonnative plants severely reduces and degrades habitat for the region's natural biotic communities. These weeds are becoming a significant component of habitat, and recent arrivals have yet to make their mark. Although the region's

forested lands appear to be mostly native, studies show that the extent of nonnative growth in the forests of Oregon and Washington is continually expanding; British Columbia has among the highest numbers of invasive plant species of the Canadian provinces.

Invasive plants are able to compete with and often eliminate native plants because whatever kept them in check in their native land is lacking here. They often release chemicals that adversely affect native species and form dense monocultures that shrink habitat, depriving wildlife throughout the food web. Some seem innocuous enough, such as nonnative shrubs or trees that offer berries that attract wildlife. However, these types of plants may be problematic because fruit-eating birds can easily disperse their seeds elsewhere, leading to displacement of native flora that can't compete.

Prickly leaved English holly (*Ilex aquifolium*) is one example: Although it supplies berries for birds, it is subsequently seeded easily in forests and, once established, can expand by suckering to create thickets that suppress native species. Such nonnatives are also deficient in providing insects for birds during the time they need it most—in springtime, when adults require tremendous amounts of protein and fat to produce eggs, feed their remarkably fast-growing young, and take care of themselves. So be sure not to grow any plants on invasive plant lists (see Appendix C for websites).

Of course, many plants from our region are invasive in other places. Take the lovely large-leaved lupine (*Lupinus polyphyllus*). Introduced to the United Kingdom by famous plant explorer and collector David Douglas, it was grown widely as a striking garden plant in its own right. Used as one of the parents

Native western maidenhair fern (*Adiantum aleuticum*) and hosta (from Northeast Asia) make a cute couple but haven't developed a functional relationship.

in hybrid crosses such as the popular Russell hybrids (*Lupinus* x *regalis*), it became a popular garden ornamental in Europe, eastern Canada, and New Zealand, where it is now considered an invasive species.

## Being Flexible

Your garden certainly doesn't need to be exclusively native to be beneficial, and there are many reasons to keep mature vegetation whether it's native or not. While the quantity of native species a garden supports is important, depending on a gardener's prerogative a functional and sustainable garden may (and usually does) also contain exotic species—

especially if you like growing edibles and favorite ornamentals. Moreover, plants not adapted to your conditions, native or not, are poor choices. Grow as many natives as you can, but keep in mind that replacing every plant in your yard is not required. Adding just a few dominant plants is much better than none at all, and may be all that is possible if you have a very small yard.

Not all exotic species wreak havoc in places they've been introduced to, and there are times when a suitable native species cannot be found at nurseries or situations in which a noninvasive exotic species may do just as well. Here's one: There is a two-foot-wide, sunny strip of

Some plants grown for food also appeal to wildlife, such as cedar waxwings, who love ripe figs. Keep a balance by growing native species as well as cultivated edibles.

and nonhybridized types that Grandma may have grown. When herbs like rosemary and sage begin flowering, I see a steady stream of visitors, from little native bees to hummingbirds. Allowing annuals like lettuces, herbs, and brassicas to flower will also attract pollinators, but to attract even more to your veggie beds to pollinate plants like tomatoes that require bumblebees, grow native species nearby.

When growing edibles, it's important to keep things balanced. Very few native creatures thrive on cultivated vegetables and fruit trees—most native insects find them unappealing, their blossoms are fleeting, and they take up space where natives could grow. Although the mature fig trees in our yard appeal to quite a few birds and some small mammals, our sweet cherry tree, Stella, attracts only a few bees and birds during the flowering and fruiting period; the rest of the year it appears to lack visitors of any kind.

## How to Use This Book

This book is intended as a practical reference for increasing biodiversity in urban, suburban, and rural yards in Oregon, Washington, and southern British Columbia, west of the Cascades, though its principles are applicable nearly everywhere. Essentially, it takes an ecologist's view and translates it into something usable in the garden. Rather than managing for individual species, it incorporates some of the principles of ecosystem restoration, which work at the level of the ecosystem itself. Elements that benefit a wide diversity of wildlife are integrated, rather than focusing on separate theme gardens for creatures like butterflies, birds, or bees. You will find advice for designing various-sized gardens that feature a variety

soil near the south side of my house along a pathway. The plants I chose for it needed to be able to tolerate drought and not grow too far into the path, and I wanted them to provide for pollinators; it seemed to be begging for a row of lavender. I obliged, the lavender thrives, and some native bumblebees like it, too. Of course, when I figure out a native spin I'll replace it as it nears the end of its days.

My garden contains other ornamental perennials and culinary herbs that provide good foraging for pollinators, especially the heirloom of native plants, suggestions for alternatives to invasive or common exotic plants, and some dispelling of native plant misconceptions.

If native plants have won you over—but before you rush off to the plant nursery—take a deep breath and realize that creating a functional garden from a blank slate or within a previously landscaped yard can be a bit challenging. You will need to do some planning, especially if you're new to gardening. However, one of the things to love about gardening is that even small steps you make toward reconciling the needs of nature and those of people are steps in the right direction.

And you can always expand later on. For instance, simply choosing native grasses to use as ornamental accents, instead of the exotic grass species that are so popular, is one step that takes very little effort and creates similar effect. If you need a rather narrow, evergreen hedge, instead of trying to create one out of English or Portuguese laurel shrubs that strive to be twenty-five feet tall and wide, arrange tall Oregon grape (*Mahonia aquifolium*) in an imperfect line—it not only needs little pruning, it's an overachiever when it comes to providing berries and blossoms for our feathered friends and pollinators.

In Chapter 1 you will learn a little practical ecology, such as the nutrient cycles and energy flows within ecosystems of which your yard is a part, and come to terms with biodiversity and habitat. Chapter 2 discusses some basic wildlife- and human-friendly landscape design principles to assist you in creating a new plan or enhancing an existing garden. You'll learn how to do a realistic site assessment of your current local conditions and discover the right and wrong reasons to remove existing plants.

Sample plans will help you visualize the steps. Since plant selection is often confusing, Chapter 3 discusses vegetation zones and plant communities and assists you in plant selection and arrangement, including how to create connected layers and green corridors, and how to keep pollinators consistently well fed. Chapter 4 presents a crash course in soil ecology and provides tips on improving soil health and maintaining it. Advice for the installation process and a review of optimal planting procedures will get your plants off to a good start. Gardening is not a one-time project, so Chapter 5 offers information for successfully establishing and sustaining your native nirvana, using organic, earth-friendly methods.

Chapter 6 is for when you want to propagate new native plants at home, and following it is a compendium of 100 of the most gardenworthy, ecologically valuable, undemanding, and gorgeous Pacific Northwest native plants in text and photographs, organized according to light requirements. Appendix A further categorizes the 100 plants for specific situations such as acidic soil, sunny slopes, and very wet conditions. Appendixes B and C offer references and a resources section with recommended reading material, useful websites, nonprofits to support, and a directory of plant nurseries and seed companies.

## Aims and Ambitions

The major goal of this book is to make gardening with native species more mainstream. The photographs are intended to illustrate how gorgeous native flora and fauna are and elevate them to the status they deserve. You may never get down on hands and knees to take in the almost otherworldly look of a wild ginger

(*Asarum caudatum*) flower, examine the tiny, exquisite blossoms of piggyback plant (*Tolmiea menziesii*) with a macro lens, or get close to the resplendent plumes of an American kestrel, so we've done it for you.

If you find yourself smitten with native plants, I encourage you to become an advocate for them. Even if you don't have a place to garden, you can further the cause by helping build awareness of and receptiveness to the advantages of replacing exotic plants and lawn with native vegetation.

→ Talk to gardeners who don't know of the benefits of natives to not only the local ecosystem, but also themselves. People will generally lend an ear when you mention that native plants require amazingly little maintenance.

→ Urge local garden shops and nurseries to increase their inventory and variety of native plants, especially those that once grew in the vicinity.

→ Give native plants as gifts, if you know the site conditions of the recipient (if you don't, there are gift certificates).

→ Join and support organizations like the Native Plant Society of Oregon, Native Plant Society of British Columbia, Washington Native Plant Society, Xerces Society, Center for Biological Diversity, land trusts, and others that promote habitat conservation.

→ Be aware of public land use changes in your neighborhood, town, and state. Voice your habitat conservation concerns during public comment periods for developing and managing public lands.

→ Watch for areas scheduled for development that contain native plants, and get involved with groups that salvage them.

→ Volunteer with native plant restoration projects through land conservancies, botanic gardens, parks departments, and other organizations.

→ Take part in "citizen science" projects, such as bird counts and the monitoring of pollinators and dragonflies.

→ Speak out on social media, write letters to the editor, and comment online whenever you see articles about habitat loss, how to tend a lawn, and dealing with pests and diseases of exotic plants.

→ Teach young people about the devastating decline of biodiversity. Helping people, especially young ones, make a connection to the natural world will increase their appreciation of it.

We are as capable of positive change as negative, and perhaps the easiest and most direct way to participate is at home. Giving back to wild creatures what was taken from them is urgent and essential if we want to halt their continual and insidious loss. In doing such crucial conservation work, we'll be doing ourselves a favor as well, because everything—even the human animal—is connected to everything else.

RIGHT American kestrel

aims and ambitions

# CHAPTER 1
## *crucial conservation work begins at home*

"First law of ecology: Everything is connected to everything else."
—Barry Commoner, *The Closing Circle: Nature, Man, and Technology*

**THERE IS NATURE IN EVERYONE'S YARD, OR AT LEAST** the potential for it. I'm reminded of that every time I watch the swallows, bats, and dragonflies share the sky over my yard as the light fades on warm summer evenings. Their random flights seem almost choreographed—not just because they skillfully manage not to fly into each other, but because each species has a niche or a role, and the loss of one would be a loss to the entire system. Each of their lives is important, no more or no less than another.

A mated pair of western screech owls once graced my neighborhood, but they left forever when a mature tree they used was drastically hacked back during breeding season, a time when birds are intensely sensitive to disruption. I still think of them and how they softly called to each other in the impending dusk, and wonder if they were able to find a more peaceful place to nest.

Their eviction symbolizes what can happen when human ignorance and thoughtlessness intervene. Indeed, recognizing that every front, back, and side yard—even those within urban areas—is a part of an intricate ecosystem (even a damaged one) that could host a number of species is the first step toward encouraging rich, natural

Each species appears separate, but connects functionally and intricately to others.

A pine white butterfly feeds on a native aster plant.

as the ancient Greeks. In his famous work *On Airs, Waters, and Places*, Hippocrates clearly saw the big picture. Way ahead of his time, he spoke of an intricately connected system of natural causes and effects that should be considered an ally, instead of something to be conquered and destroyed. Nature must be understood and respected, he reasoned. Although there is still much we don't know, this we do know: There is only one earth for all living organisms, and what affects one affects all. Naturalist John Muir may have said it best in *My First Summer in the Sierra*, when he wrote, "When one tugs at a single thing in nature, he finds it attached to the rest of the world."

What we call an ecosystem can be defined as a unified, natural community with all its living component organisms (plants, animals, and microorganisms) and all their interactions with each other and the world around them, as well as nonliving factors like soil and water. Every component is linked to others by energy flows and nutrient cycles. The sun supplies energy for photosynthetic organisms such as green plants, which use light to produce carbohydrates from carbon dioxide and water in chlorophyll-containing cells. These carbohydrates can be stored in chemical bonds and used later to supply energy for growing cells. Oxygen is released during the process.

As animals consume plants directly or eat other animals that eat plants, energy continues through the system. When organisms die, decomposers such as bacteria, fungi, and worms break down dead matter and convert nutrients into a form that may be used by plants and other microbes. This nutrient cycle is completed when carbon is released back into the atmosphere. Essentially, all processes

diversity. When they are in good shape, these natural systems are incredibly complex and support fascinating interdependent relationships, the majority of which we never notice. Albert Einstein once advised us, "Look deep, deep into nature, and then you'll understand everything better." If you want to create a garden that flourishes and is reflective of the natural world, it's helpful to know a little about how ecosystems work.

## Ecology Short Course

Although ecology—the study of the earth's living systems and how they interact—is generally regarded as a new science that developed around the turn of the twentieth century and attained public prominence in the 1960s, there was substantial ecological thinking as far back and organisms—like pine trees, pollinators, and people—are interrelated.

An ecosystem has been compared to a complete structure, of which species are functional building blocks and their integrated relationships are the mortar. Every element plays a role in keeping the structure standing; if one species or network is weakened, the stability and vitality of the whole is affected. To varying degrees, each species has the potential to hold it together or cause collapse. Even small changes can create significant effects.

When gardening magazines and books refer to a plant's "performance," they're talking about how it pleases us aesthetically, not its ecological function. Instead of performance, it's helpful to think about how each plant is connected functionally to other plants and animals. "Function" refers to the roles that each species play in an ecosystem.

Just as plants, animals, and microbes are a function of their habitat, habitat and other environmental conditions are influenced or altered by roles that they play. Some examples: Birds that evolved to eat fruit help to disperse seeds that influence the regeneration of fruit-bearing plants. Insectivorous bats, like the little brown bats (*Myotis lucifugus*) I see foraging over my yard, are the primary predators of night-flying insects and can eat over a thousand mosquito-sized insects in just an hour, serving to keep those insect populations in check. A few mammals can girdle trees, thereby creating snags for cavity nesters like woodpeckers and owls to occupy. Less obvious functional relationships occur at the soil level or within soil. The majority of birds, amphibians, reptiles, and mammals help aerate soil and incorporate organic matter by digging and tunneling,

or they may speed up the decay of wood or bark by helping to break it apart on the ground. In the winter and spring I often see thrushes and other birds looking for lunch underneath leaf litter in my yard; as they flip leaves over, they help speed decay—somewhat like turning compost bin contents to increase aeration and make composting happen faster.

## Diversity Matters

Biodiversity is the vast variety of life on earth, from genes to species to ecosystems, that

Mammals like this northern flying squirrel fill many roles, including assisting in the decay of wood.

results from four billion years of evolution. All the ecological processes, patterns, and interactions that link them together generate a spectacular tangle of intent and a little mayhem. Biodiversity strongly affects the function of ecosystems, along with *disturbance* and *succession*, and is affected by natural disturbances, such as windstorms and volcanic eruptions (as well as human-induced disturbances like logging or introduction of invasive species), that may result in temporary or long-lasting change. Ecological succession, which follows disturbance, is the change in species over time. The process begins with a few pioneering plants and animals that, over time, create favorable conditions which change and increase species composition and complexity until a stable community is reached. Like all life on earth, ecosystems are dynamic—subject to disturbances from which they need to recover, so that a relatively stable balance is maintained. Even our highly manipulated urban ecosystems are in constant change to varying degrees, depending on the extent of impermeable surface.

Counting the number of species on the planet is difficult, since fewer than two million have been named and described, and estimates vary widely; the most recent educated guess is just under ten million. Though our ecological knowledge is vast, there is much we don't know, and the estimated 85 percent of species yet to be encountered and described leads scientists to believe that many are disappearing without ever being recorded. To preserve the known and unknown, we ought to protect the whole, not just the few charismatic plants and animals we find attractive or know to be stabilizing species.

More definite numbers come from studies showing that species have recently begun to go extinct at rates unimaginable a century ago—as many as 140,000 a year—and that those rates are increasing. Unlike the five other mass extinction events in the past half billion years, the current one—known as the Holocene Extinction (named for the Holocene geologic period, which began about 11,550 years ago)—is attributed to human activity. Its rate is thousands of times greater than the unassisted "background rate," which is one to five species a year; the current rate is estimated to be dozens a *day*. Although most biodiversity—and habitat loss—worldwide occurs near equatorial regions, the Pacific Northwest's richness and variety have been feeling the pressure of an expanding human population for a long time. Any such threats come at a high cost to wild fauna and flora that cannot be replaced.

Biodiversity, then, should be high priority in your garden. One way to realize the importance of maintaining it is by taking a close look at a native plant and its flower. The shape, color, and scent tells you who it partners with, that is, who consumes its nectar and distributes its pollen. Other clues will tell you about other dependents, such as birds that eat its seeds or bugs that feed on its leaves. If the plant vanished, these creatures would lose sustenance, the soil would be unprotected, and other organisms would lose habitat.

Another lesson to learn from nature is how wide a variety of species is packed into an ecosystem. While hiking in a healthy natural area, you might at first notice only the dominant species—a few large trees, some shrubs, and ubiquitous ground cover underneath. Take a closer look, however, and you begin to see

A decomposing log provides habitat for ground-dwelling species.

how much more complex it is. There are young, middle-aged, and declining plants of the same species, which attract different fauna at their different life stages. A great variety of plant forms are arranged in layers: trees that reach into the sky to form the canopy, smaller trees that occupy space below them, large shrubs growing above perennials, dying or broken trees and moss-covered logs supporting young plants, and squat, ground-hugging plants under taller ground cover.

Nature abhors bare soil because, when soil is exposed to sun, wind, rain, and other disturbances such as tillage, it degrades by erosion and loss of nutrients and structure. To protect it, nature covers soil with plants that stabilize, insulate, and shield, along with leaf litter and other plant debris (more on this in Chapter 4). Your garden can emulate this natural proclivity for plant diversity, density, and soil protection, resulting in a rich tapestry of cover that will also help keep weeds at bay.

Not every gardener, of course, will have the space or the time to create an exceptionally diverse garden. If that describes your situation, here's what you can do: If you're going to grow anything native in your yard, let it be trees and shrubs that are known to have once

# who will come?

Iridescent rufous and Anna's hummingbirds, chartreuse tree frogs, jewellike yellow warblers and swallowtail butterflies, and awe-inspring red-tailed hawks are just a few of the many wild species native to the Pacific Northwest that may drop by for a visit to your yard. Though it's impossible to predict which species will pass through or live there, your yard's location and size, the time of year, and food availability have much to do with it.

The more urbanized the area, the lower the species diversity. In dense urban areas, where there is the most disturbance, noise, and predation, you will see mostly nonnative wildlife, but also some natives that can handle human presence and may not be very territorial or particular about food. There may be English sparrows, rock doves, and European starlings, while in nonindustrialized, noncommercial areas you may also see song sparrows, gulls, chickadees, robins, crows, house finches, mallard ducks, and raptors. Swifts, swallows, and peregrine falcons often nest in urban bridges. Mammals include squirrels and possibly bats, and, if green travel corridors are in place, raccoons and opossums.

In less densely developed areas with smaller amounts of impervious surface, such as older suburbs and residential neighborhoods with mature trees, parks, and other green spaces, you will notice additional species—birds like juncos, nuthatches, towhees, jays, grosbeaks, hummingbirds, waxwings, and flickers and other woodpeckers, and possibly great blue herons, kestrels, and Cooper's, red-tailed, and sharp-shinned hawks. Mammals may include voles, moles, rabbits, coyotes, and additional species of bat. Turtles, salamanders, and frogs may live in remnants of wetlands.

In the least developed rural areas, native species diversity increases, possibly even close to historic

TOP Western brush rabbits live in areas of brushy cover and seldom venture into the open. BOTTOM Song sparrows are common in urban residential areas.

levels, according to studies. Tanagers, thrushes, kinglets, warblers, vireos, and an abundance of raptors, including owls, are but a few of the additional species you may see. The nesting activity of woodpeckers leads to secondary cavity nesters like bluebirds, wrens, and chickadees. Mammals such as bobcats, chipmunks, native squirrels, foxes, and black bears may appear, as do a greater diversity of amphibians and reptiles.

Northern flickers often stop by our garden in search of ants and other morsels, or just to take a rest.

flourished in your area and genuinely belong in the ecosystem—even one or two can make a difference. This is certainly not to say that ferns, vines, bulbs, and other types of plants are not important, but they generally don't offer the range of attributes that many woody plants do—trees are a major factor in increasing garden biodiversity.

Those that contribute generously aren't always large in stature—usually it comes down to how much a species can support insect herbivores at the base of the food chain. Such plants might offer leaves for insects to munch on, sustenance for those who eat the

herbivores, flowers with nectar and pollen for pollinators, fruits and seeds for other wildlife, cover and nesting sites, decaying matter that protects the soil, and other benefits. Plants like ferns do provide protective cover, enrich the soil, and support some insects, but oak, as well as willow, pine, and western redcedar, have each been found to host hundreds of kinds of insect herbivores, which in turn support a wider variety of wildlife.

How will you know you've done enough? Nature will tell you: The presence of bees, butterflies, and other beneficial creatures are all indicators of a healthy, functional garden

Fruits of false solomon's seal (*Smilacina racemosa*) provide food for woodland birds and small mammals in autumn.

ecosystem, allowing us a chance to view them and to play a crucial role in their conservation. Research shows that gardens can support an enormous variety of wildlife species, and those of us who grow more than a couple of native plants attest to it. Even though my urban yard is fairly small, since I began reducing lawn and adding native plants I see a greater variety of creatures, and as our young native conifer trees mature there will undoubtedly be even more.

Animals' appearances vary with the season. Some live there part time, some full time, but most that can be seen without the aid of a magnifying glass are just passing through in search of food, water, or a place to rest. I've seen many types of butterflies and moths, dragonflies and damselflies, and myriad native bee species busy at work. If I stand or sit still long enough, birds such as warblers, western tanagers, varied thrushes, band-tailed pigeons, and even the occasional Cooper's hawk, in addition to many more common species like flickers, chickadees, and scrub jays, enter my world. Early morning is typically best for bird viewing, with binoculars and a regional guidebook in hand. The mammals—raccoons, opossums, and the occasional coyote—tend to come during the night, but I know they've been there by the overturned rocks, scattered broken snail shells, and scat.

Considering the transients, it makes sense that the more authentic a garden is, the greater the variety of life it will attract and support, and the greater the benefit to the wider world beyond property lines.

## Habitat's the Key

The term *habitat*, sometimes used interchangeably with *ecosystem*, refers to the physical features and biological conditions that individuals or populations of species make use of to reproduce and survive in a particular place. Habitat can be huge, as in the case of a mountain range that supports everything from black bears to bobcats, or very small, like a single, slowly decomposing log in your backyard that provides nutrients and homes for countless invertebrates, microbes, and budding plants. It includes the type of terrain preferred by the species, plus food, water, and cover, as well as special resources needed by some animals, such as snags or rocky outcrops.

Different species require different amounts of habitat to survive, and some (amphibians, for example) need more than one kind of habitat within a life cycle, such as one for breeding and another for getting through the winter. Migratory species depend on additional stopover habitat, which allows for refueling during exhausting migrations. Though each species has differing needs, many coexist in the same "habitat type," such as mixed evergreen forest, herbaceous wetland, or oak savanna. Such communities of species use unique combinations of habitat elements. For example, fallen leaves in my yard are an important element for ground beetles, as well as birds like colorful varied thrushes and robins that forage at

LEFT Birdbaths with gradually sloping sides are best for all sizes of birds, which will wade in to a comfortable depth. RIGHT Brush piles can provide cover for small birds, amphibians, and other animals.

Downy woodpeckers may need as much as thirty-five acres to make a living.

ground level but nest in shrubs or trees, while my neighbor's mature trees are crucial for birds such as acrobatic bushtits that glean small insects and spiders from them and position intricately woven, pendulous nests within their branches.

Although every species has very specific habitat needs, all have four basic requirements:

→ **Appropriate food:** Provide a variety of plants that offer insects, flowers, fruit, or nuts. Poor quality habitat leads to reduced breeding efforts and malnutrition or starvation when animals—especially those with specific food requirements—can't find nutritious food.

→ **Accessible water:** Available year-round, water—everything from birdbaths to ponds or streams to moist sand for insects like butterflies—will attract and sustain wildlife in your area. Although some are able to obtain water through their diet or from dew droplets, many wild species can survive only a few days without additional water. If you have a natural stream on your property, protect its banks from erosion that leads to sedimentation, which is especially problematic for amphibian populations that live in low-gradient streams: Silt fills spaces between rocks and logs that they need for shelter and nest sites.

→ **Suitable shelter:** Plants provide three-dimensional structures in which wildlife can flee from predators, feed, build nests, raise young, roost, and simply relax. When possible, include evergreens for thermal cover, as well as prickly bushes, thicket-producing plants, logs, brush and rock piles, snags, and fallen leaves.

→ **Sufficient space:** Animals need varying amounts of space for securing the previous three elements, and in which to exhibit natural behaviors like attracting a mate. Wildlife pathways or corridors are essential for animals with large ranges.

## Space on the Home Range

A *home range* is the area that a species covers in its daily movements to avoid predators and find food, water, shelter, and a mate, and raise young. Range size depends on the size of the animal, the quantity and quality of habitat elements, and dietary, behavioral, and social needs—some animals are mainly solitary, while others are quite social. Home ranges are often smaller in diverse, high-quality habitats, where needs are met more easily, than in areas that support few plant species, such as conventional farmland, or where pesticides are applied. Range size varies immensely: A small lizard might need just a quarter acre to meet all its requirements, a downy woodpecker might find everything it needs within twenty-five to thirty-five wooded acres, while a bobcat could require as much as 1,100 acres to mature, reproduce, and survive. Some types of animals, such as amphibians, need more than one habitat type over the course of a year.

If you have a large, rural property, consider that it may present challenges to wildlife similar to those in agricultural areas. For example, grassland birds and other wildlife that nest on the ground may think your grassy meadow or roadside strip is nice nesting habitat, but mowing before breeding season is over could have deadly results. If you must mow what

## species with special needs

Every species has unique needs, and the more specific those needs and localized the habitat, the greater the vulnerability to loss of habitat to agriculture, pesticide use, climate change, and urbanization. Salamanders and other amphibians are especially sensitive to environmental changes—give them year-round water sources and moist places to live, such as piles of damp leaves, brush piles, or decomposing logs. Integrating such additions as well as elements that accumulate rainwater (such as rocks with shallow depressions), by tucking them within plantings also provides structural interest. Some shade is a must for amphibians and can be provided by trees and shrubs, as well as ground cover plants that allow the little animals to get around undercover, even on sunny days. Also leave loose mounds of rounded stones in shaded areas around the garden where a salamander or frog might seek cover.

Shallow rocks that catch rainwater are not only functional but also add beauty.

A native bumblebee forages on a native rose.

## bugs over bird feeders

Although some birds are seed eaters, 96 percent of birds, excluding waterbirds, feed their young invertebrates. Those adorable little chickadees may dine on seeds from your feeder or plants during the winter, but come spring, Mr. and Mrs. Chickadee will be frantically searching for insects, their eggs and larvae, and other morsels, like spiders, to feed their rapidly growing babies. To attract and aid such birds and other creatures, we must first provide what they need to survive, and the best way to do that is with native plants, which supply drastically more insect biomass than nonnatives. The next time you see an unappealing insect, think "bird food"!

When you provide for birds naturally with native plants, there's no need to worry about attracting rats and other undesirables, as bird feeders can, and there is little risk that food will become contaminated with pathogenic organisms such as salmonella, which, according to the National Wildlife Health Center, "is a common cause of bird mortality at feeders." Salmonellosis can happen when feeders aren't kept clean. Feeders also cause birds to congregate unnaturally in small areas, where sick birds may spread disease to others, creating epidemic conditions that can wipe out backyard bird populations. Even if birds become only temporarily ill, a sick bird is much more likely to be attacked by a predator. If you use feeders and notice lethargic, emaciated, or dead birds, remove the feeders for several weeks and clean up seeds and droppings below

ecologists call "ecological traps," be sure to wait until well after breeding season is completed. Delaying mowing will also aid pollinators and other beneficial creatures that rely on nectar or pollen. Since birds often reproduce in the same area every year, keep track of when you see nesting activity to anticipate next year's broods, to be certain they will be able to survive.

## Lost Without Space

When wild animals or plants no longer have enough appropriate food, water, shelter, or space, their habitat is said to be lost. Typically

them. If you want to use bird
feeders until your garden can
supply natural food, follow
practices that keep birds
healthy:

- Fill feeders with just the
  amount of food that will be
  consumed in one day, less-
  ening the chances that food
  will become contaminated
  or moldy. Discard damp,
  moldy food and replenish
  with fresh food daily.
- Once a week, clean feeders
  with a brush and hot, soapy
  water, rinse them thor-
  oughly, and allow them to
  dry (in the sun, if possible).

Anna's hummingbirds need nectar to get them through cold
winters. Keep food fresh and feeders clean.

Dilute, 10 percent bleach solu-
tions may be used (with a good rinse) every few
weeks, but never on hummingbird feeders.
- For hummingbirds, choose real plant nectar over
  non-nutritious sugary solutions. If using feeders,
  change nectar weekly if the weather's cool and
  the feeder is out of sunlight, but much more
  frequently if it receives sun or the temperature
  climbs above 65°F. Don't assume that a nearly
  full feeder doesn't need changing—deadly toxins
  can contaminate the solution in a short time.
  Hummingbird feeders also should be cleaned
  with hot soapy water (no bleach) and rinsed well
  each time the food is replaced.
- Avoid using bird feeders with crevices, tubes, or
  rough surfaces that are difficult to clean.

- Put trays under feeders to collect fallen hulls
  and seeds and change feeder positions every
  few weeks, to help keep down pathogens that
  may develop on the ground below.
- If using multiple feeders, place them far
  apart to minimize crowding and contact.
- Keep feeding fairly consistent: Research
  shows that birds often return to the same
  feeding spots year after year.
- Hang feeders either very close to your windows (within 2 feet) or at least 30 feet away,
  to help prevent window strikes, and 10 feet
  from shrubs to prevent predation.

# dead trees bring life

Research continues to stress the critical importance of decaying wood to biodiversity, so the next time you have logs, branches, twigs, or a dying tree, don't discard them. Interactions between wildlife and decaying wood are fundamental to ecosystem functions and processes in forests, aquatic habitats, and "real" gardens, whether they be wooded or more open. Decaying wood includes older living trees with broken branches, hollow cavities, or thick, loose bark; snags (upright dead or dying trees); stumps and large, aerial roots; and *dead wood*, such as fallen limbs and debris like bark litter.

Accumulations of decomposing wood on the ground provide food, shelter, and places to raise young, support fungi species that live in symbiotic relationships with plant roots, and influence processes such as soil and fertility development. Wild creatures interact directly as they go about their daily business: Tiny insects and fungi break down woody materials that build and aerate soil; scampering squirrels fragment wood and scatter the fungi for plant growth; small birds and mammals feed on decomposer insects and invertebrates that seek shelter and reproduce within the wood; large fauna seek small prey; woodpeckers excavate nest sites in upright wood; and frogs and salamanders use dead wood for cover.

TOP Decomposing wood is essential in a healthy ecosystem. BOTTOM Iridescently handsome tree swallows nest in natural cavities of snags, as well as in old woodpecker holes.

occurring when land or water is fragmented, destroyed by logging or draining, or degraded by pollution or impervious surfaces, habitat loss is a major cause of known extinctions and promises to be the main cause of future mass extinctions caused by human activity. Although we may not notice habitat fragmentation on the ground like we might from an airplane, it can be disruptive or devastating to wildlife. Fragmentation happens when large, continuous habitat areas are broken into isolated, small patches by roads and other development, leading to interrupted wildlife travel corridors, barriers to breeding possibilities, and other overwhelming consequences.

The more specific their needs, the more vulnerable species are to habitat damage. Although often unintentional, this thoughtless and ever-increasing destruction might well be considered cruelty to animals, since taking away habitat effectively abandons them to either an immediate or slow death or causes them to be unable to reproduce. Wild animals cannot "move on" when their homes are destroyed or food becomes scarce, since there is no longer anywhere for them to move on to!

Furthermore, with increases in rapid urbanization, intensive agriculture, pollution, and climate change, staging and stopover areas along bird migration routes—places where birds can rest, feed, breed, and recuperate from amazing but grueling life-or-death migratory flights—have been either degraded or entirely lost. In addition, competition and predation are heightened in what little remains. Worldwide, nearly 20 percent of bird species are migratory, and many are heading toward extinction; others are losing as much as 9 percent of their populations per year. An estimated one billion

birds migrate along the Pacific Flyway, which stretches from the North Slope of Alaska to Central and South America, but they are only a fraction of those that took to that flyway a century ago. For example, every spring and fall Swainson's thrush, a shy, nocturnal migrant, travels 3,000 miles between Canada or Alaska and Central or South America.

If birds can't rest and refuel en route to their wintering or breeding grounds, they won't survive. The good news is, staging and stopover habitat in even urban, suburban, and agricultural areas can provide precious shelter and nourishment for hungry, thirsty, and exhausted birds on their way to their final destination.

## Butterflies Are Free . . . or Are They?

Let's face it: We take pollinators for granted. Of the bees, birds, bats, butterflies, moths, beetles, and flies that pollinate flowers, all are important and most are in trouble. Just as we are intensely reliant on pollinators for our meals, so are flora and fauna. It's not surprising that animals such as birds that feed on fruits and seeds and possibly the pollinators themselves are intensely connected to pollination, but most other animals, even obligate carnivores such as bobcats, depend on pollinators much more than you'd imagine. Without pollinators, the intertwined species and processes functioning within an ecosystem would disintegrate and collapse.

All of the 4,000 species of bees once native to North America (which reportedly are more efficient pollinators for many crops than honeybees), from gentle bumblebees to leafcutter bees, are in serious decline. Some are already extinct (or close to it), due to severe habitat loss, modern agriculture with its vast

Western tiger swallowtail

monocultures, pesticide use, disease, parasites, and competition with honeybees (which are not native). Scientific field studies show that the loss of just a single bee species can have a negative effect on plant reproductive function, and suggest that pollinator declines seriously affect ecosystem functioning.

Those ethereal butterflies in dangerous decline face many of the same threats, plus others. Since their immature life stages dictate that they be virtually immobile for many months of the year, they can't just fly off like adults. Each life stage—egg, caterpillar (larva), pupa (chrysalis), and adult—has different

# just add water

Life is wet. Especially during the dry summer months, water will attract and sustain wildlife in your space—without it you will see fewer species. From moist, gravel-filled pie plates for insects and mud puddles for butterflies and birds, to ponds or streams for bats, water is essential. Birds use water to drink, of course, but also to keep their feathers clean and waterproof— essential for flight and insulation.

Birdbaths should slope gradually to ensure that small animals can safely use them and get out easily. If yours has steep sides, place some flat rocks or pebbles on one side so visitors can wade in to a safe and comfortable depth. Site them at least 10 feet from any hiding places where domesticated predators could lurk—if you know cats hunt in your yard, consider a hanging birdbath. Keep birdbaths as clean as possible, since birds may drink from the same water other birds have bathed in. Replace the water every couple of days (this will also prevent mosquitoes) and give them a good scrubbing every few weeks. Nearby shrubs make useful perches for preening after bathing.

To attract more wildlife, consider installing a pond. At least one side should be shallow and slope gradually, the depth should be at least 18 inches, and logs and rocks should be present to supply cover and a way out. Site ponds so they receive at least a few hours of sunlight each day, and populate them with submerged native plants, such as marsh marigold (*Caltha palustris*) for shallow areas and common cattail (*Typha latifolia*) for deeper situations. Ponds should be without fish since fish eat amphibian

Ponds provide water, food, and cover for myriad creatures, as well as beauty and serenity.

eggs; tadpoles will take care of any algae. Consult a pond specialist or books with pond-building instructions, and check permit requirements before you attempt to create one on your own.

# protecting your wild guests

Wildlife that visits or lives on your property needs to be protected, but also left alone. To be sure fauna comes to no harm and is not unnecessarily disturbed:

- Don't use synthetic chemicals such as pesticides and fertilizers, which are particularly toxic to sensitive pollinators and amphibians.
- Keep domesticated companion animals (especially predatory ones) away from wild species.
- To view wild critters with minimal disturbance, use binoculars or a large camera lens rather than trying to get close, wear subdued colors, and move slowly. Never intentionally handle wildlife, since that can lead to harm to either you or the animal. Remember that animals—snakes, for instance—only bite when they feel threatened. Leave them alone and they will leave you alone.

- Teach children to respect all species, to reduce the chance of harassment and harm from curious minds. Require that they admire wildlife from afar, since catching butterflies, dragonflies, frogs, and other relatively delicate creatures can cause harm, especially if done by inexperienced hands.
- Protect habitat, whether it be soil littered with leaves, stream banks, or mature trees. Refrain from mowing grasses that are next to bodies of water and rock and brush piles. Don't use leaf blowers, which create noise and air pollution and blast delicate and beneficial creatures.
- Apply decals that reflect ultraviolet light which birds can see (such as Window Alert and BirdTape) to the outside of windows. As many as a billion birds may be killed by collisions with windows each year in the United States. Silhouettes on the inside of windows don't work.
- Create brush shelters by arranging logs and small branches in a quiet corner of the yard. Smooth rocks left in piles are also good insect and amphibian habitat.
- Attract more native pollinators by providing nest material of horizontal hollow stems or wooden blocks drilled with dead-end holes. But be sure to phase them out every two years, to prevent parasites and disease.
- Talk to neighbors about helping to protect the wildlife in your area by creating safe travel corridors on their properties that link to yours and others.

Great blue heron

A banded woolly bear larva searches for a place to pupate.

needs: Host plants, secure hiding places, nutritious nectar, and minerals are all essential. To top it off, some rely exclusively on only one host plant. The larvae of the Oregon silverspot butterfly, which once ranged from southern Washington to northern California in grasslands such as coastal meadows, feed only on early blue violet (*Viola adunca*). By steering clear of pesticides, not being too neat, and growing plants that provide for all stages, you will be helping all of these amazing pollinators stay around and stay healthy.

# CHAPTER 2
## *designing native nirvana*

"Nature doesn't have a design problem. People do."
—William McDonough and Michael Braungart,
*Cradle to Cradle: Remaking the Way We Make Things*

**FROM THE BEGINNING, GARDENS WERE CREATED TO** sustain us, stimulate our minds, and delight our senses. Modern gardens are influenced by geography, history, and climate and focus on what we want to see and do in them. But gardens are typically unnatural places—especially those carpeted with lawn and hardscape, and manicured and ordered to such an extent that few wild creatures are motivated to enter.

You can create a more natural landscape that merges into its setting while attracting and nurturing wildlife, without giving up *your* needs, but you will need to do some planning, because gardens are never designed in isolation. It takes more than buying a few plants, digging holes, tucking the roots in, and watering. While the plants may do fine, taking time to plan will pay off in the long term, whether you're starting from scratch or enhancing an established garden. Conflicts between the needs of wildlife and our own needn't arise, because what provides sustenance and shelter for wild creatures can also satisfy our need for nature and amplify the natural beauty in our lives.

Effective landscape designs blend aesthetics and functionality, both ecological and practical.

Everyone has their own idea of the perfect garden, but there's one thing that appealing gardens always have: that special, enigmatic ingredient called *character*. Though difficult to articulate, it may be what rouses our senses and stimulates our mind and makes us want to stay awhile. The character, or feel, of a garden can and should also be beneficial to the wild visitors we want to support.

Where does character come from, and how can you get it? It's been said that character develops from the site itself, or "the genius of place," a line from a 300-year-old poem by Alexander Pope that advises that landscape designs always be adapted to their location. Character, then, stems from a garden's relationship to its ecological setting and includes the unique qualities of the land, as well as the house that sits on it. In the old days, gardens were mainly influenced by an area's geology—which affects its drainage, soil, and subsoil—and the materials contained in them were usually local, since moving materials like rock could be difficult. Gardeners had to make do with what they had on hand—a great idea today as well, as we try to lessen our dependence on fossil fuels. Having an appreciation for local geologic history and regional flora and fauna can help inspire your own authentic garden. No matter where you live, it is the sense of place—conveyed strongly through native plants and animals that evolved together, from the tallest tree to the tiniest spider—which should pervade a design in order to stay true to the character of the natural surroundings.

This chapter focuses on design and is multifaceted, like an ecosystem composed of many parts that contribute to the whole. Its intent is to widen your focus beyond individual plants and help you come up with a purposeful, holistic garden plan that is guided by your inspiration and creativity. First, we'll take a quick peek at the historical progression of gardens, to see how they evolved and to learn about the international plant trade. Then we'll tackle issues and design principles that mainly affect people, followed by a discussion of elements that are key for naturalistic, or informal, gardens meant to welcome wildlife. Finally, you'll learn how to go about planning and drawing your own design and view some examples. For our purposes, the term *garden* encompasses postage stamp–sized urban courtyards, quarter-acre suburban yards, and rural landscapes that may be dozens of acres.

## History Lessons

In the sixteenth and seventeenth centuries, particularly in Italy and France, gardens were intentionally separated from nature, domesticated and tamed into orderly, anthropocentric works of art without regard to ecological relationships. By contrast, the eighteenth century nurtured many British designers who viewed nature as something to emulate. Although the fetish for verdant lawns had begun, they often used native plants in their creations, and horticulture for exclusively ornamental purposes was frowned upon. An idea developed that demonstrated the modern architectural principle that form is inseparable from and follows function, meaning that the form a garden or building takes ought to be guided by what happens inside it. This concept contributed to the science of applied ecology, which typically uses our knowledge of landforms, soils, and plant communities to address and manage environmental issues.

Few Americans at the time gardened, and those who did were only slightly affected by this reverence for nature and mainly focused on subduing the natural world for human needs. American properties generally had a utilitarian purpose, providing food, fuel, and medicinals for survival, but as the world became more urbanized and poverty declined, gardeners began to focus less on sustenance and more on ornamentals. Such traditional gardens, primarily featuring exotic species from other countries and continents, lack a connection to the natural landscape and usually require considerable maintenance, since getting nonnative plants to thrive can be laborious and even produce anxiety.

There have been exceptions, of course, including gardens created by the Olmsted Brothers, whose firm designed Seattle's park system (among many others). Although their work (and that of their father, Frederick Law Olmsted, who introduced some of the first purposeless lawns in the country) included landscape changes not always ecologically beneficial, they strove to retain native trees and often included other native species in naturalistic settings. The senior Olmsted influenced Jens Jensen, a Danish immigrant and staunch conservationist who rallied against formal gardens and made subtle, free-form gardens, patterned after nature, his signature. His core ideas revolved around native plants in informal placement and are a major influence today.

Frank Lloyd Wright also appreciated native plants that were allowed to attain their natural shapes; his architecture demonstrated how a house could harmonize with or blend almost seamlessly into the native landscape. Other, less prominent, American gardeners used

This timeless garden elegantly melds local native flora and artful historic salvage.

some easy-to-grow and showy native species—unfortunately dug up from natural areas, with decimation the result in some cases—but the trend in North America (as well as Britain and parts of Europe) was to feature the latest foreign plant material as it was encountered on plant hunting expeditions and became available for gardeners. The global plant trade, which

Meadow checkermallow (*Sidalcea campestris*), a graceful grassland species, is tall in flower.

succeeded in bundling off many Pacific Northwest natives for cultivation and use in ornamental gardens, trade, and industry overseas. The iconic Sitka spruce (*Picea sitchensis*), brought into formerly spruceless Scotland for its timber industry, has flourished prolifically there, but at the expense of decreased biodiversity, including the loss of native oak and pine species. Camas bulbs (*Camassia quamash*) were being shipped to the East Coast and England by the mid-1800s. Ironically, many species literally made a round trip, eventually shipped back for sale in the States: Our beloved red-flowering currant (*Ribes sanguineum*) is one that received a transatlantic ticket back, earning our praise only after it had become a highly regarded shrub in British eyes.

This is not to say that every country is fixated on imported plants. In many places, local plants with a natural affinity with their settings are widely used. The resulting native gardens, which may appear naturalistic or formal, often successfully blend into the surrounding ecosystem and make the concept of the native garden a valuable norm, rather than an oddity.

Nevertheless, it's reasonable to want to experiment with styles and techniques from another time or another country to complement the style of a house, like English cottage gardens, Arts and Crafts Movement designs of the late nineteenth century (which, incidentally, encourage a connection with nature that can be achieved through the use of native plants), or the more modern drought-tolerant designs of California and the Mediterranean. It's not unusual for designers to borrow from the past and other locales, such as Italian Renaissance or French Baroque gardens, although that type of adopting has declined lately.

continues today, has also transported damaging diseases, insects, and invasive species that have wreaked havoc on many ecosystems.

Pacific Northwest flora has accumulated as many frequent-traveler miles as the plants we import from other countries. Almost immediately after America was "discovered" and the colonists began arriving, plant expeditions

"Period" gardens don't have to contain plants of that era or locale—elements from the past can and ought to be converted into components for a modern, eco-conscious garden. If a historic style appeals to you, such as a simple but high-maintenance *parterre*, or knot garden, adapt it by filling it with native species no one could have known about during that time. Mix, match, and adapt whatever you want from period designs, but remember that whatever you choose, it should be beneficial. Besides, making an exact re-creation of a garden style from the past is virtually impossible and would look contrived. Revive and reinvent, but always with today's ecological crises in mind.

## Ecology by Design

To help you create a garden plan that is appealing and matches your idea of the perfect garden, there are quite a few good, albeit conventional, landscape design books available. But most of them focus on how to design a garden that looks pretty, without addressing biodiversity and the special qualities of the individual site. To establish a balance between the needs of wildlife and those of the people who use the yard, it's important to mimic nature as much as possible, by combining an artistic process with an ecological point of view.

### Aesthetics for Humans

The most difficult phase of garden design may be the beginning, organizational stage, because you need to put specific plants out of your mind for the time being and think instead of visual qualities such as shape and line. How these elements relate to each other and bind the functions of the garden together is the basis of good garden design and will help you decide what you do with your space.

**Shapes** within gardens result from the forms of buildings, beds, topographical features, and plants that may be upright, rounded, or spreading. Deciduous plants' shapes sometimes change with the seasons, as when a tree's craggy winter branches become softly rounded clumps of leaves in spring, or ground-hugging perennials send up 4-foot-tall floriferous spikes in summer.

**Lines** are used to create shapes and forms, develop cohesiveness, define and connect spaces, and control our movement. Common landscape lines include fencing, walls, plants with strongly vertical or horizontal branching patterns, and, most important, pathways to get us around. The most frequently used paths are best situated where they are most direct, such as from sidewalk to front door and back door to patio. Although nature isn't fond of straight lines, they do come in handy in tight areas to not only lead us on foot, but to draw our eyes through a space, with unbent lines moving our vision quickly and curving ones slowly. Harsh lines and hard edges can be softened or hidden with full, lush plantings. Hardscape—especially the impermeable kind—is not ecologically beneficial and should be minimized as much as possible.

Generally, what is most appealing to the human eye is when shapes and lines within a garden resonate with the surrounding area, whether it's a country landscape's gently rounded hills echoing in the flowing shapes of a rural garden, or the strong lines of urban architecture and infrastructure repeating in city gardens through geometric patterns of angular or curved forms. Plants, the locale's topography, and nearby structures all supply shape and line.

A salal shrub (*Gaultheria shallon*) softens the edges of this stairway and fence.

### Principles to ponder

One goal of a "real" garden design should be for all its parts to cohere in a unified whole, and look as though nature created it.

When we look at a beautiful scene in nature we don't analyze details, and rarely are there distractions. Instead, we take in the whole and all its relaxing effects. "Simple style is like white light. It is complex, but its complexity is not obvious," wrote Anatole France a hundred years ago. Think in terms of the whole garden—rather than this plant and that stairway—with the details being just a part of the entire picture.

A handful of underlying design principles can help guide you with visual and spatial organization. Though these principles may be named, organized, and defined slightly differently by different designers, I'll refer to them as *unity, proportion, balance,* and *rhythm.* There is quite a bit of overlap and interaction among them, and their effects are often not obvious, and *that* is the objective: to keep details subtle and gradual. Also keep in mind that these basic, suggested design guidelines are not inalterable requirements: Garden design is an art form, and it can be more enjoyable to not adhere too closely to formal "rules"!

**Unity** comes from the use of simple but strong elements and patterns that give a landscape wholeness, structure, and consistency. To be most beneficial and naturalistic, plantings should be diverse and not strictly ordered, while the repeated use of simple shapes and lines for things like pathways and beds will help create a design that feels interconnected. The type of pattern or patterns you choose will depend on suitability to the site's topography, its views, and the style of the house that the garden will surround.

The simplest shape in garden design is the square or rectangle. These easily resonate with walls and property lines, which are usually at ninety-degree angles. These shapes can serve to link the house with the rest of the yard, but less severe, nonlinear shapes create a more natural feel. Curved shapes work especially well in planted areas since plants' outlines are usually rounded. Repeating a single type of shape, in differing sizes, produces a pattern and a sense of movement; eyes may be guided to a garden feature or perhaps a view, rather than bouncing around various shapes or from point to point. Shapes can also be vertical, in varying heights, adding definition and structure. Multiple shapes may be used to break up monotony when enough space is available, but avoid creating confusion by combining too many.

Shapes should connect with each other, but subtly if possible. For instance, a vine-covered pergola might lead from a rectangular patio between two large, sunny pollinator beds and up to a woodland space with relaxed, curved edges and stepping-stone paths. Not only does the pergola connect the spaces, it creates an intriguing tunnel effect that accentuates the contrast of the naturalized woodland area. It also may act as a blind from which to view woodland birds, and provide habitat.

**Proportion** refers to the size relationship between objects or parts of the whole, and is as important in garden design as in any design field. Creating a balanced composition from shapes and objects (including plants) that are proportionate to the size of the house and the yard is the most visually agreeable and is mainly determined by a trained eye or intuition—that is, what looks and feels right. Don't be afraid to be bold. Some examples: A tall, two-story house will appear to loom above only three-foot-tall shrubs and perennials surrounding it. Adding appropriately placed trees and tall shrubs that frame and will eventually meet or exceed the house height will better fit the house into the landscape. Freestanding

pergolas and arbors should fit the situation and be sturdy enough that they don't topple over in the next windstorm (or look like they could). On large decks and patios, small containers will look like they're meant for Alice when she was small, so choose pots that have some amplitude. But big isn't always better, such as when big shrubs are grown within very small gardens or placed close to paths, entryways, or foundations: They will look out of place due to inappropriate scale, and/or cause mobility and maintenance issues as they mature.

To achieve a feeling of **balance**, you have two options. *Symmetrical* balance occurs when forms on opposite sides of a dividing line or axis are the same, such as when a front yard is

## intrigue in the garden

Beauty is most powerful when it's unexpected, so a certain amount of mystery should guide our designs. If interest is to be piqued and exploration invited, not everything should be visible at once. I'm not talking mazes and bread crumb trails: Even fairly small gardens can supply some suspense with the use of vertical trellises or simply tall plants that create divisions, keeping a portion of a garden—such as a quiet sitting area—hidden until the last minute. Unexpected microhabitat can be created as well, with little plants growing enchantingly out of crevices in walls or steps without mortar. Keeping parts of the garden hidden also benefits wild creatures, who need to be left alone.

Texture, on a small-scale

split in half by a walkway to the front door, and the plants on either side mirror each other. This tends to look formal rather than naturalistic, but it may be useful when trying to tone down a "wild" look that doesn't appeal to everyone. The human eye likes symmetry. Think Celtic designs: Although their fine detail is captivating, their symmetry is also appealing.

In contrast, more natural-appearing *asymmetrical* balance uses different sizes, textures, or colors to create equilibrium—for example, counterbalancing a large tree with two smaller trees or large shrubs on either side of a stated or implied axis. Photographers are familiar with the "rule of thirds," by which a frame is divided into nine sections by two imaginary, equal-spaced vertical lines and two horizontal lines. Objects placed near those lines or where the lines cross generate a more interesting and dynamic impression. What works well for an image is also suitable in the garden: Rather than centering a tree or water feature smack dab in the middle of a front yard, place it to the left or right of center. You may also want to use asymmetry when siting objects or plants outside a favorite window.

Strongly symmetrical houses benefit visually from the addition of asymmetrical elements to tone down formality. Although my own house isn't strongly symmetrical, a previous owner must have wanted it to be, since the front yard shrubs were paired up like critters from Noah's ark, a half dozen of them lined up two feet from the house on either side of a large, first-story front window. To add to the effect, they were sheared into lollipops and popsicles. My remedy was to remove all but two non-paired shrubs, thin those out so they looked more natural and could grow normally, then add other plants around them.

Another design principle is **rhythm,** in which the repetition of patterns—like shape, line, color, and texture—adds interest, quiets a chaotic look, and draws the eye through the site, creating a feeling of motion. Too much repetition, of course, can cause monotony, as in the case of an abundance of plants with similar leaf sizes, which results in homogeneous texture throughout. But when not overdone, repetition creates harmony. It can also help reduce the patchwork effect that results when we give in to a lust for collecting single specimens of a plant species.

## salvage is sustainable

Using durable and found materials is an important green principle when creating sustainable gardens. When such materials are locally available and truly belong in a place, energy use is minimized or even eliminated. Whether it's a mass of rocks dug up from your backyard for a cobblestone pathway or some reclaimed lumber and bricks for an arbor and patio, giving a second life to items that seem to have little value is time well spent. Incorporating salvaged materials like antique metalwork or outdoor lighting as focal points can also tone down the austere newness of a young garden, lending a patina of age and increasing the curiosity factor. Practically speaking, such reuse of materials also lessens the burden on our landfills and minimizes the demand for natural resources and toxic materials used in the processing, manufacture, and transportation of new items.

A reclaimed piece of widow's walk from a demolished nineteenth-century house in Portland now adds a beautiful focal point and historical interest to this shady front yard.

Focal points, like a bench, can draw eyes through a pathway.

Rhythm may be more than just visual: Pleasant sounds can be rhythmic, such as aspen leaves fluttering in the breeze or a babbling water feature that also provides for birds. Pathways and steps can create rhythm, whether they're varied or irregular patterns that allow for more movement and stimulation, or regular patterns that create a sense of restfulness. The distance between stepping-stones influences the rate at which we travel through a garden: Wide placement increases our speed, while close placement tends to slow us down. Crunchy gravel or filbert-shell paths also break our speed because they're more difficult to walk on. Such speed limits allow us to notice the finer details and maybe even motivate us to stop along the way.

You can also use rhythm to make a garden appear more natural. By repeating specific plants—particularly larger ones that offer year-round interest, such as interesting structure, bark, foliage, or long-lasting flowers—throughout a bed or throughout the yard, you'll create continuity and a more natural effect. For example, red-twig dogwood shrubs (*Cornus sericea*) offer structural interest in fall and winter, as well as beautiful flowers, leaves, and berries during the rest of the year.

A design element that affects unity, proportion, balance, and rhythm is **texture**, which usually refers to leaf and flower size, shape, or arrangement, as well as branching or bark characteristics. Besides the aesthetic qualities, supplying a variety of flower shapes and sizes will accommodate a greater diversity of pollinators, from birds to bees and other insect species, which come in all shapes and sizes and have different tongue and proboscis sizes. Some need tubular flowers, while others mainly feed from clusters of teeny-tiny flowers.

Boldly textured plants may best fit into large landscapes. The massive trunk and branches of a Garry oak (*Quercus garryana*), coupled with the small leaves and delicate flowers of shrubs such as oceanspray (*Holodiscus discolor*) and serviceberry (*Amelanchier alnifolia*), and the spiky fronds of western sword fern (*Polystichum munitum*), together create a varied and attractive planting while providing food and cover for wild fauna. Smaller gardens also benefit visually from a variety of textures, such as when the tall and frothy flowered goatsbeard (*Aruncus dioicus*) is paired with the upright fronds of deer fern (*Blechnum spicant*) and the heart-shaped leaves of wild ginger (*Asarum caudatum*).

### Tricks of the trade: dimension, views, focal points, and color

Designers sometimes use visual tools to manipulate the perceived dimensions of a garden. For example, the parallel borders of a straight pathway will appear to come together toward the end, making a yard appear longer than it really is, while staggering the shape of the path from side to side will slow the pace and add interest by causing the eye to travel laterally. The use of calming horizontals can make a narrow site or pathway appear wider, while incorporating tall elements adds vertical strength.

Views may be "borrowed" so that even small yards can be visually expanded. For example, if privacy is not an issue, replacing a solid, fortresslike fence with a more open trellis will allow light to enter and offer a glimpse into a neighboring area. Allow a colorful native flowering vine such as orange honeysuckle (*Lonicera ciliosa*) to weave through it, and birds and pollinators will be provided with food and cover.

The stunning and fragrant western azalea (*Rhododendren occidentale*) illuminates a woodland garden.

Directing how the eye travels around a garden is accomplished by creating not only lines but also focal points that act like little stop signs to attract attention and offer interest. An inviting bench, exceptionally beautiful plant, birdbath, sculpture, or view are all examples of focal points. Though especially suitable at the end of a line of sight, they can also be used to divert attention from things we want to downplay in the yard or within view of the yard, such as trash cans or a pile of junk next door. Regardless of their intent, focal points can add both character and visual strength, but don't overdo them or make them too obvious. Use just a few, since too many will clutter and distract and lessen their effect, and keep them in scale with the immediate area—a group of small, interesting rocks is much more suitable for a thirty-square-foot rock garden than a gigantic piece of pottery.

Color is a favorite element for some gardeners and a very important one for pollinators (see Chapter 3). Colors that are close to each other on the color wheel, such as red and orange or blue and purple, are said to harmonize, while opposite ones, such as yellow and purple or orange and blue, will contrast or complement. If color lights your candle, consider using mostly harmonious ones in naturalistic gardens, with only occasional contrasting colors as accents. Whites look good with just about anything. Glossy leaves reflect light and tend to stand out, while dark colors recede. Deep-green trees that are sometimes employed to create an illusion of depth also make the perfect background for white or pastel flowers like western trillium (*Trillium ovatum*), goatsbeard (*Aruncus dioicus*), and western azalea (*Rhododendron occidentale*).

## Essentials for Wildlife

A fundamental goal of gardening for biodiversity is meeting the requirements of wildlife—from the obvious and charismatic bees, butterflies, and birds to the much more abundant but nearly invisible creatures—and balancing them with human needs and enjoyment. A successful naturalistic design comes not only from good plant selection, but also from clearly identifying your objectives and goals early on.

That said, naturalistic, "real" gardens aren't created overnight, and what will work best for your site may not be apparent right away, but will expand as your awareness and knowledge grow. To begin restoring natural functions that assist and mimic nature, we need to explore a few more principles, this time relating to wild species and ecology. These include minimizing disturbance and providing secluded wildlife habitat, conserving and enriching diverse vegetation and structure, and preserving and enhancing natural topography, transition areas, and wildlife corridors. We'll also look at yard size and how it affects sustainable gardens.

### Please do not disturb

Human activity can negatively impact wildlife and reduce the quality of the habitat you provide. Many wild creatures need heavily protected habitat and cannot adapt or survive

RIGHT Mature trees, even nonnative ones, are important for structure. Twittering little bushtits weave their remarkable, stretchy pouchlike nests in older trees and shrubs. Often taking over a month to build, they can accommodate the mated pair, their brood, and helpers (often male) who attend the nest.

in the presence of human development. The changes we have wrought make it impossible for many animals to survive, and those that do remain are subjected to many stresses. Besides introduced nonnative species, pollution, impervious surfaces, land fragmentation, and the elimination of important habitat like snags (to name a few), fauna in urban (and, to a slightly lesser extent, suburban) areas have constant noise to contend with. Researchers have found that communication interrupted by noise negatively affects reproduction and can cause unnatural nervous system stimulation, resulting in chronic stress that in turn leads to squandered energy, inadequate feeding, and poor health.

Densely populated areas are also higher in predation and parasites, and natural food can at times be scarce. Other disturbances that may seem small to us can have a devastating impact on biological and behavioral rhythms that are guided by natural cycles of light and dark. For instance, excessive artificial lighting can seriously disrupt the rhythms of animals (and plants). Nocturnal and migrating birds may become disoriented by lights, and the effects on bats are many, including altered feeding behavior, roost abandonment, and a possible increase in being preyed upon. The effects of human activity are immense and have been compared in scale to geographical effects; climate change is beginning to generate additional challenges.

In residential areas, feeding, nesting, and travel are typically affected by how a property is used by people, not merely their presence. The more human activity, the less likely the site will appeal to wildlife, even if the habitat otherwise meets their needs. Though most raptors aren't commonly seen in residential areas, one study found that bald eagles were more stressed by pedestrian activity than by cars, boats, or aircraft. Many other species likely react similarly, since wild animals see people as a potential threat. Other garden-related activities include the air and noise pollution caused by maintenance equipment (gas-powered lawn mowers, whackers, blowers), the presence of companion animals, and the use of pesticides and other poisons.

The species that seem to tolerate our presence well are relatively few, such as gulls and crows. I like to think that the little hummingbird who swoops down to check me out is being friendly or curious, but much more likely she's concerned about her nestlings or her territory. Then there's the pair of chickadees that so diligently bring food to their babies each spring in a nest box nestled in a mini aspen grove in our backyard. Chickadees are known for their tolerance of people, so perhaps they are comfortable with my adoring gaze from just a few yards away, but keeping that distance and moving slowly and quietly certainly helps keep their stress level down.

Of course, most of us enjoy being outdoors and using our outdoor spaces, so compromise is necessary and, fortunately, possible. By concentrating human activity in areas close to the house and using motorized tools only when house maintenance demands it, we can provide wild animals with secluded space away from noise, prying eyes, and pavement. For example, in my urban lot of just under 7,000 square feet—only slightly larger than the average—the intent is to share with other species. In the front yard, we've chucked our lawn and instead grow native and nonnative ornamental plants, as well

# inside the box

Nest boxes are used to provide temporary housing for cavity-nesting birds that normally would reside in snags or decaying live trees. Primary cavity nesters, like woodpeckers, excavate holes themselves in decayed or dead wood, while secondary cavity-nesters (such as bluebirds and tree swallows) use abandoned cavities or cavities formed naturally by decay.

The best way to help cavity-nester populations that are dwindling due to loss of natural habitat is to preserve aging habitat that includes snags. If there are no old trees to preserve in your area, your garden is young, and you've seen these birds and other cavity nesters, like nuthatches, owls, wrens, wood ducks, and chickadees, you may be able to offer them a place to raise their young right now.

Not all cavity nesters will use boxes (or it may take a year or two for them to take advantage), and the boxes can't be just any "birdhouse." They need to be of a size and type appropriate to the species and placed in a situation (usually away from human activity and in morning sunlight) and at a height appropriate to the species; for example, boxes for flickers are much larger than those intended for chickadees or nuthatches, and need to be placed higher. Boxes should be made of thick wood (without preservatives) with ventilation and drainage holes, a perchless entry suitable to the occupants (that also keeps out competitors and predators), and be easy to mount and clean. Boxes for roosting may also be placed to help birds stay warm and dry in winter. Russell

A fledgling chickadee musters up the courage to leave the safety of the nest as mom attempts a feeding. Properly sited, species-appropriate nest boxes can provide nest sites for cavity-nesting birds when mature trees and snags are scarce.

Link's *Landscaping for Wildlife in the Pacific Northwest* provides detailed information on purchasing and building nest boxes for particular species, where and when to site them, and more.

as a couple of espaliered fruit trees parallel to the driveway. Each spring we attach a large nest box for flickers fifteen feet up a towering elm tree, and a birdbath offers water for additional wild guests. In the backyard close to the sunny south side of the house, we have a vegetable and herb garden, small fruit trees, both native and nonnative plants, and gravel pathways edged in reclaimed bricks.

Further south in the backyard, where it is usually the most tranquil, we grow almost nothing but natives, including two (still youthful) native conifers. It's also the location of a second birdbath and a couple of nest boxes for small birds; the little bit of lawn that has escaped my handiwork is cut infrequently with a push mower. Unsurprisingly, it's also where we witness the most wildlife activity—birds foraging, dragonflies and bats hunting, raccoon

Descended from giant relatives 250 million years ago, dragonflies are skillful and efficient hunters of invertebrates. Usually found near water, some, like this female cardinal meadowhawk, venture away to search for prey.

families passing through—viewed mostly from the house with binoculars, or outside when we behave like statues, to cause the least disturbance.

### Conserve existing habitat

Before you decide to remove every plant in your yard because it isn't a Pacific Northwest native species, be sure to keenly evaluate the function of all mature trees and shrubs, even if they are not native. Exotic but noninvasive plants already providing wildlife with food, cover, or a valuable connection to another area should be kept, but phased out gradually, when possible, to minimize disturbance. Large, mature trees, especially conifers, provide structure for roosting and nesting, as well as shade and possibly food; existing understory shrubs may provide food and cover as well. Removing them from green corridors may force animals to find other means of crossing an area, possibly leading them into harmful obstacles.

Preserving such plants still gives you ample opportunity to garden with natives. For example, if an area beneath existing trees and shrubs lacks ground cover or you have removed invasive vegetation in the area, you can quickly develop beautiful woodland garden beds using some of the region's ferns and other shade-tolerant perennials.

### Preserve terrain and enhance transitions

Shady areas, rocky edges, intensely sunny slopes, and wet areas all supply different micro-habitats, and should be viewed as opportunities for increasing diversity and retained whenever possible. Unless an area poses a safety issue, it's best not to significantly alter the natural terrain and instead preserve your yard's contours and landforms. Minimize additions of hardscape (driveways, walks, patios) and make them permeable to water whenever possible.

In sites where the natural terrain has been bulldozed into expanses as flat as this book, however, think about adding some slight elevations and depressions, not only to make things more interesting but to diversify what you will be able to grow. For example, if you've been dreaming of a Garry oak (*Quercus garryana*), which needs quick drainage, siting it on a large berm that prevents water from pooling up may help it thrive. In the low areas surrounding the berm, choose shrubs and perennials that like extra moisture, such as twinberry (*Lonicera involucrata*) and western columbine (*Aquilegia formosa*).

In nature, habitats shift gradually from one to the next, each of them supporting different flora and fauna. Areas where one habitat type blends into another are called *transition zones*, where living conditions appeal to species in both habitats. They are often richly diverse in plants and animals that are known as *edge species*. Creating such gradients in our yards not only accommodates a wide variety of plants but also attracts a diverse range of wildlife that is drawn to those plants.

Most common on residential sites is the transition zone from tree canopy, tall understory shrubs, and low shrubs to ground cover or lawn—somewhat reminiscent of the zone where forest meets meadow or savannah. To mimic this transition area, plant in gradual layers—from tall trees to small trees, to shrubs and ground species—avoiding sudden change. The inclusion of plants that flower and fruit at various times of the year will add to the diversity.

Create privacy and connecting corridors with layering or unclipped hedges.

If you're lucky enough to live next to or near a protected natural area such as a wildlife refuge or conservation area, growing natives on your property will also serve as a *buffer*, an area at the periphery that enhances protection from human activity and perhaps connects fragments. Repairing and preserving such buffers helps wildlife safely travel from one area to another to obtain food, rest, hide from predators, and avoid harsh weather. Such green corridors are of utmost importance on properties in rural areas

Life flourishes in tangles of stems, roots, leaves, and lichens in one seamless passage.

next to wilder terrain, but they are also crucial in urban and suburban areas that have suffered the most ecological damage.

The greater the number of connecting properties, the more an area will facilitate safe travel. Corridors also occur vertically, at all levels—from treetops to lower tree canopies, to shrub and ground layers—and interconnect. Conventional garden designs, which usually include large expanses of lawn, often have few connections between plants, resulting in few linkages for wildlife.

Corridors are best located in quiet zones, away from human activity and well-traveled roads. If your property is on or close to busy or noisy streets, much megafauna activity will likely be lacking, although this can be countered to some extent by the addition of dense plantings away from the street. Often the best place for corridors in suburban or urban areas is toward the back of adjoining yards. The easiest way to provide or add to corridors that offer living space for myriad tiny creatures and undercover routes for larger ones is by simply leaving your yard—especially the wooded areas—untidy (more on this in Chapter 4).

### The hedge connection

Often used as habitat elements in rural and agricultural areas to border fields, hedgerows are usually linear and are immensely superior to fencing because they provide food, shelter, structure, and wildlife travel corridors. We can take lessons from farmers who are increasingly using hedgerows to provide pollen-rich flowers from spring to fall to boost the diversity of native pollinators. In residential situations, we also gain privacy and visual interest. The idea is to think outside the box—boxwood, that is—and not prune (or keep pruning to a bare minimum), to make them most attractive to wildlife.

If you have a large yard, use several different types of shrubs that mature at roughly similar size. Choose species that are native to your area, have similar needs, and have a dense structure. Include at least one evergreen species and others that offer blossoms and berries. The possibilities are almost endless and include serviceberry (*Amelanchier alnifolia*), black hawthorn (*Crataegus douglasii*), red-twig dogwood (*Cornus sericea*), and oceanspray (*Holodiscus discolor*). Traditional hedgerows are much too massive for smaller, urban gardens, but smaller shrubs, like tall Oregon grape (*Mahonia aquifolium*), red-flowering currant (*Ribes sanguineum*), mock orange (*Philadelphus lewisii*), and huckleberries (*Vaccinium* spp.) might work in partly shaded situations. Add a vine that climbs among them for more interest and attraction, and if you have the space, grow smaller plants in front of the hedge to provide for even more species.

## Size Matters

The size of a yard has a great deal to do with how naturalistic you can get. Larger sites with dense and diverse plantings will be most beneficial, but every yard has potential. Although many wild species have space requirements beyond our wildest dreams—even bumblebees can forage up to a mile away—your yard, even if it's small, may be able to provide a home range and a bit of the diversity needed by many species. And what you cannot offer might come from neighboring yards, parks, or more natural spaces. No matter the size, all sites can be functional and attractive.

### Small urban gardens

Typically, unless you rarely leave the house, a small lot—roughly less than 7,500 square feet—will have the most human activity by area. Nevertheless, by organizing activity areas, plants, and other elements, you should be able to provide a retreat for some wildlife. Siting patios and decks, basketball hoops, any lawn you can't live without, and high-maintenance plantings (such as vegetable beds) as close to the house as possible will help allow a quiet spot for birds to feed, bathe, roost, and possibly nest. Edible gardens can serve a dual purpose when used to grow a little food, like sunflowers, for seed-eating birds, and many plants that we value for food, such as blueberries, supply nectar for hummingbirds and native bees.

Wherever possible, plant native species—to provide food and shelter for wildlife and to add shade, privacy, and beauty for you—preferably in a layered effect, as space allows. Native plants can be grown near vegetable beds to invite even more pollinators. The western columbine (*Aquilegia formosa*) seeds that volunteer in my veggie beds are welcome not just because they're gorgeous and provide for hummingbirds, but also because they attract native bumblebees that are needed for optimal pollination of tomato blossoms.

You can also add small brush and/or rock piles in quiet corners and allow fallen leaves to remain on bare soil to provide shelter for small creatures. Ponds don't usually fit in small yards, but consider incorporating a shallow birdbath placed away from predators' hiding places. In immature gardens, post nest boxes for native bees such as mason bees and birds that don't mind human presence, like chickadees (site boxes to receive early morning sunlight and clean them at the end of each season to prevent disease).

If your backyard feels cramped or seems excessively noisy, don't overlook the front (and side) yard as a good place for native plants. Even if the front porch is a summertime hangout and you park your car in the driveway, the remainder may be rarely used and could support much more than just lawn and a few foundation shrubs. Front yards are often fairly quiet, but even if they're not, natives will provide for insects and possibly a few madcap species undaunted by human ways. Although some people don't like the look of edibles in their front yard, native plants seldom look out of place.

If you don't want to revamp the whole thing, consider enlarging your existing beds or borders and adding natives. Beds along foundations are often so narrow that they look poorly proportioned; improve them by adding depth and not situating plants too close to the house. More ambitious? Remove all front lawn, and plant layers of trees, shrubs, and perennials, with stepping-stones for weeding and pruning access. Place a shallow birdbath in a safe, open area, and you will have feathered friends enjoying your front yard in no time.

## Medium-sized yards

Although a medium-sized yard—generally anything from a double city lot up to an acre or so in suburban or rural areas—will likely have quite a bit of human activity, it should be able to support everything a small garden can and then some. Local native plants should replace lawn when possible, particularly if the site is near a natural area. If there is space, small native trees and flowering and fruit-producing shrubs grown into large, unpruned hedgerows will add food, shelter, and nesting potential. Create structural diversity by preserving any snags on the property and adding plentiful brush and rock shelters and dead wood. Consider also adding nest boxes that are size and shape appropriate for the birds and bats in the area. Water is crucial, so provide a birdbath or two, a pond, or a wildlife-friendly drainage area.

## Large gardens

Larger spaces (over an acre) have the most potential for undisturbed habitat, especially if native plants are already in residence. If your acreage has much lawn, it will be best to remove most of it and plant the majority of the site with local native species. Any natural water—streams, wetlands, or ponds—must be preserved in its natural state due to its tremendous value to wildlife. Add groups of large native trees, shrubs, and hedgerows to add privacy, supplement whatever woodland is on the property, and extend connections to aid the safe movement of wildlife. If you're an avid birdwatcher, consider adding a blind so birds won't be bothered by your presence—and for your comfort in inclement weather. To create snags that will offer nesting sites for cavity-nesting

Dominant in many plant communities, oceanspray (*Holodiscus discolor*) is a stunning addition to sunny or partly sunny spots in medium to large gardens.

birds like woodpeckers, consider girdling any invasive, nonnative trees on the property that are safe distances from your house. Minimize the amount of pathways, whether created with stepping-stones, wood chips, straw, or filbert shells (a byproduct of Oregon's filbert industry), to help keep human disturbance to a minimum. If your site is in close proximity to a natural area or was once part of a wetland, consider hiring a qualified botanist or ecological consultant before you attempt any major restoration on your own.

## Best-Laid Plans

Whether you just want to add a few native plants to an existing garden, or restore a whole landscape to its approximate former habitat, you will need to do some planning. An organized approach is important for many reasons and doesn't need to be elaborate, unless you're redesigning your entire yard. Even, and especially, small yards benefit from planning and preparation, since details (and mistakes) are much more visible close-up. Advantages of planning include determining priorities, recognizing issues and ecological relationships you may not have previously considered, allowing for an integrated approach rather than a piecemeal one, and eliminating potentially costly errors in plant choice and placement—mistakes are much cheaper on paper! If you do most or all of the planning yourself, the garden will have your signature, which means it is distinctly yours—no cookie cutters allowed. It will reflect your locale, your inspirations, your likes and dislikes, your needs. Planning should be done before plants are purchased, whenever possible.

## Getting Started

Before you begin your design, spend some time at a nearby natural area that contains native plants, for some inspiration. Depending on where you live, this might be a large urban nature park, a restored greenbelt, a wildlife refuge with hiking trails, or a wilder area; the latter two, in particular, will allow you to see which native species are thriving together and the natural arrangement of the plants. Nurseries, native plant organizations, and soil and water conservation districts may also host demonstration areas and garden tours. Native plant societies offer field trips to see plants in their native settings, where you may also notice nuances in the way some species grow. For example, red huckleberry (*Vaccinium parviflorum*) is usually found growing in partly or mostly shady areas on decaying wood like old stumps or "nurse logs." Many plants that aren't especially drought tolerant, such as alumroot (*Heuchera micrantha*) may survive during the dry months by spreading their roots under large rocks that help retain moisture in the soil. Mimicking such conditions may help your own plants thrive.

In addition, be aware—especially if your property is rural or suburban—that there may be rare plants or animals on your property that could be harmed by landscaping activities. If you are unsure, consult a botanical or restoration professional—it's always safest to err on the side of caution when it comes to vulnerable species.

LEFT Visit nearby natural spaces to learn which plants grow in your area and how they are arranged in nature.

Finally, it's important to do a little reality check to make sure you have a grasp of the variables that determine how much you can do. Both time and money can be saved in the long run if you deal with these issues up front.

**Think about the degree to which you want to change your yard.** Perhaps all your schedule can handle right now is replacing a couple of shrubs, and adding a tree or two and some ground cover. Alternately, you may want to revamp your entire yard, or maybe you've just acquired a yard that is a virtual blank slate. Also think about the purpose of your high-maintenance lawn, if you have one. Front lawns in particular are rarely used, and if that's your situation, shrink its extent by enlarging beds or leaving just enough to act as pathways. Better yet, replace an area of lawn altogether with much more useful habitat—when it comes to lawn, less is better. Install vegetable beds and fruit trees only if you will have the time and energy to tend them.

**Come to terms with your budget.** Start by pondering how much you can spend now versus how much you can invest later on for additional improvements. You'll need funds to prepare the site, buy plant material, and implement the design, as well as for future maintenance. Since the biggest cost of implementing a design is usually labor and because sustainability implies self-sufficiency, consider doing all or some of it yourself. Undertake the tasks incrementally, one part of the yard at a time, to prevent that awful overwhelmed feeling that can come with taking on a large project. Informal native gardens require little long-term maintenance, so unless you plan on a high-maintenance formal design, those costs will likely be very low. Even if finances are not a concern, consider doing at least some of the work yourself—it will bring you closer to sustainability and make your unique garden even more decidedly yours. Of course, gardens are never really finished. No matter how hard you plan, changes will need to be made due to unforeseen issues and conditions, and because of the ever-changing nature of gardens (more on this in the next chapter).

**Consider whether you need or want an irrigation system.** Although many native plants, once established, will not need much supplemental water during the summer months (depending on your location) and may even respond adversely to it, adequate irrigation will be necessary for the first two to five summers, especially if the plants are planted in the spring rather than fall. See Chapter 5 for information about the options.

**Research any homeowner association (HOA) rules and regulations.** HOA rules, which can involve things like color restrictions, fence styles, and plant sizes, may seem set in stone, but could be worth challenging if you feel they are extreme or unreasonable.

### Replacement and Renewal

If you are satisfied with the general layout of your yard and just want to replace a few plants, you won't need to draw up a detailed plan. Whatever existing, nonnative plants you want to replace can simply be swapped with locally adapted substitutes that have similar characteristics (each plant description in the "100 Native Plants" section includes an example or two of what it might replace). You can put together a very basic plan and then install it plant by plant, as they die out, or all at once. It should be possible to make just about any of these changes without a huge investment of time, cash, and sweat, depending on the size of the yard.

Which plants get the pink slip? First on your list should be invasive species, which have been found to be detrimental to the environment. Check your local and/or state or province's list of invasive species if you are unfamiliar with

## stash the cash

You can save money by obtaining healthy plants from friends, buying small-potted plants (which, except for slow-growing trees, will catch up to their bigger siblings in little time), and acquiring seed and propagating plants yourself. Another idea is to install plants on a portion of the site and then use the seeds, seedlings, cuttings, or divisions from those plants to expand to the next area later on (see Chapter 6 for propagation tips). Never collect plants from the wild, unless a site is being developed and the plants growing on it are doomed (in which case you should obtain permission from the landowner or developer). Note, though, that plants dug from the wild often don't survive transplantation. Keep an eye out for discarded plants, too: On several occasions I've rescued large, mature clumps of licorice fern from patches growing on the bark of trees that had been cut down in my neighborhood. And, sometimes people have extra plants that have self-sown in less-than-perfect circumstances—I've potted up and given away quite a few sword ferns that popped up in inappropriate places.

# on cutting down a native tree

Changes in the garden can be wonderful and unexpected, especially when they're natural and so gradual they're barely noticed, or when new plantings lead to new life. Changes can also be nightmarish when they are harsh, sudden, and unnecessary. One day last summer I heard an odd sound near my backyard. I noticed a young man making his way up a neighbor's majestic, eighty-foot-tall ponderosa pine tree with a chainsaw strapped to his body. I asked what he was doing and my worst fears were realized. Shocked and panicking, I called my husband at work, who dropped everything and sped home. A next-door neighbor was already calling his city-employed partner to find out how this atrocity—felling a beloved, perfectly healthy, nondangerous tree that had 200 more years to live—could be happening. I had bumped into a city tree inspector a few months earlier who'd mentioned that he was asked to take a look at the native pine. He found the tree to be healthy and safe and denied the owner's request to eliminate the awesome conifer.

Unfortunately, Portland's tree code had few teeth at the time, and the neighbor had it butchered anyway (Portland's new tree code prevents trees larger than 12 inches in diameter from being killed; this pine's trunk was 4 feet wide). The owner's excuses were nonsensical, and it finally came down to this: The magnificent pine that offered nest sites and food to myriad species and beauty for many humans lost its life because it shed needles.

I couldn't look out my windows without tearing up for a long time—that tree and others nearby were a major reason we had chosen our house. Hardly a day had gone by when we and many others hadn't looked for wild ones on its branches or just given it a smile. Moonlight through the pine? Never again. Birds nesting on its boughs? Never again. Glistening sunlit needles after a spring shower? Never again.

Emotional? You bet. Bottom line: If you're thinking about or know someone who's thinking about taking out a large tree that wild ones or neighbors might value, communicate with the neighbors and consult a trusted, reputable tree expert (not someone who could benefit financially from the removal) and take their advice. There are usually options to prevent the loss of mature trees that are invaluable ecologically and aesthetically.

> *... Its cutting down plundered us all*
> *The comely shrub whose bounty fed the birds,*
> *Its like never grew out of the ground;*
> *Till my very death it will cause me grief.*
>
> —from *On Cutting Down an Ancient Tree,*
> by Laoiseach Mac an Bhaird

# let it rain

As landscapes become more urbanized, impervious surfaces like roofs, driveways, roads, and parking lots prevent rain and storm water from infiltrating underground aquifers and springs. Runoff and toxic contaminants from such hardscape overwhelm sewer systems and pollute waterways, harming aquatic life. Rain gardens help counteract this by collecting and absorbing runoff, filtering and cleansing it in the process. Intended to withstand moisture extremes, rain gardens are typically designed as shallow depressions with deep-rooted plants that like to have their feet wet. Strategically sited near the source of the runoff, they allow water more time to seep into the soil and release it slowly, preventing erosion and flooding.

Rain gardens can provide wildlife habitat, particularly for insects like bees and butterflies, as well as birds. They can be crafted into beautiful features or be integrated almost seamlessly into a landscape. Plants in the lowest, central portion (where water may temporarily accumulate) must be tolerant of flood conditions as well as some dry periods. Wetland plants that have adapted to living in saturated soil, and riparian species that grow adjacent to rivers and streams, are often suitable candidates for these areas of the rain garden. Plants on the upper edges should thrive in drier soil but tolerate seasonal wet conditions.

Like all thoughtful landscaping, rain gardens may increase your home's value. Incentive programs and educational workshops, available in many areas, make rain garden installations

ABOVE Streetscapes: Urban rain gardens collect, slow, cleanse, and filter storm water from streets, parking lots, and sidewalks. The first of its kind, this award-winning storm water retrofit in Portland brims with native plants. RIGHT This swale directs and absorbs water from a downspout disconnected from a city sewer system.

easy. For technical information on creating a low maintenance rain garden, consult the guides in the Resources section; check local and state requirements that may apply to your project.

A disconnected downspout leads to a planter.

- Are diseased or dying (although consider retaining dying trees as snags)
- Take up space where a larger, more useful tree or shrub could grow
- Represent no emotional bond (it's not the rose you planted when your beloved kitty died)

And which do you keep? Preserve mature trees that aren't invasive species. Never take out large, healthy trees—especially native species—for frivolous reasons, like wanting more sunlight or tiring of fallen leaves. There are exceptions, of course. Every fall, fruit ripening on our two large fig trees (or not, depending on the weather) drops from count-less branches out of our reach—it makes a goopy mess, but it breaks down quickly and eventually enriches the soil below. Though the ripening fruit attracts many species for about a month each year, everything from wasps to flickers to huge flocks of cedar waxwings, I'm in the process of replacing one of the trees with a native tree that provides year-round food and cover. The other one will stay, since removing it would eliminate privacy, the woodland plants underneath that depend on it for shade would suffer, and the birds would miss it.

which ones are problematic in your area (see Resources). When deciding which additional plants should be removed and replaced, choose those that are nonnative *and* fall under one or more of the following categories:

- Offer little or no habitat for wildlife and are not part of a wildlife corridor
- Require large amounts of water and/or maintenance
- Grow in an inappropriate place (such as a huge shrub growing into a walkway)

Noninvasive shrubs and perennials that aren't native also may not need to go, as long as they have value to wildlife or yourself. Keep those that provide habitat for wildlife, and those that you are madly in love with. Also keep snags, which provide tremendous value to wildlife as nesting and perching sites, as well as food; potentially dangerous limbs may be removed for safety purposes. Fallen trees on large properties should also be left as shelter for wildlife.

Here are suggestions for what to do, when to do it, and in what order, if you're mainly replacing some existing nonnatives with native species:

1. **Remove all invasive plants.** Some, like Himalayan blackberry, may need to be dug out more than once before replanting is possible. If the area is relatively small, you can cover it with light-blocking, weed-barrier fabric between removals (which gets easier each year!). Don't use water-impermeable plastic—the idea is to shade out the plant, not kill the soil organisms.

2. **Determine soil type and pH.** Knowing your soil type and how acid or alkaline it is may help you choose plants and assess whether you will need to amend the soil with anything other than organic matter (see Chapter 4).

3. **Make a list of the plants you've decided to remove, and come up with native replacements** (see Chapter 3 and "100 Native Plants"). Generally, if you liked the look and size of what you removed, choose a native species that possesses some of the same attributes, such as fall color, flower color, leaf texture, and branch pattern, but only if conditions match the replacement plant's needs.

4. **Remove the plants you've decided to take out,** preferably in fall, when the soil is still warm and unsaturated, to minimize damage; working cold, wet soil destroys its structure.

5. **Amend soil with organic matter** (or simply apply it as a mulch, after planting), as described in Chapter 4.

6. **Plant trees and shrubs first, then perennials including ground cover.** For proper planting instructions, see Chapter 4. If vines are on your list, be sure ample support is in place before plants are tucked in the ground.

7. **Water well, then mulch the newly planted areas.** A couple of inches of compost will provide nutrients along with other benefits, but aged bark or fallen leaves may be used instead. Placing fallen leaves on top of compost is even better, as the leaves will further protect the soil during winter. Keep all mulches several inches from tree and shrub trunks and off the crowns of perennials, to prevent rot.

8. **Leave some logs and branches in piles on the ground** in out-of-the-way places, to provide structural habitat and to slowly return nutrients to the soil as the wood decays.

## The Whole Nine Yards

If you are starting with a blank canvas, there is little existing plant material in your yard, or you will be removing a large section of lawn, it is best to draw up a planting plan for the entire yard. Though you may not implement the whole plan at once, it's a good idea to design the whole area—front, sides, and back—on paper, at the same time. Creating a full design will help you maintain unity and determine the best placement for all the features you want to include. Otherwise, you may end up playing musical chairs with plants and other garden elements later on.

I recommend drawing up a series of four plans—each with a specific purpose that leads to the next plan—which culminate in your planting plan. In addition to the following descriptions of each plan are sample illustrations, which should help you visualize what

## sun maps

Some plants need quite a bit of sun to thrive, while others need nearly full shade; many fall somewhere in the middle. To help you decide what types of plants you will be able to grow in particular locations, and to determine the best site for items like compost heaps or bins that should be shielded from prolonged direct sun and excessive rain, add a north arrow to your drawings, to help determine your site's exposure to sunlight. If you have trouble figuring out sun patterns, draw a "sun map," recording where the sun is every four hours or so. Keep in mind that the sun's position will vary with the seasons, so sun and shade patterns will vary seasonally too.

### *Base map*

The creation of a base map or plot plan is the initial step in your design process. It should consist of a scaled, bird's-eye-view drawing (what designers call *plan view*) with the following elements in reasonably accurate placement:

→ Property lines
→ The house, with windows and doors indicated
→ Hard surfaces such as driveways and walkways
→ Any dramatic elevation changes
→ Water sources
→ Utility meters and poles
→ Fences or walls
→ Any other permanent features or obstacles

yours might look like and perhaps even give you some ideas.

To draw your plans, you will need a steady work surface, paper (graph paper is helpful), pencils and eraser, a ruler, and a triangle or T-square (if not using graph paper). Tracing paper will help you create subsequent drawings, or you can simply make several photocopies of your first drawing—the base map—for later use. (If you already have and are proficient in a CAD program, or you enjoy learning new software, you may prefer to use it rather than hand drawing.)

Choose a scale of ⅛ to ¼ inch for each foot of outdoor space, the latter for small gardens. If using graph paper, let one square equal a certain number of feet. Draw it large enough that there is space for labels, symbols, and other notations.

To save time and effort, or if you're unsure of your property lines, try to locate site plans, surveys, or accurate plats that may have been done in the past—such information should be available from your city or county's property records department or, for newer homes, from the builder or developer. There may also be physical survey markers in the ground at the corners of your property from previous land surveys.

If you think you will be building anything on your property, even just a shed, a short retaining wall, or a blind to view wildlife, check zoning ordinances and building codes for setback regulations and other issues that may affect your plans—you may need to obtain a variance. Zoning and building codes often revolve around safety issues such as fire equipment access and placement of railings on elevated balconies and decks. Also check to see if your community has guidelines for tree planting: Many municipalities require permits to remove, plant, or prune (above and below ground) trees in parking strips (that public strip of land between street and sidewalk) and on private property.

It also helps to communicate with your neighbors, especially if you think there could be "issues." We had an interesting situation arise when a former neighbor decided, unbeknownst to us, to take down a mature vine maple tree and build a garden folly at the extreme far end of his lot, which borders ours. Besides considering the 14-foot-tall structure visually intrusive, we were surprised to learn that the neighbor had not researched the property line location and actually intended to build the structure partly on our lot. Had our properties been in a historic district it would have been illegal to build such a structure at all; we had to settle for the legal setback requirement of 5 feet from the property line.

### Site inventory and analysis

Next, take some time—possibly as long as several months or seasons—to get to know your property, as well as the surrounding area. Grab a clipboard, pencil, and paper and do what designers call a *site inventory and analysis*, which will give you an opportunity to take stock of what is currently in place and make observations of existing conditions that may be helpful when drawing your plans. As you become familiar with your yard's issues and potential, you'll be prepared to respond to the unique conditions of the site.

First, make a list of any special physical qualities of your site that you think will influence the design and directly affect wildlife, such as nest sites or burrows, wildlife pathways, dead wood, water sources, and mature trees and other plants that are used for food or cover. If you need help identifying plants in your yard, consult a guidebook or take samples to a nursery, botanic garden, or native plant society event.

Second, jot down the physical things that may affect you and others who live on the property, including issues that you think should be addressed, such as lack of privacy, an eyesore that you want screened from view, or soil considerations, such as poor drainage or erosion (note that retaining walls over 3 feet tall require a structural engineer). Also note positive elements or qualities that you think should be retained or enhanced, such as a view you would like to preserve, mature trees that provide shade for your house and yard, or shrubs that attract native bees and other pollinators to your vegetable beds. If you notice anything positive or negative in adjacent yards or streets, such as an ugly fence or street noise that needs to be buffered, include that as well. Also decide whether it's feasible to disconnect downspouts that transport rainwater from your roof to a sewer system that can become overwhelmed during storms, leading to overflows of raw sewage and other pollution into waterways, killing wildlife. Rain gardens, slightly sunken areas of various size that are planted with flora that tolerate wet conditions, are one way to mitigate excess storm water.

Be sure to also note any *microclimates*, areas where temperature and light may differ—sometimes dramatically—from other areas just a few feet away. Microclimates vary from cool, shady, dry spots (often the result of dense shadows from neighboring trees, buildings, or hedges) to hot areas that are exposed to prolonged, direct summer sunlight. A slope that receives sun most of the day will dry out faster than a flat area in sun. Light colors reflect heat, so houses painted white tend to increase the air temperature nearby, particularly in sheltered locations. Walls, fences, and hedges may also encourage frost pockets or erratic winds, or may decrease air circulation in some situations. Low-lying areas can be damp or wet, especially in very heavy soils, and dry bands usually occur under houses and other buildings with wide eaves. If you have any of these situations, be sure to note them. In windy areas, determine which direction prevailing winds come from, to help decide whether windbreaks might be necessary.

Figure 1. Base map with inventory analysis

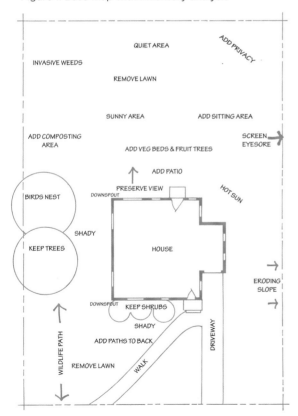

Now, analyze what you want from your site by listing activities you enjoy regularly outdoors or plan to in the future, like dining, entertaining, bird watching, or hosting badminton tournaments. Do you want a kitchen garden in a sunny spot, other edibles like fruit trees and shrubs, a play area for children or companion animals, a quiet retreat for reading, or space for a clothesline? Don't forget about a service area for recycling bins and those all-important compost bins. All these items—the special physical qualities you want to address, microclimates, and the things you want to be able to do in your yard—should be added to your base map (Fig. 1)

### Functional diagram

The next step in the design process is the functional diagram (Fig. 2). You will likely want to make several of these, by tracing over your base map or photocopying it. These drawings will help you brainstorm different configurations and circulation pathways and ways to subdivide your yard into smaller areas. Colored pencils may be helpful for delineating these components. Play around with "bubble diagrams" in which rough circles are drawn around spaces and then labeled with your ideas. For example, you may want to have bubbles that delineate where there will be human activities, such as a patio area surrounded by a berry patch where fruit is just an arm's reach away, or that propose protected, quiet areas for wildlife.

Other ideas might include a rock garden in a sunny spot to attract pollinators, or a rain garden that accepts water from a disconnected downspout. Also consider traffic patterns, including existing primary pathways and whether they will be kept or eliminated.

A few more tips for creating your functional diagram:

→ Keep the most frequented areas (dining areas, herb gardens, children's play areas) close to the house, for convenience and to allow quiet areas for wildlife.

→ The most practical pathways are the shortest ones, such as from kitchen to herb garden or front door to mailbox; the most interesting ones, on the other hand, meander through and offer a tour of the garden.

→ Secondary, infrequently used pathways may be needed to access areas for weed-

ing and other purposes, but keep them to a minimum to increase seclusion for wildlife.

After you've come up with at least a couple of scenarios of how to lay out your property, think them over awhile. One configuration might seem perfect right away, or you may want to blend parts of one and parts of another into something that works best.

### Preliminary plan

With your final functional diagram done, you can now create the third drawing, the more detailed preliminary plan, a refined functional layout (without all the bubbles) that also indicates the general location of plant material (Fig. 3). The purpose of this plan is to decide on the location of new plant groupings, pathways, and other garden elements.

At this point you still aren't selecting specific plants, just the *types* of plants. For example, there may be notations for several tall evergreen shrubs in an area that needs screening from a neighbor's outdoor light, a shade-tolerant perennial bed on the north side of the house with a stepping-stone path through it, a couple of conifer trees to add privacy from the street, and a chickadee nest box on a pole (to keep predators at bay and for easy cleaning) in a native bed near an existing birch tree that receives morning sun. You can also draw in symbols for any benches, birdbaths, arbors, and that sundial you picked up at an estate sale last year, some of which could be used as focal points.

In addition to working at a bird's-eye view, some people find they can visualize things more dimensionally and work on scale and balance more easily by combining photographs and

**Figure 2. Functional diagram**

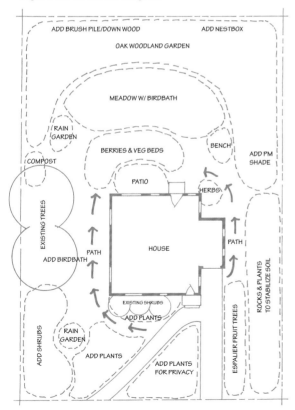

Figure 3. Preliminary plan

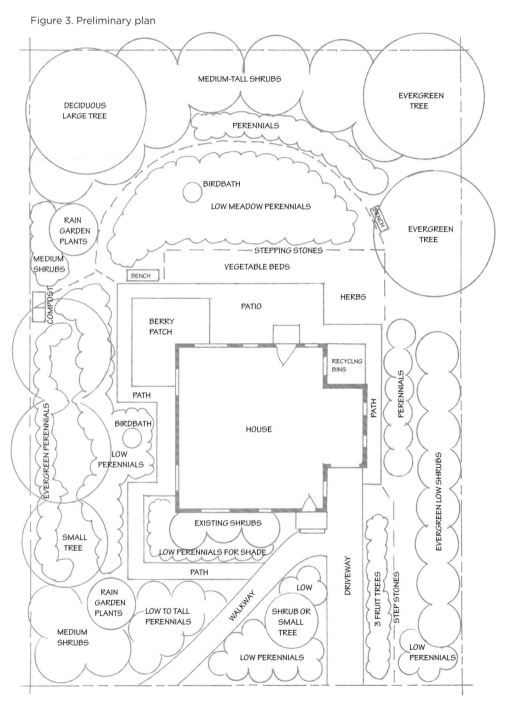

MEDIUM-TALL SHRUBS

DECIDUOUS
LARGE TREE

EVERGREEN
TREE

PERENNIALS

BIRDBATH

LOW MEADOW PERENNIALS

RAIN
GARDEN
PLANTS

BENCH

EVERGREEN
TREE

MEDIUM
SHRUBS

STEPPING STONES

VEGETABLE BEDS

BENCH

HERBS

COMPOST

PATIO

BERRY
PATCH

RECYCLNG
BINS

PATH

EVERGREEN PERENNIALS

BIRDBATH

PATH

PERENNIALS

LOW
PERENNIALS

HOUSE

EVERGREEN LOW SHRUBS

SMALL
TREE

EXISTING SHRUBS

LOW PERENNIALS FOR SHADE

PATH

RAIN
GARDEN
PLANTS

LOW TO TALL
PERENNIALS

LOW

WALKWAY

SHRUB OR
SMALL
TREE

DRIVEWAY

3 FRUIT TREES

STEP STONES

MEDIUM
SHRUBS

LOW PERENNIALS

LOW
PERENNIALS

drawings. Simply print out some of the photographs you've taken of your yard and sketch over the photos to figure out how different plant forms and other features might look. You can also take a pair of scissors to a print and cut out what you want to alter and then draw in, on attached paper, what you intend to add. It's low-tech but easy, and a good supplement to plan views.

This is also a good time to think about materials for patios, paths, arbors, fencing, or other nonliving elements. Check the source of any new lumber bought for the garden to be sure it comes from sustainably managed plantations. Avoid chemically treated products, tropical hardwoods, or any lumber that may contribute to the loss of natural forests. Whenever possible, create paths, driveways, and patios out of materials that allow water to be absorbed rather than run off, such as stones, bricks, or other pavers set in sand, instead of impermeable materials like concrete slabs or mortared stone. Secondary paths that are seldom used might be stepping-stones, grass that is mowed infrequently, or filbert shells. To help visualize things, get outside and note potential locations for these elements, along with the larger plants. Be sure to take the time to explore all the possibilities now, since making changes on paper is much easier and cheaper than doing it later, after the plan is implemented. Plants are usually easy to transplant or replace within a year or so, but other materials require much more effort.

Confused? Overwhelmed? That's perfectly natural, considering all the information and elements you need to review. But once you move toward the finer details, it will likely come together. If things aren't moving smoothly, you may need to reevaluate something discussed earlier or take a long break and come back to it later. You might even ask someone else to look at your plans and sketches—sometimes all it takes is a fresh pair of eyes to sort things out. Don't give up now, because you are almost at the point of selecting your plants. You can do this!

### Final planting plan

Your final drawing is the eagerly awaited planting plan (Fig. 4), which indicates the location and approximate spread of the plants, as well other elements on your base map. A dot at the center of each plant marks its planting position. Tree outlines should be simple (since plants under trees need to be shown), but thick, to indicate their size. Plants that are grassy or heavily textured are typically drawn as spikey or zigzaggy outlines, and other plants' outlines can be varied to differentiate them. Bulbs

## garden photos

Snap some photographs—for use when you're indoors drafting your garden plan on a rainy day, or to enlarge and trace over if you decide to do some ground-level views (known as *side elevations*) from selected vantage points. Such views might include the front entrance area, your yard as seen from the street, and the back of the house as seen from the rear of the yard. Also take shots from the patio, porch, or deck, and from the interior at your favorite or most commonly looked-through window. "Before" photos are also fun to look at later, to see how far you've come.

## Figure 4. Final planting plan

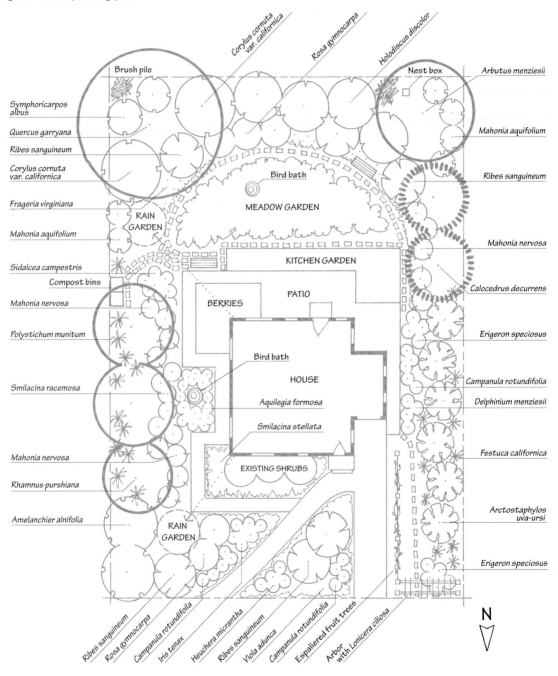

Corylus cornuta
var. californica

Rosa gymnocarpa

Holodiscus discolor

Brush pile

Nest box

Arbutus menziesii

Symphoricarpos
albus

Mahonia aquifolium

Quercus garryana

Ribes sanguineum

Ribes sanguineum

Corylus cornuta
var. californica

Bird bath

Frageria virginiana

MEADOW GARDEN

RAIN
GARDEN

Mahonia aquifolium

Mahonia nervosa

Sidalcea campestris

KITCHEN GARDEN

Compost bins

Calocedrus decurrens

Mahonia nervosa

BERRIES

PATIO

Polystichum munitum

Erigeron speciosus

Bird bath

Smilacina racemosa

HOUSE

Campanula rotundifolia

Aquilegia formosa

Delphinium menziesii

Smilacina stellata

Mahonia nervosa

Festuca californica

EXISTING SHRUBS

Rhamnus purshiana

Amelanchier alnifolia

Arctostaphylos
uva-ursi

RAIN
GARDEN

Erigeron speciosus

Ribes sanguineum

Rosa gymnocarpa

Campanula rotundifolia

Iris tenax

Heuchera micrantha

Ribes sanguineum

Viola adunca

Campanula rotundifolia

Espaliered fruit trees

Arbor
with Lonicera ciliosa

N

or other flora planted "*en masse*" are usually shown only roughly, using dots, Xs or hatching.

I like to initially do a rough planting plan on tracing paper over the preliminary plan, sketching in only approximately sized circles for plants. For example, for an area that is located just north of some fifty-foot-tall conifers within a fairly large site near the Columbia Gorge, I would draw in circles that stand for smaller deciduous trees that can tolerate the shade cast by the evergreen trees, interspersed with slightly smaller circles representing a mix of understory evergreen and deciduous shrubs, followed by circles that stand for shade-tolerant perennials at ground level. Ground covers that will spread would be represented by some consistent symbol like squiggles or stipple marks.

Next, I'd decide which locally adapted, associated plants with similar needs will do best in the current conditions. In this case, it might be vine maple trees (*Acer circinatum*), California hazelnut (*Corylus cornuta* var. *californica*),

LEFT This sample planting plan for an upland Willamette Valley site uses mostly plant community members that likely existed pre-development. If extensive disturbance has resulted in soil and water conditions that can no longer support such plants, consider choosing a plant community that fits those conditions. Plants in the meadow garden include *Achillea millefolium* var. *occidentalis, Allium acuminatum, Camassia quamash, Delphinium menziesii, Dodecatheon hendersonii, Erigeron speciosus, Erythronium oregonum, Festuca californica, Penstemon serrulatus,* and *Sidalcea campestris.* The rain gardens contain *Aquilegia formosa, Carex aurea, Deschampsia cespitosa, Iris tenax, Potentilla gracilis, Polystichum munitum,* and *Symphyotrichum subspicatum.*

salal (*Gaultheria shallon*), and red huckleberry (*Vaccinium parviflorum*) shrubs, and perennials and ground cover like goatsbeard (*Aruncus dioicus*), deer fern (*Blechnum spicant*), false solomon's seal (*Smilacina racemosa*), inside-out flower (*Vancouveria hexandra*), and western trillium (*Trillium ovatum*). With the plants decided upon, I'd retrace the final plan onto heavier but translucent paper that's easier to work with (such as vellum), using more exact circle sizes that indicate the mature spread of each chosen plant. For example, using a scale of ⅛ inch = 1 foot, a large shrub that will mature at about 16 feet wide would be represented by a circle that is 2 inches wide. This step ensures that growing conditions won't get too crowded or remain too sparse; when in doubt, err on the side of closeness.

Plants should then be labeled, either by printing in the plan's margins and using arrows to point to the circle that represents the plant or, more simply, with a key. To do this, make a list of your chosen plants and give each a letter or symbol, then mark each circle that represents a plant with the appropriate letter or symbol. Your plant list, which should include botanical names, can also be used as a shopping list when you're ready to buy plants.

## Naturalistic Composition

In the next chapter you'll learn about choosing plants to mimic natural plant communities, but how do you arrange the plants to make your site look appealing and be ecologically functional? Once again, look to nature, this time to borrow from nature's beauty secrets and ingenious compositions. Although we tend to arrange plants according to human aesthetics and usually want to have more seasonal

# designing with less

If your design includes a new patio, deck, arbor, or pathway, take a minimalist approach. Using salvaged or recycled materials, responsibly removing waste, and avoiding chemically treated materials are all important parts of sustainable gardening. And as your needs and the garden's needs change over time, be adaptable and willing to reconfigure the areas that may require it.

- Reuse and recycle: Figure out if there are any materials that can be reused or recycled, from pavers and rock to lumber and hardware.
- Waste less, gain more: When using new materials, reduce waste by measuring carefully and, whenever possible, using whole pieces of milled lumber or sheet materials. Instead of a solid wooden fence, consider a more open design that uses less lumber and allows plants, such as vines, to grow on it; open fencing also allows more air circulation, which is important for plants. Making pathways narrower in the wilder parts of the garden will require fewer materials. Setting bricks or stone into sand negates the need for mortar and the waste that accompanies it, and horizontal surfaces will be more permeable to rainwater as well.

- Contemplating an outdoor kitchen or firepit? If just a grill would suffice, let it go at that, and use the space for plants instead.
- Minimize and plan waste removal: If you need to remove unwanted materials like concrete, communicate with your waste hauler or contractor about the most environmentally responsible way to manage such waste. And remember that one person's trash may be another's treasure.
- Be adaptable: Consider how a garden might evolve over time and be configured so that it can be used in several ways to minimize impact. For example, situating your popular vegetable garden and a toddler's grassy play area (which will later be turned into a native pollinator garden) near the house keeps that space functional while allowing for quieter areas.

interest than the arrangements found in natural habitats, we can still emulate nature through informal and natural patterns of growth that will also help out wildlife much more than a conventional garden would.

In open areas such as prairie or meadows, plants are mixed with many other species in what is termed a mosaic effect—it looks random but isn't. Wildflowers often grow in drifts, with one species dominant in some areas and other species dominant in others. This is counter to conventional planting, in which plants are often grouped in rows or stands of single species. Whether we plant in clumps or more irregular-looking drifts, it's best for plants like perennials and small shrubs to be placed so that there is a high density of a species within a small area, rather than spreading them out over a wide area. Research has shown that siting numerous plants of the same species close together is more obvious to pollinators and provides better forage than when they are placed far apart.

Sometimes plants will pick themselves to be the dominant type. In damaged areas such as roadsides, deforested land, and urban zones, some plants are able to take hold and begin the process of ecological succession, which leads to a more diverse and balanced system. Some of these native pioneer types can be a bit assertive when used out of their historic range or in gardens that are irrigated in summer, such as fringecup (*Tellima grandiflora*), which may shade out small plants that begin growth later in the spring. But many are not: I continually cheer on my little pioneering evergreen violet plants (*Viola sempervirens*), which spread at a snail's pace each year (unlike the nonnative violets that I can't seem to discourage). Although enthusiastic pioneer species are part of the ecosystem and shouldn't be considered weeds, it's often a good idea in small gardens to choose plants that don't have a strong tendency to spread quickly.

Other ways to make gardens look less artificial is by the placement of rocks that look like they belong. Place large, indigenous rocks in naturalistic groupings in rock gardens, on slopes, or anywhere you want to prevent erosion, add a little solid interest, or break up lines. Smaller rocks arranged together can give a worn and weathered impression. Bury rocks at least halfway in the ground to make them look like they've been there awhile and to keep them stable. Grow irregular drifts of plants that will eventually meld into the gaps and crevices between the rocks.

## How Far Apart?

When considering how far apart to space plants, remember that nature is not a minimalist! Aim for continuous cover—so there is more vegetation for wildlife and to lessen the space in which weeds can sprout. The two exceptions: Leave some bare soil for ground-nesting bees, and keep at least a 3-foot plant-free radius around young trees that are just getting established, because other plants in their root zone compete for moisture and nutrients. Site new plants a few feet from established trees and shrubs as well, and minimize damage to existing roots at planting time; some plants, such as serviceberry (*Amelanchier alnifolia*), don't do well with close competition.

A few placement tips:

→ Group plants with similar light, moisture, and soil needs in the same area.

→ Tree placement is dependent on mature size and type. Most trees need at least 15 feet of space to achieve an ample root system and a natural form, and to prevent the shading of other trees nearby that need sun.

→ Place trees at least 5 feet from property lines and sidewalks, farther away from walkways if the tree produces messy fruit. Large trees should be at least 10 feet from buildings.

→ To provide shade and keep your house cooler in summer, optimal tree placement is 10 to 25 feet from the west or southwest side of your house. Trees planted to the east or southeast will be second best. Since most heat enters through windows (not roofs and walls) when the sun isn't at its peak, placing trees directly to the south of a house doesn't provide shade when it's

needed most. The taller your house, the taller the trees will need to be.

→ For continuous cover, place shrubs and perennials their mature width apart. For example, 6-foot-wide shrubs would be placed roughly 6 feet apart from center to center.

→ Ground cover plants may be placed 1 to 3 feet apart, depending on how vigorous their rate of growth is.

→ Shrubs at the end of driveways and in urban parking strips near intersections can be safety hazards, so limit plants in these areas to those that mature at no more than 3 feet in height. Trees may be fine if their trunks are free of vegetation below 7 or 8 feet.

To help you decide which plants to choose, read through the next chapter, which describes different types of plants and their roles, regional choices, and some things to keep in mind when choosing plants. Return to the natural area you visited at the beginning of the planning process, if necessary, to refresh your memory about which native plants are growing there. Then review flora in the 100 Native Plants section that will thrive in the light, soil, and moisture conditions of your site, taking into consideration any microclimate and topography issues.

LEFT Native meadow garden wildflowers bump heads but keep a balance.

# CHAPTER 3
## *selecting the right plants*

"It never will rain roses: when we want
to have more roses we must plant more trees."
—George Eliot, *The Spanish Gypsy*

**CHOOSING PLANTS CAN BE ENJOYABLY PERSONAL, SINCE** we all have unique likes and dislikes, as well as different conditions in our yards. But it can also be confusing, or even frustrating, due to the gigantic array of plants available at garden shops and nurseries. Or downright boring if you shop for plants at big-box stores that sell only the dozen nonnative plants that seem to be in every yard.

In some ways, native or partially native gardens make the selection process much easier. First, not all Pacific Northwest native plants thrive in garden settings—some, like orchids, need such exacting conditions that growing them at home is difficult if not impossible. Second, nurseries generally offer a fraction of the species that exist naturally in the region, leaving us with hundreds of choices instead of thousands. By basing your choices on what will thrive in your yard's conditions and be size appropriate for your space, you reduce the selection even further.

When you choose to grow species that are part of your area's historic plant community, the field is narrowed further. I find that it also helps to choose plants—at least the dominant ones—that

Nootka rose (*Rosa nutkana*)

make my heart go pitter-patter. Good relationships, whether within ecosystems or between humans, require some chemistry. If you choose plants that for some reason don't appeal to you, or someone gives you a plant that doesn't grow on you, you won't be as inclined to give it whatever care it needs, however low maintenance it may be.

With all these limitations, it may sound like there are few plants left to choose from, but that's far from the case. "100 Native Plants for the Garden" presents the most garden-friendly and ecologically beneficial natives that are fairly easy to grow and find, along with many related species, many of which might be members of the natural plant community that originally took root in your area. And there are other contenders that just didn't make it to these pages.

## It Takes a Community

The region this book pertains to is bounded on the west by the Pacific Ocean and on the east by the crest of the Cascade Mountain range in Washington and Oregon and the Coast Mountains in British Columbia, and reaches from southwestern British Columbia to the northern Californian border. Although there's a general similarity in climate throughout the region due to the ocean's influence and prevailing westerly winds, it is somewhat diverse in precipitation, topography, and soil composition.

For these reasons, a wide variety of plants grow in various habitats. Much of what is indigenous to and thrives in the Victoria, BC, area, will be different from what is found in Camas, Washington. Some plant species, however, occur nearly everywhere in the region, but at varying elevations and latitudes—typically a species that is found at low elevations in British

Columbia or northern Washington will be found at higher elevations farther south. Other species are exclusively local or rare, such as certain wildflowers that are found only in the Columbia Gorge, and those that grow at narrow elevation levels.

Knowing something about the places where native plants grow naturally may help you select plants and play matchmaker. To describe and delineate general plant communities, ecologists have come up with vegetation zones, designated with varying terminology and categorized in many ways. These zones are determined by their climate, soils, and geography, as well as relationships among living things.

In our region there are interior valleys, forested areas that can be further subdivided, timberline and alpine areas, and transitional wetlands. Each zone is named according to the general plant material that occurs there naturally, or to the characteristic plants it supports, especially one or several of them that are dominant under certain conditions (Map 1). Such "climax species" are at the tail end of species succession; they compete well with other plants because they are often shade tolerant, and they stay dominant until a site is disturbed. Here is information, historic and current, on each zone west of the Cascades:

**Sitka Spruce Zone:** A fog-shrouded, coniferous zone extending at low elevations from Vancouver Island to southwestern Oregon, within about fifty miles of the coast and its inlets. Originally dominated by Sitka spruce (*Picea sitchensis*), this extensively damaged area is now dominated by Douglas-fir (*Pseudotsuga menziesii*) and western hemlock (*Tsuga heterophylla*). Wetter areas may support

## Map 1: Historic Vegetation Zones

- Mixed Conifer / Broadleaf Evergreen Zones
- Western Hemlock Zone
- Subalpine Forest Zones
- Sitka Spruce Zone
- Grand Fir / Douglas-Fir Zones
- Coastal Douglas-Fir Zone
- Western Redcedar Zone
- Engelmann Spruce Subalpine Fir Zones
- Wetlands (herbaceous or riparian)
- Savanna / Prairie / Wetland Zones
- Alpine Province Zone
- Oak & Douglas-Fir Woodlands Zone
- Steppe Zones
- Desert Shrub Zone
- Big Sagebrush Zone
- Western Juniper Zone
- Rogue and Umpqua Forest / Shrub Zones
- Ponderosa Pine Zone

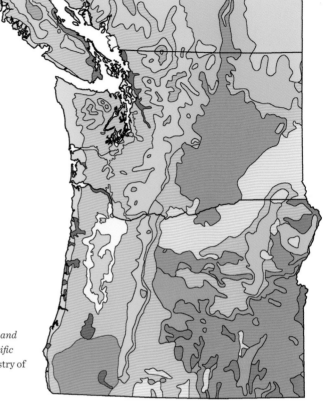

Adapted from *Wildlife-Habitat Relationships in Oregon and Washington* (Johnson and O'Neil 2001), *Atlas of the Pacific Northwest* (Jackson and Kimerling 2003), and BC Ministry of Forests, Lands, and Natural Resource Operations.

western redcedar (*Thuja plicata*), bigleaf maple (*Acer macrophyllum*), shore pine (*Pinus contorta*), vine maple (*Acer circinatum*),and red alder (*Alnus rubra*). Shrub layers include salal (*Gaultheria shallon*), salmonberry (*Rubus spectabilis*), Oregon grape (*Mahonia aquifolium*), and red and evergreen huckleberries (*Vaccinium parviflorum* and *V. ovatum*). Herbaceous species include sword fern (*Polystichum munitum*), deer fern (*Blechnum spicant*), vanilla leaf (*Achlys triphylla*), and sorrel (*Oxalis* spp.). Urbanized areas and Douglas-fir plantations are prevalent in this intensively logged and managed landscape.

**Western Hemlock Zone:** Comprising the Coast Range and the western Cascades from British Columbia to southwest Oregon, this zone is characterized by both western hemlock (*Tsuga heterophylla*) and Douglas-fir (*Pseudotsuga menziesii*). Ponderosa pine (*Pinus ponderosa*), incense cedar (*Calocedrus decurrens*), western redcedar (*Thuja plicata*), red alder (*Alnus rubra*), and bigleaf maple (*Acer macrophyllum*) may succeed in disturbed sites. Grand fir (*Abies grandis*) is found in some sections and Pacific silver fir (*Abies amabilis*) grows only in the wettest part of the western Olympic Peninsula. Shore pine (*Pinus contorta* var. *contorta*) and Douglas-fir with madrone (*Arbutus menziesii*) are found in the Puget Lowland. Associated subcanopy species include cascara (*Rhamnus purshiana*) and vine maple (*Acer circinatum*) on moist sites and Pacific yew (*Taxus brevifolia*) on well-drained sites. Salal (*Gaultheria shallon*), Pacific rhododendron (*Rhododendron macrophyllum*), red elderberry (*Sambucus racemosa*), huckleberries (*Vaccinium* spp.), Cascade Oregon grape (*Mahonia nervosa*), deer fern (*Blechnum spicant*), beargrass (*Xerophyllum tenax*), inside-out flower (*Vancouveria* spp.), and sorrel (*Oxalis* spp.) may appear in the understory. Industrial logging greatly damaged this zone, resulting in Douglas-fir plantations with low tree canopy diversity and the removal of trees in early growth stages. Just a fraction of old-growth forest remains, and it continues to disappear.

**Subalpine Forest Zones:** This complex of zones occurs in the upland forests of the mountains of British Columbia, the Cascades, and the Olympics. It is dominated by evergreen conifers including Pacific silver fir (*Abies amabilis*) and noble fir (*Abies procera*) from central Washington to central Oregon at lower subalpine elevations, with mountain hemlock (*Tsuga mertensiana*) and subalpine fir (*Abies lasiocarpa*) occurring sparsely in high-elevation open meadows. Dominant understory shrubs include huckleberries (*Vaccinium membranaceum*, *V. ovalifolium*, and *V. deliciosum*), Cascade rhododendron (*Rhododendron albiflorum*), salal (*Gaultheria shallon*), Cascade Oregon grape (*Mahonia nervosa*), Pacific rhododendron (*Rhododendron macrophyllum*), and Oregon boxwood (*Paxistima myrsinites*), and in the southern Cascades, trailing snowberry (*Symphoricarpos hesperius*) and baldhip rose (*Rosa gymnocarpa*). Ground cover species include sedges (*Carex* spp.), bunchberry (*Cornus unalaschkensis*), twinflower (*Linnaea borealis*), oak fern (*Gymnocarpium dryopteris*), deer fern (*Blechnum spicant*), sorrel (*Oxalis* spp.), and false lily-of-the-valley (*Maianthemum dilatatum*). Although many areas in these zones have been clearcut and logging and road building continue in unprotected areas, much is relatively undisturbed and there are still some areas of old-growth forest.

**Mixed Conifer / Mixed Broadleaf Evergreen Zones:** This group of diversely vegetated zones is found in the Klamath-Siskiyou and southern Coast Range mountain regions of southwestern Oregon. Conifers like Douglas-fir (*Pseudotsuga menziesii*), ponderosa pine (*Pinus ponderosa*), white fir (*Abies concolor*), and incense cedar (*Calocedrus decurrens*) are dominant or co-dominant. A broadleaf subcanopy occurs on the western slopes with madrone (*Arbutus menziesii*), tanoak (*Lithocarpus densiflorus*), canyon live oak (*Quercus chrysolepis*), and others. Coast redwood (*Sequoia sempervirens*) forests grow at the southernmost region of the Sitka Spruce Zone. Understory shrubs include Douglas maple (*Acer glabrum*), vine maple (*Acer circinatum*), Pacific rhododendron (*Rhododendron macrophyllum*), serviceberry (*Amelanchier alnifolia*), baldhip rose (*Rosa gymnocarpa*), oceanspray (*Holodiscus discolor*), sticky currant (*Ribes viscosissimum*), evergreen huckleberry (*Vaccinium ovatum*), kinnikinnick (*Arctostaphylos uva-ursi*), pinemat manzanita (*Arctostaphylos nevadensis*), prostrate ceanothus (*Ceanothus prostratus*), snowbrush (*Ceanothus velutinus*), Idaho fescue (*Festuca idahoensis*), beargrass (*Xerophyllum tenax*), and others. Portions of this zone have

Restored Garry oak savanna, a grassland ecosystem

dry, rocky "serpentine" soil that lacks some essential nutrients and gives rise to plants that are tolerant of such soil conditions. These zones have been greatly degraded by clearcut logging and timber management practices that suppress natural fire, decreasing frequency but making fires more severe. Other threats include development, grazing, and invasive species.

**Rogue and Umpqua Forest / Shrub Zones:** These zones lie in the interior Rogue and Umpqua Valleys of southwestern Oregon at low elevation. It is considered chaparral habitat, with a variable canopy and understory. Wooded areas contain Garry oak (*Quercus garryana*), black oak (*Quercus kelloggii*), and Douglas-fir (*Pseudotsuga menziesii*), often in association with incense cedar (*Calocedrus decurrens*), ponderosa pine (*Pinus ponderosa*), sugar pine (*Pinus lambertiana*), madrone

(*Arbutus menziesii*), and bigleaf maple (*Acer macrophyllum*). Understory shrubs include deer brush (*Ceanothus integerrimus*) and manzanita (*Arctostaphylos* spp.) on slopes and burned areas, as well as tanoak (*Lithocarpus densiflorus*), gold chinquapin (*Castanopsis chrysophylla*), Cascade Oregon grape (*Mahonia nervosa*), salal (*Gaultheria shallon*), sword fern (*Polystichum munitum*), and many others.

**Savanna / Prairie / Woodland / Wetland Zones:** These zones encompass the richly diverse and unique habitats of the Willamette Valley, Puget Trough, and Georgia Basin. Originally a mix of forest, riparian wetland, savanna, and wet and dry prairies dominated by Garry oak (*Quercus garryana*), within the past century these habitats have been consumed by agriculture, livestock grazing, logging, invasive plants, fire suppression, and urban and suburban areas that abound

## turtles in trouble

Wetland species like western painted turtles are listed as imperiled in Oregon; western pond turtles are also endangered in Washington. Wetland and upland habitat loss, human recreation, road mortality, and invasive species such as Himalayan blackberry, which choke out native plants, take a heavy toll. Turtles need two habitat types: shallow, slow-moving, or still bodies of water with muddy bottoms, vegetation, and quiet basking places such as rocks and logs, and nearby terra firma for nesting.

in nonnative plants. Only a few patches remain: The Willamette Valley has lost over 99 percent of its historic wet prairie habitat. Many of the zone's plants and animals are found nowhere else and are listed (or need to be listed) as endangered or threatened species. Moist woodlands may contain Oregon ash (*Fraxinus latifolia*), willows (*Salix* spp.), black poplar (*Populus nigra*), Garry oak (*Quercus garryana*), quaking aspen (*Populus tremuloides*), cascara (*Rhamnus purshiana*), serviceberry (*Amelanchier alnifolia*), red-twig dogwood (*Cornus sericea*), licorice fern (*Polypodium glycyrrhiza*), and inside-out flower (*Vancouveria* spp.), among others. Drier areas may include such species as Garry oak, madrone (*Arbutus menziesii*), ponderosa pine (*Pinus ponderosa*), oceanspray (*Holodiscus discolor*), mock orange (*Philadelphus lewisii*), wild rose (*Rosa* spp.), snowberry (*Symphoricarpos albus*), Oregon grape (*Mahonia aquifolium*), red-flowering currant (*Ribes sanguineum*), yarrow (*Achillea millefolium* var. *occidentalis*), columbine (*Aquilegia formosa*), and shooting star (*Dodecatheon hendersonii* and *D. pulchellum*).

**Wetlands (herbaceous or riparian):** These are transitions between aquatic areas and dry land that carry a rich diversity of species. They may be seasonally saturated or continually saturated. The Pacific Northwest has lost nearly 40 percent of its freshwater vegetated wetlands, mostly drained for agriculture; in the Willamette Valley less than 1 percent remains. Changes to coastal estuary habitat have also been dramatic and extensive. Although there are federal and state regulations to protect wetlands, they continue to disappear, slowly and catastrophically, due to development. The only type of wetland that has increased is artificial ponds.

Grasses or grass-like plants dominate herbaceous wetlands, while alders (*Alder* spp.), Oregon ash (*Fraxinus latifolia*), bigleaf maple (*Acer macrophyllum*), western redcedar (*Thuja plicata*), Sitka spruce (*Picea sitchensis*), willows (*Salix* spp.), spirea (*Spiraea* spp.), and salal (*Gaultheria shallon*) dominate riparian wetlands.

Within these unique vegetation zones are many smaller plant communities. These collections of various *associated species* growing

A mature evergreen tree can intercept more than 4,000 gallons of rainwater each year, about 80 percent more than deciduous trees.

naturally near each other can be differentiated from communities next door that contain other species. Because these plant pals have similar needs, they flourish together. Some interact with other species in synergistic ways that benefit both, such as by boosting soil nutrients or moisture. Such interactions ultimately result in more food and shelter for insects and other wildlife. There is overlap between different communities that results in a blending of species, rather than abrupt boundaries.

In your garden it's not crucial to include all of the plants that a natural plant community might support, and in a small yard that would be impossible anyway. Since there have been

dramatic changes in plant distribution and content from what originally existed here, and because most of our yards have been drastically altered, it will only be possible to approximately replicate the natural plant community. In urban areas especially, heat reflected from roads, buildings, and other hardscape, along with small lots, narrow planting strips, and limited permeability, create conditions that many native plants will not be able to tolerate. Grow plants that *can* tolerate those conditions in parts of your site that can't support local species.

Whenever possible, intermingle plants with their associates, so that your garden begins to resemble a mini-version of your area's historic

Mature trees provide habitat for wildlife such as cavity-nesting woodpeckers, which excavate holes in trees.

native plant community that is able to impart the most benefits to the ecosystem. Visit nearby natural areas to acquaint yourself with growing conditions and compositions and patterns of plants that thrive together and contribute to a natural balance. You can also seek information on plant communities from websites listed in the back of this book, native plant societies, nurseries, and 100 Native Plants for the Garden, later in this book.

## At the Root: Trees Rule

Although the region's unique wetlands and grasslands carry the greatest diversity of species, it is the forests that dominate and most distinctly characterize the Pacific Northwest. Structurally complex, dense, and immense ecosystems, forests sustain trees that substantially outgrow and outlive other plants and tolerate temperature variation and soil differences better. When the first European settlers arrived, conifers covered nearly the entire landscape of western British Columbia and Washington, and northwestern Oregon—from coast to Cascade crest—including the Puget Trough and parts of the Georgia Basin and Willamette Valley.

These conifers (and other dominant species) are known as *keystone species* because of their strong and often unique effects on their ecosystem. Though they are greatly outnumbered by smaller plants in the forest, their contributions are mammoth. Cool, wet winters and mild, dry summers, along with rich soils, have made for optimum evergreen growing conditions.

Conifers are able to photosynthesize during much of the year and are essential for watershed stabilization. Some species are the most massive on earth, often growing over 200 feet tall and living for more than 500 years. Worldwide, conifers represent the largest terrestrial "carbon sink," where carbon is packed away in plant tissue above and below ground. The wettest forests—those on the west side of coastal mountain ranges—were once especially complex, with lush layering and much variation in tree age. Logging has eliminated much of the original, most productive old-growth forests, and massive clearcutting has resulted in severe fragmentation. Today, much forested land is "second growth" that has followed logging and wildfire.

Garry oak ecosystems, where Garry oaks grow naturally, have become rare, with only a very small percentage remaining. The loss of these unique ecosystems puts all the species that rely on them in jeopardy, and indeed, some species have already been lost, while many of the remaining are at risk. If you live on land that was once part of a Garry oak ecosystem and are starting with a blank slate, consider planting Garry oaks and associated species like madrone (*Arbutus menziesii*), oceanspray (*Holodiscus discolor*), tall Oregon grape (*Mahonia aquifolium*), and baldhip rose (*Rosa gymnocarpa*). If your site is too small for large trees, grow the smaller associated species in a meadowlike garden or rock garden. Spring ephemerals include white fawn lily (*Erythronium oregonum*), Henderson's shooting star (*Dodecatheon hendersonii*), and camas (*Camassia quamash*); mid-bloomers include tiger lily (*Lilium columbianum*), nodding onion (*Allium cernuum*), stonecrop (*Sedum* spp.) and western columbine (*Aquilegia formosa*); for late blooms try yarrow (*Achillea millefolium* var. *occidentalis*), showy fleabane (*Erigeron speciosus*), and goldenrod (*Solidago canadensis*).

Most yards can support more trees, whether evergreen or deciduous, than they do. If you have the space, grow the large trees—the oaks, the pines, the firs—that are quintessential to our region and will help replace some of the habitat that has been lost to development and logging. Just one western redcedar (*Thuja plicata*) will provide dense shelter and nesting sites for various birds and small mammals, bark that can be used as nesting material, food for seed-eating birds and browsing mammals, and, as the tree matures, cavities for roosting and cavity-nesting birds.

In urban areas, street trees that grow in parking strips could be native species (as well as the other plants you grow there). Some good choices for narrow parking strips (not less than 4 feet wide) include cascara (*Rhamnus purshiana*), Douglas maple (*Acer glabrum*), and black hawthorn (*Crataegus douglasii*), and for wider strips (greater than 6 feet wide and without overhead utility wires) Garry oak (*Quercus garryana*), incense cedar (*Calocedrus decurrens*), and Oregon ash (*Fraxinus latifolia*). Always check with your city's urban forestry office before planting.

## Making Choices

There may be plants that you already know you want to include in your plan. Before you make any final decisions, though, take a little time to make certain they are the right choices. And if you haven't a clue what to plant, here are some things to keep in mind:

→ To ensure that any plant—native or nonnative—thrives in your garden, always select according to your site conditions. Plants that are native to your immediate area will be most suitable, but since your yard may bear little resemblance to what it once was, be sure to double check that the plants' needs will be met. The light, moisture, soil, and nutrient requirements (if known) of every plant need to be compatible with the conditions of the site.

→ Come up with little want ads in your mind for various areas of your yard. Here are some examples from a client's front yard:

*Wanted: Short plants that can handle shade on north side of house. Must be willing to share space with two tall, nonnative rhododendrons. Evergreen a plus.*
*Wanted: Shrubs for mostly sunny conditions, to provide screening of street and create vertical interest. Drought tolerance mandatory.*

*Wanted: Low, evergreen plants (less then 3 feet tall) for partly shaded parking strip. Must get along with a mature, handsome oak tree, be drought tolerant, and be able to stabilize eroding soil.*

→ Choose new plants with existing plants in mind. For example, a Garry oak that has been growing in well-drained soil that stays fairly dry during the summer months might die a slow death if suddenly underplanted with moisture-loving plants that are heavily and consistently irrigated. Instead, choose from the palette of plants that naturally grow with Garry oaks in drier areas.

→ Be aware of microclimates—zones whose temperature and light may differ wildly from those of other areas just steps away—and how they can affect the type and range of plants that can be grown. Although the shady parts of my yard can accommodate many plants that likely grew there centuries ago, like Cascade Oregon grape (*Mahonia nervosa*), the sunny spots—the bright space surrounding the vegetable garden, for example—cannot. In these warmer, sunnier areas I've chosen, along with some nonnative species, natives that thrive in this microclimate, such as stonecrop (*Sedum spathulifolium*) and Cardwell's penstemon (*Penstemon cardwellii*).

→ The amount of space you have to work with may rule out some plants, simply due to their mature size. The distance you should set your plants away from other plants, buildings, or walls depends on how big they will eventually grow. A very common mistake, and we all do it, is mis-

judging a plant's mature height and—often more problematic—width. Any shrub that's 2 feet tall and 1 foot wide when brought home in a gallon-sized pot looks great when you plant it 3 feet from the house or 3 feet from a walkway. But fast-forward eight years, when it's on its way to becoming 10 feet wide and tall, and it will have to be either brutally hacked back, or dug up and thrown away. There is no such thing as an "overgrown" plant: Problems with size happen when plants are placed by someone who didn't consider their mature size. Every plant needs space to stretch its limbs and attain a natural size and shape so extensive pruning won't be necessary. Sheared or otherwise drastically pruned plants are not nearly as attractive to wildlife, and repeated pruning can even be harmful. Nursery labels offer very limited information, and they seldom tell you how wide a plant will become, so it pays to double check with a reliable source before planting (if you choose something other than the plants in this book, which does note width!).

→ Some species, including silk tassel bush (*Garrya elliptica* or *G. fremontii*) and Indian plum (*Oemleria cerasiformis*), have male and female flowers on separate plants and so require both to produce fruit. More common are self-fruitful species with both types of flowers on the same plant, such as serviceberry (*Amelanchier alnifolia*) and

RIGHT Western hazelnut will produce more nuts when grown near another of its kind.

evergreen huckleberry (*Vaccinium ovatum*), which require only one specimen to produce fruit. Still, some that are self-fruitful will be more fruitful when more than one plant is present—a western hazelnut (*Corylus cornuta* var. *californica*) will satisfy nut eaters much more when grown with another.

→ Give ground cover plants some company, because they will be most beneficial and natural looking when grown alongside other species. Take a stroll through a relatively wild, shaded woodland and you will see not one, but often over a half-dozen different ground-hugging species growing in the same area. Several may be blooming at once, or they may bloom sequentially, which results in prolonged flowering that benefits native pollinators. In mostly shady, moist woodland settings, try the varied textures and forms of bunchberry (*Cornus unalaschkensis*), wild ginger (*Asarum caudatum*), inside-out flower (*Vancouveria* spp.), and western white anemone (*Anemone deltoidea*). In sunnier, drier areas, try Idaho fescue (*Festuca idahoensis*), prostrate ceanothus (*Ceanothus prostratus*), and kinnikinnick (*Arctostaphylos uva-ursi*).

→ Not all perennials are long-lived. Some, such as western columbine (*Aquilegia formosa*), may live only a few years but will be replaced by their seedlings a few inches away.

→ Fragrance is often a welcome addition to gardens, but it's not there just to please us. Plants with scents are also important ecologically. Some insects, especially pollinators like butterflies, are attracted to plants with alluring aromas, particularly those with large clusters of flowers, like milkweed (*Asclepias* spp.), ceanothus (*Ceanothus* spp.), and oceanspray (*Holodiscus discolor*).

→ When selecting nonnative plants, choose species or heirloom varieties that have proven not to "naturalize" (those that self-sow everywhere), rather than new plants on the market that have yet to show they won't pose a problem to the natural environment. For example, if you love clematis, choose one of the many hybrids that have been around for decades or longer and have demonstrated they will not encroach on native species. Or, if you have a large site, choose our native *Clematis ligusticifolia*. To keep plants from spreading their seeds cut the spent flowers off before they go to seed (which may also promote a second bloom). But it's much less work to grow native plants that are no real threat to the ecosystem if they spread. Avoid nonnatives that spread rapidly by underground runners or rhizomes, and those that root easily or are wind-dispersed. Besides possibly endangering native plants in the surrounding ecosystem, they create much more weeding for gardeners.

## Putting It All Together

It's best to start your plant list with the dominant plants, then choose the smaller species that will associate with the big guys:

1. **Choose trees.** Trees should be chosen carefully, since they have the most potential to live very long lives if planted in appropriate conditions and will very likely outlive us. Choose fast-growing species such as

Choose ground cover plants that grow together naturally to create a living embroidery on your landscape, such as *Cornus unalaschkensis, Oxalis oregana,* and *Smilacina stellata*, which thrive in moist forests.

Douglas-fir (*Pseudotsuga menziesii*), cascara (*Rhamnus purshiana*), or Oregon ash (*Fraxinus latifolia*) if you want relatively quick shade, privacy, habitat, and beauty. If you prefer that those attributes inch their way in, consider the slowpokes (that store more carbon): Garry oak (*Quercus garryana*), black hawthorn (*Crataegus douglasii*), or mountain hemlock (*Tsuga mertensiana*).

I recommend planting conifers whenever possible (depending on your location), and other trees that will grow to be large, except for nonnative fruit trees such as cherry,

apple, and plum (choose dwarf forms or espalier semidwarf varieties on supports to minimize the space needed to grow fruit). Keep in mind that most cultivated fruit trees that we grow for food need annual or semi-annual pruning and often require plenty of other maintenance due to their susceptibility to disease in our moist region. Stone fruits such as cherry, apricot, peach, and plum are all prone to fungal diseases, and it's a given that most apple trees will be attacked by scab, as well as insects like apple maggot and codling moth, which are very difficult to get rid of.

2. **Decide on the understory.** Choose smaller trees, shrubs, and vines to fill the space between the top canopy and the lower shrubs and perennials. They should associate well with your chosen trees or those already in residence, and be placed so they will be able to handle whatever shade their taller neighbors create. Select these midrange plants in a variety of heights to give wildlife different layers of canopy to hide and feed in. This middle layer also excels at providing insects, seeds, berries, and other fruits year round; willows (*Salix* spp.) in particular offer a smorgasbord of insects. Vines can tie everything together, but remember that they will need some sort of support. While smaller vines like orange honeysuckle (*Lonicera ciliosa*) can wind their way through existing, openly branched shrubs or small trees, or be coaxed to grow on a large trellis or non-solid fence, western clematis (*Clematis ligusticifolia*) requires a strong and lengthy support—perfect for hiding an unattractive chain link fence.

3. **Finally, select your ground cover.** What you choose to grow under new trees and shrubs—the perennials, bulbs, and very low plants known as ground covers—will depend on your current conditions, not what it will be like ten years from now. Choose a variety of associated plants that will eventually mingle and evolve into a rich tapestry of foliage and flowers.

## Never Twice the Same

Since plants are living and growing, landscapes are never static, and the changes that occur over the years will likely require you to respond. For instance, the shade that newly planted trees and shrubs eventually provide may require a later change in the plants growing beneath them and possibly nearby. How quickly this happens is contingent on the size and type of the tree at planting time: Slow-growing trees like oaks probably won't cast much shade for decades, while fast growing Douglas-firs can change a sunny situation into a fairly shady one in a half-dozen years.

Fortunately, there are ways to plan ahead. Let's suppose you have a mostly sunny site now but will be planting trees and/or shrubs that will eventually supply shade that woodland perennials thrive in. Because the young trees and shrubs will not cast enough shade for ground cover such as ferns and inside-out flower (*Vancouveria hexandra*) for quite a few years, you could choose species that need part sun, like showy fleabane (*Erigeron speciosus*) and monkeyflower (*Mimulus* spp.). Years later, when the shade finally arrives, the fleabane and monkeyflower can be gradually replaced with shade-loving species. Alternatively, you could opt for ground cover that tolerates some sun (with extra water) as well as shade, like salal (*Gaultheria shallon*) and small-flowered alumroot (*Heuchera micrantha*).

Yet another option is simply to phase in your plantings. Install the trees and shrubs that need sun first, then wait a few years until there is sufficient shade to grow understory plants that can't tolerate much direct sunlight. (The downside of this is that the ground will need to be covered with a thick layer of leaves or weeds may take over.) You can also grow sun-loving annual natives such as *Clarkia amoena* and *Lupinus bicolor* as you wait for the shade to come.

A much more sudden decrease in sunlight can occur due to human activity, such as a new addition on a neighboring house. Or the opposite situation, when a shady spot suddenly is inundated with bright sunlight—this can happen after a storm takes down a tree or a neighbor decides to part with something that has provided shade in your yard. Remaining plants may do fine if they're of a type that can tolerate a range of light conditions, but most that require shade probably won't make it unless something else shields direct sunlight.

Another reason to edit the garden is that we all make mistakes. I need more than one hand to count the times I've had to relocate or replace plants because conditions changed much more rapidly than I had anticipated, or I failed to take something into account that affected a particular plant. Plant large shrub too close to path? Check. Plant sedum in too much hot afternoon sun? Check. Kill madrone seedling by moving it? Check. Kill second madrone seedling with too much love (i.e., water)? Check.

Be careful about transplanting: Not all plants can handle being moved. Many can be relocated within a year or two, especially if their roots are not disturbed too much and it's done during cool weather, but others should not be moved at all. The sweet little one-year madrone seedling that I carefully moved just one month after planting might have died because I didn't know at the time how notoriously sensitive madrones are to relocation. It pays to do a little research before you decide to put plants on the road again.

Plants sometimes don't make it if their genetic material originated in a very different geographic setting, and sometimes we just make poor plant choices. This happens to everyone, and the best thing to do is just accept it, learn from what didn't work, and find something that does.

Then there is the attrition factor: Plants don't live forever, and you will be called upon to replace them now and then. If it is a non-native plant you have no attachment to, the loss is a gift that will allow you to grow yet another enticing native plant. Seeing change as an opportunity to create, rather than a problem, goes a long way. If a tree is dead or dying, though, keep it as a snag if there are no safety issues involved.

If there are any plants pictured in this book that beguile you but don't fit the conditions you have, remember that you may have the right conditions later on. For instance, if you're captivated by the understated beauty of western white anemone (*Anemone deltoidea*), a sweet little woodland species that needs a fair amount of shade, but your site is baking in sunlight now, include a fast-growing western redcedar or two in your plan and in a few years you will probably have the partial shade that your heartthrob needs. If you're enthralled by plants such as *Lewisia columbiana* that require speed-of-light-draining soil, you may be able to grow them in somewhat heavy soil (or in containers) if you amend it with gravel or pumice or create a rock garden with the appropriate conditions. "Real" gardens are all about choosing what will grow best naturally, but it's OK to cheat a little.

## Providing for Pollinators

If you plan to grow a variety of species native to your area, you won't need to worry about whether you will provide for dwindling pollinators. Research suggests that native plants

Butterflies and moths often obtain nutrients and moisture in mud puddles, but they also may be attracted to perspiration on skin, like this green comma butterfly.

are four times more alluring to native bees, for example, than exotic flowers. But there are additional steps we can take, even in small spaces, to lend a hand to these fascinating, hardworking animals. (For more detailed information, please refer to the Xerces Society's website, www.xerces.org).

→ **Leave your garden a little "wild" and delay spring cleanup.** Undisturbed ground nesting locations are essential, and gardens that aren't too neat and provide log piles, mounds of smooth stones, exfoliating tree bark, and patches of bare, well-drained soil will help. Avoid extensive tilling or anything that prevents access to soil, like plastic mulch. Nest sites for bees that nest aboveground can be supplemented

by placing hollow or pithy stems or dead wood with narrow tunnels drilled into it horizontally. Some species also utilize the vegetative parts of plants for food and cover while nesting.

→ **Steer clear of insecticides.** Even those approved for organic gardening, such as rotenone, can be harmful. Systemic insecticides, like neonicotinoids, that are absorbed by plants produce toxic nectar and pollen. Studies show that residues may persist in woody plants for up to six years following application and may persist in soil for several years.

→ **Turn roadsides native.** Studies show that native pollinators are much more prevalent in native stretches of roadside habitat—often the only connection between patches of remnant habitat—than in weedy, nonnative stretches. If you own rural land, plant natives at your roadside and if you need to mow, do it infrequently to prolong bloom.

→ **Transform exotic lawn with natives.** Whether you have a large or small lot, consider replacing lawn with native grass and wildflower mixes in sunny areas, or mosses in shady areas. Beware of some "eco-lawn" mixes which may contain seeds of weedy nonnatives like foxglove or Queen Anne's lace.

→ **Provide variety in flower color, shape, and size for pollinators with different needs.** Bees tend to prefer yellow, purple, and blue flowers—anything but red, which they can't see—while hummingbirds can see and do use reds (and other colors) although one study suggests that their preference may not be innate, but rather

# natives contained

Even those with microscopic yard space or limited mobility can grow natives. With a bit of planning and time, many native species can be grown in pots or other containers. Some—the low, drought-tolerant ones like sedums—can also be grown on green roofs.

For bright situations, try yarrow (*Achillea millefolium* var. *occidentalis*), blue-eyed grass (*Sisyrinchium* spp.), nodding onion (*Allium cernuum*), monkeyflower (*Mimulus* spp.), stonecrop (*Sedum* spp.), camas (*Camassia* spp.), or lewisia (*Lewisia* spp.), the latter with extra-sharp drainage. Partly shaded containers might grow Douglas iris (*Iris douglasiana*), leopard lily (*Lilium pardalinum* subsp. *vollmeri*), columbine (*Aquilegia formosa*), alumroot (*Heuchera micrantha*), beach daisy (*Erigeron glaucus*), mock orange (*Philadelphus lewisii*), or oceanspray (*Holodiscus discolor*). For shady areas, choose piggyback plant (*Tolmiea menziesii*), maidenhair fern (*Adiantum aleuticum*), deer fern (*Blechnum spicant*), or snowberry (*Symphoricarpos albus*). Keep in mind that any potted plant will need more pampering than those in the ground; your watchful eye and experience will tell you what works and what doesn't, but for starters:

- Group plants with similar needs together to make watering easier.
- Keep plants—even those that like sun—out of scorching sunlight during summer.
- Arrange larger pots in the center, with smaller pots at the edges, being aware that small pots may need more shade since they dry out more quickly.

Many native species, like heucheras, do well in pots and other containers.

- Repot plants every few years to keep them healthy and growing, pruning roots as necessary. Donate those that have outgrown your space to someone with a yard, before their bound roots give them a "prognosis negative."
- Protect plants from winter rain and cold. Excessive rain leaches nutrients out of soil. Never let pots sit in saucers full of water for long periods. Roots are subjected to colder temperatures in pots than in the ground, so insulate them from damaging cold.

Many native pollinators are in steep decline and in need of protection. Providing late-blooming native plants such as asters helps conserve pollinators in the changing dynamics of our world.

they choose reds since bees don't. Butter-flies need clusters of short, tubular flowers with a wide landing pad, such as yarrow (*Achillea millefolium* var. *occidentalis*), various native bees need a variety of generally shallow flowers, while hummingbirds like relatively large, tubular or urn-shaped flowers. Experts recommend planting clusters or drifts of at least three different plant species so that each plant is next to or within a few feet of another of its kind, to supply enough forage and to make them easy for pollinators to find.

→ **Keep it blooming.** From spring through fall, something should always be in bloom, preferably several species at a time. Both early and late forage may aid in bees' reproduction. Early spring pollen and nectar producers, like Indian plum (*Oemleria cerasiformis*), willows (*Salix* spp.), and red-flowering currant (*Ribes sanguineum*), are particularly important to bees emerging from hibernation, while late-season nectar sources such as various asters (*Symphyotrichum* spp.) help overwintering adults get through the winter. Many native species bloom for extended periods, such as charming foamflower (*Tiarella trifoliata*), which produces flowers from spring to late summer. Learn when plants bloom to be sure you've got it covered, and aim for some overlap in bloom times. Remember that trees and shrubs without obvious flowers can also provide nectar and pollen.

→ **Moisten sand or loose soil to help adult lepidoptera.** Butterflies and moths ingest only liquids like flower nectar, from which they obtain sugars, minerals, and other nutrients. They also "sip" from muddy or sandy puddles, sap, decaying fruit, sweaty humans, even manure piles, to hydrate themselves and obtain dissolved minerals, including salt. Such minerals are vital for many physiological functions, including reproduction: Male lepidoptera often transfer "nuptial gifts" of sodium and amino acids to the female during mating (along with other donations). Before you say, "He shouldn't have," consider how evolving toward generosity might generate rewards: More gifts mean more nutrition and better egg survival. To assist, add a dash of salt to containers of moist sand or soil, to be sure lepidoptera get what they need.

→ **Grow butterfly host plants.** To become adults, butterflies in earlier life stages— egg, larva, chrysalis—require host plants that provide habitat and food. Find out which butterflies frequent your area, and grow the plants that provide for all their stages (see Appendix C for sources of information on butterflies and other lepidoptera).

→ **Forgo hybridized and "double" flowers.** When choosing plants, keep in mind that hybridized varieties may lack sufficient pollen nutrition—pollens vary in protein content, and bees need a wide variety to fulfill their protein requirement. Research

also suggests that some commonly used garden plants, especially those hybridized for features valued by gardeners, like disease-resistance or flower size or color, may not provide sufficient or appropriate nutrients in nectar, needed for carbohydrates. Frilly double-flowered varieties (those with extra petals that make a flower look inflated and flouncy) are usually inaccessible to pollinators simply because they can't get through the mass of petals to the nectaries. It's a bit sad to watch a bumblebee try earnestly and fervently to get inside an overly dressed flower, but fly away empty.

## Going Shopping

Plants and seeds are available at specialist native plant nurseries—which may also provide consultation services—but some natives can also be found at retail garden shops (see Appendix C for shops that carry a selection of native plants). All purchased seeds and plants should be obtained from reputable nurseries and not taken from the wild, to be sure we don't further deplete natural areas. Native plant societies, nature centers, botanic gardens, and arboretums may also occasionally hold native plant sales, often in spring and/or fall.

Particularly if you live close to wild populations of native plants or are involved in a large-scale restoration effort, determine the original source of plant materials (the geographic area where seeds or cuttings were first collected, not where they were propagated, such as a nursery). This is important for maintaining genetic fitness and to give the plant the best chance to thrive. Plants grown from source material at different elevations and latitudes will have different growth rates and cold tolerance. Whenever possible, obtain plants and seeds that have been grown relatively close to your site and in similar terrain; they will be best suited to your conditions and won't contribute to outbreeding. Outbreeding depression happens when plants with different genetic forms that normally would be separated spatially are brought closer together, resulting in plants that are unfit or poorly adapted to the local conditions. This is especially troublesome for rare plants—if less fit genes appear, a small population of plants could vanish. Plants propagated from specimens in northern California will not be adapted for Washington's climate, just as the genetic material in plants growing on Vancouver Island isn't meant for Oregon. Restoration projects have demonstrated that failure to use

## native plants in the kitchen

When I first started gardening, it was in a Seattle P-Patch community garden plot. Plant choices then were simple: All I had to do was think about what I enjoyed eating and what would taste supremely better than the same food found in the grocery store—things like tomatoes and raspberries, which need to be picked when completely ripe to realize their full, mouthwatering potential.

I often chose heirloom types, mainly because they sounded so much more interesting than the standard varieties. Purple carrots and potatoes pushed my fascination button, but I had no idea then that they were also remarkably more nutritious than commercial produce. Crammed with even more degenerative-disease-fighting phytonutrients are the nonhybridized, nonengineered wild plants, which most humans stopped foraging for around 10,000 years ago. If you want to use part of your yard to grow edibles as well as natives, consider, along with common vegetables and fruits, wild species that excel in the taste and nutrition categories *and* are virtually pest- and disease-free, like huckleberries, blackcap raspberries, serviceberries, and hazelnuts. If you grow enough, the birds will gladly allow you a portion.

Serviceberries (*Amelanchier alnifolia*) can be delicious, but you'll have to beat the birds to them.

seed or plants from similar, nearby areas can result in poor outcomes.

## What's in a Name?

Both botanical and common names are used throughout this book. But why use botanical names rather than the often charming nicknames assigned to plants over the years? People who use botanical names usually aren't just trying to show off their grasp of the nomenclature—it's usually best to use more scientific terms for several reasons. Although common names are sometimes reliable, many plants have more than one, often due to language or regional differences. What we call serviceberry (genus *Amelanchier*) is known as shadbush, Saskatoonberry, or juneberry in other places. Fawn lilies (genus *Erythronium*) are called trout lily, avalanche lily, glacier lily, dogtooth violet, snow lily, lamb's tongue, and possibly other names in other countries.

While a common name like "trout lily" could refer to any of twenty-five species of *Erythronium* found worldwide (four of them indigenous to our region), the botanical name *Erythronium oregonum* always refers to one and only one plant species. Some common names can even refer to more than one species. "Bluebells" might refer to our native *Campanula rotundifolia* or some other *Campanula* species, a *Muscari* species (also commonly known as grape hyacinth), or the invasive *Hyacinthoides hispanica* (Spanish bluebells), and more.

To create a more universal understanding and foster clarity and stability, Carl Linnaeus, an eighteenth-century Swedish botanist, physician, and naturalist, developed a model for scientifically grouping and classifying plants known as *plant taxonomy*. Still in use today, it uses a binomial system of botanical nomenclature that prescribes the words that apply to each plant.

The first word indicates the *genus*, which is the name given to a group of organisms with similar characteristics that are mostly restricted to that group. The second word is the *epithet*, which may help describe a plant (if you understand Latin or Greek) or it may not. Sometimes an epithet honors a person, such as in *Iris douglasiana*, for the famous nineteenth-century Scottish botanist and plant explorer David Douglas, whose name has been incorporated into almost 500 botanical and common names. The common name for *Pseudotsuga menziesii*, Douglas-fir (which is hyphenated because it isn't a true fir), refers to Douglas even though its botanical name honors his contemporary Archibald Menzies, whose name you will also recognize in the madrone's botanical name, *Arbutus menziesii*, among others.

Combined, the genus and the epithet classify the plant and sometimes describe it as well. *Iris tenax*, the botanical name for what is commonly called Oregon iris, derives from the Greek *iris*, which means rainbow (in reference to the wide variety of flower colors found among its many species), and the Latin *tenax*, which means tough or tenacious (in reference to the tough leaves that indigenous people braided to make cord). When referring to more than one plant in a particular genus, the abbreviation "spp." is used, so if you see *Lupinus* spp., it is referencing more than one lupine species. When multiple species of the same genus are used in text, the first initial of the genus may be used (after the first genus name in the list is spelled out): *Lupinus polyphyllus*, *L. rivularis*, and *L. littoralis*.

There is variation within species, so some plants may be further classified as *subspecies*, *varieties*, or *forms*. These result from evolution and natural selection—which means that the plants that survive are the strongest or best suited or adapted to the environment—and usually occur due to isolation in the wild. Subspecies may differ significantly from the original species, while varieties and forms differ only slightly. A variety of red-flowering currant (*Ribes sanguineum*) found along the coast from Oregon to central California is *Ribes sanguineum* var. *glutinosum*, while the more common variety you will find in nurseries is *Ribes sanguineum* var. *sanguineum*.

A *cultivar* is another subclass, usually selected by a plant breeder for some pleasant characteristic, which is then propagated in such a way as to maintain it. Popular nonnative ornamental garden plants such as rhododendrons, roses, and hydrangeas are typically cultivars produced by breeding and selection for flower color or size, leaf characteristics, or other attributes. But some native cultivars are special selections from the wild. A red-flowering currant named *Ribes sanguineum* var. *sanguineum* 'Pokey's Pink,' a bright-pink-flowered cultivar, was found growing on the slopes of the Columbia River Gorge. *Ribes sanguineum* var. *sanguineum* 'White Icicle' is a white variety that was cultivated at the University of British Columbia Botanical Garden. Older cultivar names are in Latin and newer ones in modern languages; all are enclosed in single quotation marks.

LEFT The botanical name *Iris tenax* describes the flower's range of color and the toughness of its leaves.

Some species are able to interbreed, naturally or in a nursery, and their offspring are called *hybrids*. They result when one type of plant is pollinated with the pollen of another, genetically different, variety. The seeds that result from the two parents will produce plants that carry traits from both. Naturally occurring hybrids occur from natural selection. A hybridized plant may be given a new name, as in the case of *Prunus* x *pugetensis* (note the x, which denotes a hybrid), a practically sterile and fruitless cross that occurred in the Puget Sound area between the native *Prunus emarginata* (bitter cherry) and *Prunus avium*, of European origin. Or, a hybrid may simply be named with the cross of its two parents.

Some plants, including the eleven species of Pacific Coast irises, hybridize very easily when growing in the same area, making the possibilities of flower color almost endless. To duplicate a hybrid plant exactly, it must be propagated by division or other means other than seed, since seeds usually grow to be replicates of the parent plant. Columbine (genus *Aquilegia*) is another plant that will hybridize freely, so if you want purity, keep your western columbine (*Aquilegia formosa*) away from marauding garden-variety species!

Botanical nomenclature is not without its quirks. Sometimes plants are classified under one genus and later reclassified under another, or sometimes the same plant can have more than one binomial name (although this isn't common). Rote memorization of botanical names is hardly necessary, but it's a good idea for your plant list to include them, to be certain you are buying the plants you want. As for pronunciation, you're on your own.

# CHAPTER 4
## *soil that's more than dirt*

"A cloak of loose, soft material, held to the earth's hard surface
by gravity, is all that lies between life and lifelessness."
—Wallace H. Fuller, *Soils of the Desert Southwest*

**ALTHOUGH MOST OF US DON'T THINK OF SOIL—IF WE** think of it at all—as fascinating, there are some incredible things going on beneath our feet. The stuff we call dirt is the most biologically diverse part of the earth. What grows from it aboveground is really just a covering for an intricate ecosystem so full of life and so closely linked to us that we and most other earthly organisms would perish without it. Essential for our food, clothing, and fuel, soil also filters water and helps regulate climate, since there is double the amount of carbon in soil as in the atmosphere, and triple the amount in plant matter. In many ways, it is the basis of life.

In the natural world, organic matter such as leaf litter accumulates on the soil surface, the liveliest layer of soil. This natural mulch continually decomposes with the help of fungi, bacteria, worms, and other creatures into a brown, carbon-rich material called humus. Slowly incorporated into the soil beneath it by soil organisms, humus contributes to the light, fertile layer known as topsoil. Typically a couple of inches deep, topsoil has an open structure that invites oxygen for growing roots and soil-dwelling organisms, and allows toxic gases produced by respiration to escape.

Decomposed organic matter helps restore and revitalize depleted soil.

But topsoil is fragile and quickly becomes depleted or degraded when it erodes or its original organic matter is used up or removed. Most degradation is due to poor agricultural practices such as overtillage, livestock ranching, and chemical applications, but it is found closer to home when earth is moved to prepare for new development. When topsoil is removed (and often compacted) during major construction projects, the remaining soil is seldom amended with organic matter before any landscaping is done. Subsequent use of synthetic fertilizers and pesticides further damages what little soil life is left, and root growth is impeded.

Topsoil can also be degraded by excessive wind, rain, and heat when it is not protected by vegetation or leaf litter. When one of our neighbors replaced their wooden fence next to the slightly sloping property line, mature salal plants that had been holding on to the soil were unfortunately also removed. To prevent a cascade of eroded soil, they added large rocks on their side of the fence and we added a few on our side, interplanted with native sedum, to be sure the area was stabilized well before winter rains.

Plants grown in eroded, compacted soil that is lacking in nutrients will typically be weak and stressed by nutrient deficiencies. As a result, they'll be easy targets for insects and diseases, although this is typically more problematic for food crops than for native plants, which generally are more adaptable and tolerant of soil imperfections as long as light and moisture needs are met. Cultivating soil that is not eroded or compacted, well drained, and teeming with communities of diverse soil life is the foundation for growing healthy plants.

## It's a Big World Down There

This natural substance we walk on that holds plants in place, serves them nutrients and moisture, and provides their roots, along with billions of vital soil organisms, a nurturing place to live, is not dead or uncomplicated—quite the opposite. As in life in aboveground ecosystems, relationships between soil processes and subterranean organisms are amazingly complex. Because soil biology is a relatively new science, we are just beginning to understand how complicated it is.

An intricate mix of components—minerals, air, water, and organic matter—makes up ideal soil. Though proportions vary from place to place, by volume, minerals compose just under half, and the remaining half consists of pores that offer roots air and water, both critical for plants' survival. Organic matter makes up about 5 percent and is composed of living organisms, their waste, and the decomposing remains of plants and animals.

Healthy soil is rich in an incomprehensible variety and number of networking organisms, from producers and consumers to predators and prey. Some, like worms and millipedes, are visible to our eyes, but most are not, like the diverse population of bacteria, fungi, and other microorganisms that are critical to the long-term productiveness of the soil.

These subterranean organisms make up only about 1 percent of soil volume, yet a teaspoon of lively soil can contain a billion bacteria of thousands of types, nearly ten feet of fungal filaments, and thousands of other microscopic organisms. Their job is to decompose organic matter into a form that plants and other organisms can use, build soil structure by providing organic matter made up of their waste plus decomposing plant and animal tissue, degrade certain pollutants, and perhaps provide a meal for other beneficial organisms.

Most fungi are decomposers, living off the remains of plants and other organisms, but some have symbiotic, or mutually beneficial, associations with the roots of most plants. Mycorrhizal fungi, an ancient symbiotic type, essentially acquire carbohydrates produced by the plant while increasing the plant's access to nitrogen, phosphorous, and various other minerals.

Organic matter is essential for healthy root systems that lead to beautiful plants, for a number of reasons. First, it provides a continuous food supply for soil dwellers that need to be nurtured and fed to thrive and multiply. Organic matter also inoculates the soil with huge numbers of beneficial microbes that buffer plants' roots from pests and are able to extract nutrients from the mineral part of soil and make them available to plants. It helps maintain a balanced pH (how acidic or alkaline a soil is), improves how water functions within the soil, and stabilizes and enhances soil structure. No matter what type of soil you have, organic matter is crucial.

## Soil Texture, Composition, and Structure

Soil texture, or type, refers to the composition of the soil in terms of the size of its mineral particles (sand, silt, and clay), or how coarse or fine it feels. Texture affects the size and number of pore spaces and capillaries that allow for gas exchange and water infiltration, which determine the amount of air circulation and drainage a soil has, as well as its water- and nutrient-holding capacity. Sand has the largest particles and a coarse texture, clay has

the smallest and finest, and silt is somewhere in the middle. Few soils are one pure type; most are a combination of mineral particles in varying proportions. They are classified according to the primary particle component or the most abundant ones in a mixture, such as *silty clay* or *sandy clay*. To get an idea of what you have, take a small sample of soil and moisten it until it's slightly sticky. Roll it into a ball about the size of a golfball, and then try to roll it, between your palms, into a cylindrical sausage. The quicker it falls apart, the more sand it contains; the longer it gets before breaking, the more clay the soil has. Having a soil analysis performed on a sample from your garden (see Resources) will more accurately determine your soil type, as well as its organic matter content and nutrient levels. Soil survey information may be available from your county soil conservation district.

Sandy soil is loose and easy to work with. It drains quickly but doesn't retain much water, and is the least fertile because it doesn't retain many nutrients. Silt feels smooth or floury and has better water- and nutrient-retaining abilities than sand, but slower drainage. Clay soil, with its tiny pores, has poor drainage and aeration and is hard when dry and goopy or sticky when wet. Its fine particles can bind to water and dissolved nutrients and retain them against the pull of gravity, but nutrients are sometimes unavailable to roots because of clay's fine, heavy texture.

Loam is a combination, in varying proportions, of sand, silt, clay, and humus (decomposed organic matter), somewhat like an undisturbed forest floor. Loam is what gardeners strive for: dark, crumbly, often pH neutral, and loaded with soil life, it has a balance of large pores that are connected to the atmosphere above, and smaller pores that allow for optimal moisture and nutrient retention.

The arrangement and binding together of sand, silt, clay, and organic matter particles into tiny stable groups called aggregates creates soil structure. Particles become grouped into these aggregates in a number of natural ways, including freezing and thawing, root movement of growing plants, fungal activity, and the burrowing of small creatures like worms and moles. Aggregates provide a good place for root development because they keep carbon and minerals accessible, help hold air and water near the roots, and improve both drainage and moisture retention. Aggregates are *not* clods of compressed soil caused by human activities such as plowing or working the soil while it is wet. Soil should not be worked until it is just moist enough to crumble easily in your hand. Digging, walking, or driving on any soil when it is wet, but particularly clay soil, destroys structure by reducing or eliminating pore spaces, leading to compaction. When rain or irrigation hits such hard soil it tends to run off, carrying away topsoil and nutrients. As with soil covered by impermeable pavement, roots in compacted soil become deprived of oxygen, drought-stressed, and stunted.

Soil that has a loose, granular structure is said to have good *tilth*, which means it has the ideal physical qualities for supporting plant root growth and is easy to work with. Healthy soil works somewhat like a sponge—it allows water from the soil surface to easily infiltrate the large pores, while at the same time it absorbs and retains moisture in small pores. Excess water then drains away and is replaced by air, which is essential for plant roots and most soil organisms.

## Improving Your Soil's Health

The key to promoting and maintaining good tilth in your garden soil comes back to those two magic words: organic matter. Even so-called problem soils can be improved by the addition of organic matter. Applied at planting time and as mulch, it's the most effective and sustainable way to build and maintain good structure and consequently grow beautiful and healthy plants. In gravelly soils, such as some in the Puget Sound area, organic matter protects plants against drought by helping to retain water and nutrients that would otherwise drain below the reach of plant roots. In my yard, which is primarily clay, it helps promote aggregation of tiny clay particles into larger ones, which increase air spaces within the soil, creating better drainage.

In the wild, natural topsoil is impeccably lively and rich, but it takes hundreds of years to form. Gardeners don't have quite that long, so we improvise by adding soil conditioners that contain organic matter. For quick effect, you can dig them in before you plant. A less invasive way is simply to spread a few inches of a soil conditioner over an area—it's easier, won't expose the soil to moisture loss, and kinder to soil dwellers who can't handle having their world turned upside-down. Applying them as mulch after planting will keep down weeds, slow surface moisture evaporation, and add decomposing material as it is worked down into the soil by macro- and microorganisms. Materials that are homemade and close at hand are the best options. However, new or large gardens, particularly those with damaged soil, may require large amounts of soil conditioners to be trucked in (a more earth-friendly option than buying it in numerous plastic bags).

Homemade composts are rich, dark, and full of life and nutrients.

Here are the best soil conditioners:

→ **Leaf mold** is a type of rich compost that many believe is the best ingredient for any soil. Although not particularly rich in nutrients, it does contain trace minerals and is an excellent soil conditioner that improves soil structure and increases moisture retention. Use it (screened) in place of peat in potting and seedling mixes. It's easy to make: Rake up leaves from walkways, driveways, and lawns in the fall and place them in a heap or round chicken-wire cage situated in a shady spot. The pile will rot slowly and be ready for use in one to two

years, but it's important to keep it moist all year round to accelerate fungal break-down. The wire cage can be removed and reused the following autumn. Another option, if you have the space, is to create two permanent pits placed side by side that can be filled and emptied in alternate years. Shredding large leaves first with a push mower will speed up the decomposition process but is not necessary.

→ **Homemade compost** is another rich soil conditioner that costs nothing but your time and is fundamental to organic gardening. Many materials can be composted, including fallen leaves, grass and garden clippings, vegan kitchen waste, sawdust, soot, charcoal, and noninvasive weeds. Try to keep the volume of high-nitrogen materials (wet "greens," such as fresh grass clippings, garden cuttings, and kitchen scraps) and high-carbon materials (dry "browns," such as straw, fallen leaves, sawdust, and brown paper) roughly equal. Varying the ingredients diversifies the microhabitats of the little decomposers—from bacteria, fungi, and nematodes, to millipedes, mites, and snails—providing all a good meal and leading to more nutrient-rich compost. If you have very little to compost, try worm composting, or vermicompost, which may be done inside your home. The end product, called worm castings, is an extremely rich material that can be added to potting soil or used as top dressing for plants that need rich soil. *A few composting tips:* To speed up decomposition, chop or cut up large or dense ingredients and aerate the pile by frequent turning with a pitchfork. Keep the compost out of hot sun and excessive rain, and about as moist as a wrung-out sponge. Don't compost chemically treated wood products, diseased vegetation, animal waste, animal products, fats and oils, invasive weeds, or anything with viable seeds (small compost piles may not get hot enough to kill unwanted seeds).

→ **Mushroom compost** is the composted material that is left after a mushroom crop is harvested. This compost has few weed seeds, insects, or pathogens because it is pasteurized. The addition of mushroom compost to garden soil can result in increased microbial populations and nutrient- and water-holding capacities, and better soil structure. Be sure the source of your compost is a certified organic mushroom grower, as it could contain fungicide and pesticide residues otherwise. One possible disadvantage of mushroom compost is an increase in the soil's pH if applied too often, so don't use it around acid-loving plants.

## Making Do With What You've Got

Your site may already have adequately fertile soil, such as in parts of the Willamette Valley, and unless the plants you choose require

## cover crops to the rescue

If you will be planting in degraded soil, such as areas that were once chemically treated lawn, under impermeable concrete, or heavily compacted, or a soil test reveals that your soil is imbalanced or lacking in nutrients, you may need to do even more to nourish it than adding organic matter. Cover crops, also called *green manure*, are easily grown plants that improve soil aggregation and fertility. Most commonly used in vegetable gardens, they are suitable for all types of gardens except shady ones. Seeded in the fall or spring, they improve air and water movement, protect bare soil from erosion and nutrient leaching, and increase organic matter in the soil. Some also "fix" atmospheric nitrogen by taking it out of the air and converting it into a form that plants can use the following season. The nitrogen fixers are legumes like clover, field peas, and fava beans, which use bacteria that colonize the nodules on their roots.

Nonleguminous crops such as winter rye, buckwheat, and oilseed rape don't add nitrogen to the soil, but they help maintain levels; they grow faster during autumn, giving better weed suppression than legumes, and tend to rot more slowly than legumes and add more organic matter to the soil. For winter cover crops, broadcast seeds by October (or at least four weeks before the expected frost date), tamping the soil gently. If it doesn't rain, sprinkle the area to keep the seeds moist. Summer cover crops such as buckwheat, red cowpea, and flax seed should be seeded from late spring to early summer and will need summer irrigation. Whether you plant in spring or early fall, cut or dig and turn over your crops just as they start to bloom. Allow three or four weeks before planting, to let the crop break down. Cover crops shouldn't be allowed to go to seed, since they have a tendency to become weedy.

Some birds, like this fox sparrow, feed mostly on the ground in tangles and thickets, hopping and flicking through fallen leaves for insects, snails, spiders, seeds, and fruit.

especially rich soil, you may be able to make do with what you've got. In large gardens in particular, it may be most realistic to just apply a one-time mulch after planting and then let nature take its course, allowing all future leaf litter to remain where it falls on the soil. You can also rake leaves from lawns, walks, and driveways, and toss them onto bare areas to protect the soil and provide habitat for overwintering beneficial insects. Allowing leaves to stay on the soil also provides essential food for birds who rummage through leaf litter in search of slugs and insects to eat.

## Preparing Your Site

Your design is on paper (or perhaps etched in your mind), you've chosen the plants, the weather's fine, and now it's time to plant. Almost. Preparation is key to most worthwhile projects we want to last, and the garden is no exception. The best time to prepare your yard for installing your design? Yesterday. Perhaps more realistically, last year—especially if your site is occupied by invasive weeds that will compete with native plants if they aren't removed, or if there are drainage problems. Taking the time to address both issues is crucial for the health of your new plants and to prevent headaches later on.

When we bought our house we noticed a fairly extensive patch of English ivy (*Hedera helix*), the well-known tree-strangling scourge of parks, gardens, and natural areas west of the Cascades and officially listed as a noxious weed in Washington and Oregon and as invasive in British Columbia. You can't blame the plant; it was intentionally imported from Europe and planted by many, decades ago, and it likes it here—a lot. It not only covered a slope in our backyard, it tangled itself around every shrub and tree in that area. If we hadn't removed it, it would only have grown more—invasive-plant removal is not something to put off.

Early in the first summer, when the soil was still moist, we manually dug out its roots as much as we could, working around a tree, a few shrubs, and large rocks in the area. To make the eradication a little easier, we decided to remove a few nonnative shrubs that had a huge amount of ivy growing from beneath them and a couple more that were in poor health due to a lack of adequate sunlight. After removing all the ivy we could, we covered the area with black land-scape fabric to cut out light but allow water to permeate the soil, and to prevent erosion from the winter rains.

In late spring the following year, we pulled the fabric back to find a small amount of growth. We removed that and replaced the light barrier, and by fall I was ready to plant, after adding several inches of compost and strategically placing large rocks found onsite to prevent erosion. A few vines came back, mostly next to a tree, but with persistent cutting-back, it eventually died and the area became completely free of ivy.

Keep your tools handy!

Because ivy is fairly shallow rooted, manual removal is feasible and much better than chemical control, which is detrimental to surrounding plants, soil life, and other creatures and is reportedly less effective. Though the removal took nearly two years, it was well worth the wait. I then moved on to eliminating the more intractable morning glory (*Ipomoea* spp.), also known as bindweed. The twining vine had apparently been hiding out underground during the ivy seizure, and while my back was turned, tried to take over a coast silk tassel bush (*Garrya elliptica*). Unlike the ivy, morning glory roots are *not* shallow, but periodic yanking and cutting to prevent photosynthesis is having some effect (at least I like to think so). For some invasive plants you may need to seek competent professional advice to control or eliminate them before planting natives. Even if you don't need to eradicate particularly noxious weeds, before you plant, it pays to remove and control any plants that can get out of hand.

Another issue you may have to deal with is abnormally poor drainage. A very wet soil could be the result of being rich in clay, but an excessively wet soil could be due to a high water table—the level below which soil pores are always saturated with water—that sometimes extends into the soil above. Continually wet soils can also be caused by what is commonly called a "perched" water table, which comes about because of a layer of rock or sediment within the soil that prevents or slows the downward flow of water. The best solution, if it's not close to your house and causing a wet basement, is to go with a damp garden, rather than fighting it. Simply grow plants that thrive in wet conditions, such as natives that evolved in wetland or riparian areas and are deemed good "rain garden" plants. Other options are to raise the level of the roots farther above the water level by building up a wide mound of soil, or berm, on which to plant, or to lower the water level by directing it to lower ground using ditches or trenches with buried perforated pipes.

A percolation test will tell you the rate at which your soil absorbs water. To perform one, simply dig a hole about 12 inches deep in the poorly drained area. Fill it with water and let it drain to saturate the soil. Fill it a second time and observe how fast it drains. If it drains 2 or more inches in an hour, you have adequate drainage. For extensive drainage problems close to your house's foundation, it may be best to consult a civil engineer.

## Tools and Materials Checklist

You will need to gather some tools before you start on your installation. Secondhand tools offer great value if they are sound. When buying new tools, invest in well-made ones that will last. Some urban areas now have tool libraries, so check to see if you have one in your area if you need a tool that won't be used often. Be sure that the size and weight of the tools are right for you.

Some things you will need:

### Tools:
→ Gloves
→ Hand trowel
→ Old buckets
→ Pitchfork
→ Pruning shears (secateurs)
→ Spade
→ Stakes and string
→ Watering can and/or hose with nozzle
→ Wheelbarrow

### Materials:
→ Composting system (bins, chicken wire enclosure, etc.)
→ Irrigation system, such as soaker hoses or driplines (optional)
→ Loads of compost, preferably organic (*To calculate how many cubic yards of compost or mulch you'll need, multiply the size of the planting site in square feet by inches of compost desired and divide by 324. For example, 1,000 square feet x 3 inches ÷ 324 = approximately 9 cubic yards.*)

→ Mulch material, if not using compost

→ Path material (gravel, hazelnut shells, reclaimed or new outdoor bricks, pavers, or stepping-stones)

→ Selected trees, shrubs, perennials, vines

→ . . . and of course friends or family to help

The following sequence of steps will help you organize the implementation of your plan. If you have a choice, install areas that are at the farthest reaches of your yard first and work inward, so that previously planted areas won't be trampled on.

1. Have your soil analyzed to determine whether it is low in any nutrients, or at least check its pH, which is calculated on a scale of 0 to 14. One of the most important considerations in plant cultivation, pH influences nutrient availability for plant growth. If you're concerned about toxins in your soil, have that tested too.

2. Before attempting any digging, check with utility companies for potential underground pipes or wires. Mark any buried infrastructure to prevent damage.

3. To prevent damage to trees, take care around live tree roots, and consult a certified and experienced arborist before cutting anything more than minor roots. Never cut large roots close to tree trunks.

4. Remove any concrete not in your plan, invasive plants, nonnatives that you and wildlife are not using, and other plants that are diseased or cannot work with the plan. Concrete chunks can be used to build low retaining walls or function as stepping-stones. Any healthy, noninvasive plants may be given away, provided enough of a root system is preserved.

5. If you need to remove a large amount of lawn, it may be easiest and quickest to use a sod cutter. Roll up the sod as you go and then compost it (stacked green side down and covered with a water-permeable cover for a year or two, until roots are decomposed—never add sod to compost bins). For small areas, simply use a spade, slicing horizontally 1 to 2 inches below the soil surface, shaking out loose topsoil. However, since removing sod also removes valuable topsoil and is laborious, there is a better way to kill sod without removing it, if you're not in a hurry: Smother grass by placing biodegradable cardboard and/or 6 to 8 sheets of uncolored newspaper over the lawn you want to remove. Overlap edges by several inches so grass can't grow through openings. Wet the paper, weight it down with several inches of leaf mold, compost, or grass clippings, and moisten again. In a few months the grass should be dead and the newspaper or cardboard well on its way to decomposition. (Don't use herbicides or plastic sheets, which will keep out moisture and air and kill beneficial organisms.)

6. Mark out your plan with stakes and string when you are ready to work on an area. Install hardscape and permanent features such as pathways, patios, stepping-stones, and arbors. Even if you will be implementing your design one area at a time, consider installing pathways that travel through several areas, all at once if possible.

7. Loosen any compacted soil in areas to be planted when the soil is not saturated and cold. When in doubt about its workability, dig up a ball of soil from 6 inches

deep and toss it 6 inches in the air. If it crumbles, it's ready to work; if not, wait until it dries further. Use a spading fork or even a pickax to loosen extremely compacted soil. Consider using a rotary tiller for large, highly compacted areas, such as those that were under concrete or well-worn paths.

8. Incorporate at least 3 inches of soil conditioner such as compost (maintaining a slight slope away from the house to promote drainage). Or, simply apply it as a mulch after planting, rather than digging in; soil organisms will bring the organic material below the surface. Soil that is compacted, such as under a driveway or lawn, will need special attention and extra organic matter to come back to life.

9. Mix in any special soil amendments, preferably at least a month before planting, per your soil tests. If the soil's pH is not under 6.5, acid-loving plants like huckleberries and rhododendrons will appreciate the addition of acidifiers, such as leaf mold, aged bark mulch, or conifer needles.

10. Install any underground drip irrigation pipes, if you plan to use them.

11. For vines and other plants that will need support, place trellises or stakes prior to planting, to avoid harming roots later.

## taking a ph test

A pH test measures the relative acidity or alkalinity of the soil, on a scale of 0 to 14, with 7 being neutral. The lower the number, the more acidic the soil is; the higher, the more alkaline. Soil with a pH of 5 is ten times more acidic than a soil with a pH of 6; a pH of 8 is ten times more alkaline than a pH of 7. Soil pH generally ranges from 4 to 8 and results from rock and mineral decomposition in the soil, rainfall, poor irrigation practices, and the plants themselves. Some plants are tolerant of wide pH ranges, while others can survive only within a relatively narrow band.

Many regional natives actually prefer soil that is a bit acidic, since many Pacific Northwest soils are naturally that way. If yours is significantly acidic (under pH 5.5), grow plants such as madrone (*Arbutus menziesii*),

huckleberry (*Vaccinium* spp.), rhododendron (*Rhododendron* spp.), bitterroot (*Lewisia* spp.), goatsbeard (*Aruncus dioicus*), false solomon's seal (*Smilacina racemosa*), western bunchberry (*Cornus unalaschkensis*), and wild ginger (*Asarum caudatum*), which can tolerate or need acidic conditions.

If you want to create a more acidic soil, adding pine, spruce, and fir needles as well as leaf mold (especially oak leaf) is a natural way to do it, but be patient—it can take years to permanently change a soil's pH. If you have alkaline soil, choose plants that don't need acidic soil or can tolerate a higher pH. Adding ground limestone to the soil can increase pH, but because it will change back over time and require future limestone additions that disturb roots, leave the alkalizers to the vegetable beds.

# to stake or not to stake

Temporarily stabilize trees (or large shrubs) only if they are in very windy areas, if they are bare rooted, or if they have little root mass—plants need to experience movement to become strong and healthy, and improper staking can cause irreversible damage.

Staked trees often have weaker trunks and less developed root systems than trees that are not staked. To test whether a newly planted tree needs staking, grab its trunk and move it back and forth; if movement causes shifting soil, stakes will help stabilize it.

If necessary, trees can be supported with two 5- to 6-foot-long stakes (on either side) driven 12 to 24 inches deep (depending on soil conditions). To stake a very large tree, space 2 to 4 stakes equally around the hole, outside the root zone. The stakes should be placed several inches away from the root ball of a containerized plant and about 24 inches from the trunk of bare-root trees, preferably before planting—if afterward, stakes should be placed just outside the planting hole to prevent damage to roots. The stakes and ties should be situated perpendicular to the prevailing wind when space allows. After planting, tie the trunk *loosely* to the stakes, about 3 feet from the ground, with a soft tie (never use wire), so that the tree is not completely immobilized and can move a bit with the wind. Very small trees can be loosely tied in a figure-8 loop to a single stake. Check ties periodically to be sure they are not too tight or causing abrasion. Remove ties as soon as the tree is stable in the ground, usually within about one year.

## Time to Plant

The best time to plant is fall, before the rains start. Spring is second best. Here's why: In autumn, plants tucked into their new homes soon go dormant aboveground. Below ground, however, they are anything but. Our wet, relatively mild winters give them a chance to produce fairly well-developed root systems before the aboveground demands of spring and summer—stem, leaf, flower, and fruit production—are thrust upon them.

When plants are planted in the spring, they have only the root system their pot allowed. And yet the same aboveground work—which can be quite taxing for young plants—is demanded of them. Spring-planted flora is more work for the gardener as well, since it usually requires much more watering the first summer to keep new plants alive and healthy—especially those planted in full sun—due to their small root systems, which haven't had a chance to grow into the surrounding soil.

Unfortunately, the available selection of plants is usually greatest in the spring, despite optimal fall planting, so be on the lookout for fall native plant sales sometimes hosted by nature centers, conservation districts, and other organizations. Although some nurseries have a decent selection in the fall, keep in mind that you may need to shop for some plants in the spring and either plant them then or keep them, well-watered, in pots until fall. You may also be able to preorder plants that are not immediately available. Many garden shops are able to order plants they might not normally carry, so if there's something you can't find, be sure to ask.

## Tucking Plants In

When it's finally time to place all your new plants in their homes, start with the larger ones, the trees and shrubs. Proper ground preparation and handling are especially important in planting and establishing them. Obtain trees and shrubs in the fall or winter when they are dormant. Plant bare-root specimens—sold without any soil attached to their roots—as soon as possible after you bring them home. Their roots should be kept moist at all times, so if you can't plant them right away, keep their roots covered with moist leaves or soil in a cool place, out of sunlight. Before planting, soak the roots for 8 to 12 hours.

Plants of all types growing in containers can wait longer, provided they are not badly root-bound and are sheltered and kept moist. Avoid buying badly root-bound plants, those that have been confined so long that their roots are growing in circles inside the pot. Such plants are often difficult to establish and may not make it if they cannot be coaxed into the surrounding soil. If a plant seems excessively large for the size of the pot or if it looks stressed, try removing the pot at the nursery to see how serious the problem may be. Let's get the planting started:

1. Mark where trees and shrubs will be planted according to your planting layout, and gather up your tools and materials. You will need a spade for digging and removing any grass or other vegetation, a watering can or hose, mulch, and possibly stakes and ties. Nearby lawn or vegetation should already have been removed (see the previous section), but if not, remove

## protecting and maintaining soil

Because soil that takes centuries to build can be damaged in a small fraction of that time, follow nature's model:

- Avoid bare soil and erosion. Grow a canopy of trees and ground cover and allow fallen leaves to remain on bare soil to shelter it from wind, rain, and sun.
- Supplement organic matter, such as compost applied as a mulch, to help aerate the soil, provide food for soil creatures, inoculate the soil with beneficial microbes, and keep the

pH close to neutral to increase microbial activity.

- Make well-drained soil that contains adequate pore spaces a priority. Avoid activities that crush aggregates and cause compaction, like working or walking on the soil when it's wet, and try not to place very heavy objects on it.
- Minimize tillage of soil, which disrupts the food web and destroys soil structure and fungal filaments.

Plant perennials, vines, and low ground cover, like wild ginger (*Asarum caudatum*), after tucking in trees and shrubs.

it in a circular pattern where each tree or shrub will be placed—4 to 8 feet in diameter or out to the *drip line* (the area directly under the outer edges of the tree's branches—not to be confused with *dripline*, an irrigation system component), whichever is larger.

2. Dig a hole twice as wide as and slightly deeper than the root system—the roots should fit into the hole without being cramped. Fracture the sides and bottom of the hole with a spade or claw tool.

3. Remove any wires, supports, or ties from the tree. Trim off any dead or damaged roots and branches with clean pruning shears. For bare-rooted plants, mound a cone of soil on the bottom of the hole and drape the roots over it, gently untangling the roots if necessary. For potted trees, massage the root ball to loosen roots that are tightly wound in the shape of the pot. Such root-bound plants may be difficult to establish if outer roots are not unfurled or, in extreme cases, cut apart.

4. Place a straight stick horizontally across the top of the hole to help judge the depth at which to plant. Since the number one cause of tree mortality is planting too deep, be sure to place it slightly above the level grown at the nursery. In severe wind

situations, plant so that the tree leans a couple of inches into the direction of the strongest winds. Otherwise, straighten the tree, judging its posture from several angles. When lifting and transporting non–bare-root trees and shrubs, always support the heavy root mass from below with your hands or a tarp. Never lift or carry them around by their stems.

5. Replace the original soil around the roots until the hole is filled about halfway, lightly firming to avoid air pockets, then water. Do not mix compost or other soil amend-ments into the soil around the tree, since that can prevent roots from growing into the native soil. Once the water has drained, adjust the depth of the tree, if necessary, and backfill with more soil, firmly tamping it down to eliminate large air pockets that can kill young root hairs. Water again thor-oughly.

6. To conserve moisture, suppress weeds, and add nutrients to the area, apply about 3 inches of organic matter as a mulch, *keep-ing it 4 to 6 inches away from the trunk* to prevent rot and potential insect damage, and thicker on the outer edge to prevent erosion. The higher a tree is mounded above the surrounding soil level, the deeper the water-conserving mulch should be. Using fine sawdust or fresh bark is not recommended, because those substances can deplete the soil of nitrogen as they decompose. Inorganic mulches, like rock or gravel, which can cause heat damage and don't improve the soil or hold water,

should be reserved for certain rock garden situations.

7. Arrange potted perennials, vines, and ground cover on the ground, according to your plan.

8. Remove them from their pots and, if root bound, massage their roots to help them grow into the surrounding soil.

9. Dig holes large enough to accommodate their roots and plant them at the same depth as they came in their pots. If they are a type that needs rich soil, such as ferns and most woodland perennials, mix in some compost into the planting hole.

10. Firm the soil so that when gently tugged on, the plants don't come out easily, and water well.

11. Optional: Attach drip irrigation emitter tubes at the drip line of trees and shrubs and over the root zones of perennials, or lay porous soaker hoses at drip lines and between perennials (but not too close to them).

12. Plant bulbs in autumn, to a depth of approxi-mately 3 times the width of the bulb.

13. Apply mulch, taking care to prevent bury-ing the root crowns of perennials.

When planting during a particularly dry autumn, keep all new plants moist until the winter rains begin. When drought returns in late spring or summer (or during unseasonal dry periods), water trees and shrubs weekly near their drip lines, where rootlets take up water, and water other smaller plants until they are doing well on their own (2 to 5 years).

# CHAPTER 5
## *cultivating a green thumb*

"It is ironic to think that man might determine his own future by something so seemingly trivial as the choice of an insect spray."
—Rachel Carson, *Silent Spring*

**ONE OF THE REASONS MANY OF US ENJOY GARDENING** with native plants—apart from their beauty and function—is that they are low maintenance. Unlike your neighbor's manicured lawn and conventional flower beds, which require frequent attention every spring, summer, and fall, your little oasis may leave you wondering what to do with all your extra time. Gone will be the hours you may have spent mowing, fertilizing, watering, and applying pesticides to plants native to faraway places. The air and noise pollution caused by lawn "care"—the repeated mowing, whacking, and blowing—will become just a memory too. Freed from the chains of conventional gardening, you will have more time for hiking, biking, tending vegetable beds, and relaxing in the hammock. You may even have time to talk to your neighbor about the joys of having a sustainable, ecologically viable space that's inviting to all.

But before you get *too* comfortable in that hammock, let's have a look at what it takes to get to the point where your yard is sustaining itself naturally, without synthetic chemicals, excessive watering, pruning, and fussing. First, it's important to realize that people are not born with the proverbial green thumb, or fingers for that matter.

Diverse, ecologically functional gardens are stable and require little maintenance.

Using natural, non-toxic controls prevents harm to wildlife locally and downstream. This native ladybird beetle's large, fake eyes and red shell defend her from predators, but not pesticides.

Although there may be some inherited tendency to having an affinity with plants, it's not either you-have-it-or-you-don't, and there's no magic or sixth sense involved.

What may be most defining is a basic inclination toward being *observant*. An observant gardener notices when a plant's moisture needs are not being met, or when a support has broken and needs to be fixed before the plant it held up gets trampled. A willingness to avoid procrastination also helps, since time is often of the essence with plants in trouble. Equally essential is a desire to learn—like discovering that it's best to irrigate well *before* the onset of a heat wave and preferably during the cool part of the morning, not after the plants have drooped or shriveled up beyond recognition. Learning why organic gardening methods are best for all types of gardening is a good place to start.

## Organic Ways

For home gardening purposes, *organic* is defined as a gardening method that takes our understanding of natural systems and applies it to growing plants so that stability can be reached without resorting to artificial controls like synthetic chemical pesticides or fertilizers. Pests and disease are recognized as being part of a living system that has an inherent balance.

If a problem should arise, nature is consulted as a guide to help work out effective solutions. Gardening organically also helps us to:

→ Reduce our negative effects on the earth by minimizing pollution and other environmental damage

→ Nurture biodiversity

→ Minimize waste by composting onsite and using locally available materials

→ Acquire a feeling of well-being and self-sufficiency that can be lacking in more artificially controlled environments.

Furthermore, organic growing can be rewarding and even fascinating when we pay attention to all the garden's little nuances. By becoming involved in the whole natural cycle, we gain greater satisfaction from our own yard, as well as appreciation for larger ecosystems.

Many of us grow edibles organically, but why stop there? Native and ornamental plants ought to be grown organically for both the health of the soil and the plants themselves, and for all the interconnected organisms that depend on them within our immediate ecosystem and beyond. Although our modern diets don't commonly include many nonhybridized native species, there are countless species that rely on them. If given a choice, we would certainly choose not to consume toxic chemicals, and if you asked some informed tadpoles or birds, they would surely agree.

## Issues with Synthetics

The general term *pesticide* encompasses insecticides, herbicides, and fungicides, and includes products like insect repellents, weed killers, disinfectants, and other poisons. Because these substances usually create noxious effects and

Killdeer have adapted to live in semiurban areas and agricultural habitats, but they are intensely vulnerable to pesticides that may be used there.

gentler alternatives are available, they are not used in ecological gardening. As the Environmental Protection Agency acknowledges, "By their very nature, most pesticides create some risk of harm—pesticides can cause harm to humans, animals, or the environment because they are designed to kill or otherwise adversely affect living organisms."

Due to abysmally extensive use, pesticides can be found almost everywhere in the environment. They often reach far beyond their intended victims with toxic secondary side effects that harm beneficial, nontarget species either in the immediate vicinity or "downstream." Pesticides can enter surface water runoff from lawn applications, or they may drift to neighboring plants and get into soil—where some persist and accumulate—and eventually into groundwater. Predators may ingest poisoned prey, with lethal results.

Spiders are our friends and benefit us every day.

It's worth noting, too, that pesticides, whether synthetic or "natural," are required by law to be tested on animals—hardly something we want our gardens to be responsible for. Although the EPA is beginning to reduce its animal testing requirements on pesticides, as many as twenty different laboratory poisoning tests are conducted on thousands of dogs, rabbits, fish, birds, and other animals to evaluate the toxicity of a single new pesticide chemical. In addition, there are high fossil fuel demands in pesticide production, including intensive processing and refining, packaging, and shipping.

## Insecticides

Millions upon millions of birds and fish and untold numbers of amphibians, invertebrates, and mammals are killed each year from heavy agricultural and residential applications of toxic pesticides in the United States (and many more birds never return from their Latin American wintering grounds, where pesticide use is even worse). Scientists have determined that the devastating decline of grassland birds, which are dying faster than birds in other ecological communities, is more the result of insecticide use than of other factors, including habitat loss. Whether they are poisoned directly or starved by a poisoned food supply or agricultural intensification, it appears that little has changed for many birds and other wild animals since Rachel Carson first documented the horrors of pesticide use in her 1962 book, *Silent Spring*.

Whether your yard borders a natural area or lies within an urban zone, it is perverse to apply pesticides (even organic ones) to kill or harm insects and other organisms that are part of the food web and are sorely needed to attract and sustain predators and pollinators.

While we're at it, let's give spiders a break. The vast majority of them never bite people, and they're brainy—researchers have found that small spiders in particular have such large central nervous systems that excess brain often spills into other body cavities. It's more well known that most spiders consume insects on a large scale, including pests that threaten food crops and those that buzz around our ears at night, but a recent study found that they have a much more extensive role than formerly realized. Besides their active consumption of insects, it turns out that the mere presence of spider silk—even after the spider that spun it has moved on—causes herbivores to feed differently, eating less plant material than if there was no spider silk around. It's not

We need to be tolerant of what others eat for dinner. Insectivorous western tanagers often catch meals in mid-air.

surprising that, for centuries, farmers in China appreciated and revered spiders' abilities so much that they built huts for spiders to live in during the winter months. Indeed, a garden with ample numbers of resident spiders is a healthy garden.

If we want to have birds and other predators of insects around to help out in the garden, we need to be tolerant of the creatures that they must consume to survive. Herbivorous insects, which eat plant material such as leaves or seeds, usually only take hold and cause problems when plants are in poor health, diversity is low, or predators are lacking. By growing a variety of plants, keeping them healthy, and

attracting wildlife that dines on insects, we can avoid the possibility that a particular herbivore species will get out of hand.

Some herbivore damage to leaves is actually a good thing, because insects keep plants healthy. How could that be? As always, it's chemical: Plants have developed an amazing array of defense mechanisms, and some create volatile organic compounds that repel harmful insects or attract invertebrate predators and parasites, which in turn help rid those plants of herbivore pests. Plants also get help from some types of birds that have been shown to be more attracted to trees with munched-on leaves than leaves without damage.

Slug poisons can harm or kill cats and dogs, as well as native banana slugs, which are voracious decomposers of organic matter. Natural slug and snail predators include raccoons, frogs, snakes, moles, ground beetles, and birds such as thrushes and crows.

The greater the diversity of insects in a garden, the more chance of predator-prey interaction. Fewer insects mean that our gardens will suffer, since studies show that low insect diversity results in fewer birds and more herbivore damage to leaves. The ecological dining service that birds and other predators provide helps keep plants healthy by keeping herbivore numbers down. So if we don't tolerate some holes in plants' leaves, the predators miss their breakfast and their young may starve. And pollination could decrease: syrphid fly larvae ravenously consume aphids, but without such juicy mouthfuls they'd fail to become pollinating adults. In short, without herbivores around, we will have fewer wild ones and much less functional ecosystems. Moreover, the entire ecosystem and planet benefit from the resulting addition of oxygen and sequestration of carbon dioxide when plants stay healthy.

## Herbicides

What about synthetic pesticides known as *herbicides*, which are used to kill or inhibit the growth of unwanted plants? These complex chemical compounds have no place in a "real garden" either, even those whose manufacturers claim they break down biologically in short periods of time. Sprayed application can drift to and affect other plants important to us or wildlife; when it reaches hardscape or disappears with the wind it can travel to waterways. While long-term toxicity to humans is still being debated, herbicides are known to poison amphibians and aquatic species as well as the animals that feed on them. And the inert ingredients (such as preservatives and solvents) in herbicides are anything but: Studies show that these often unlabeled substances amplify the toxic effects of the active ingredients.

Some organic gardeners use soaps, vinegar, and essential oils instead of synthetics, but they all have the potential to harm, so use them very carefully. I find that pulling or digging weeds is all that is necessary in ordinary garden care, and it's much safer than reaching for herbicides. To prevent something like a neighbor's bamboo patch from invading your yard, install a 2- to 3-foot-deep root barrier.

## Fungicides

Fungal diseases on native plants are not common, but any gardener who has had to deal with fungal diseases such as canker, mildew, and black spot knows that not all soil organisms are good to plants. However, most are beneficial, especially when a garden has healthy soil that supports a complete and balanced food web with sufficient diversity to keep disease-causing species in check. The soil will not be disease-free, but the impacts of the pathogen will be reduced.

Stepping back and allowing natural organisms within the soil to do the work reduces the chances that one pest will get out of hand, eliminating the need to use unnatural, dangerous fungicides. In fact, some plants may be directly harmed by the use of fungicides nearby, like bunchberry (*Cornus unalaschkensis*), whose roots are often infected with a beneficial fungus called endomycorrhizae, which helps the plant take up nutrients from the soil. Simply not growing plants that are susceptible to fungal diseases, such as hybrid tea roses, helps too. With few exceptions, native plants grown in appropriate conditions have little chance of being overwhelmed by fungal diseases.

In summary, there is no reason to add toxins to the habitat and diet of innocent wild animals who have no choice but to eat what is available, tainted or not. If we want the benefits of a naturalistic garden to extend beyond our property lines, we need to also concern ourselves with potentially harmful substances that may find their way outside.

## Sustaining Your Garden

No matter how low maintenance real gardens are, there will be tasks—like weeding, watering, mulching, and occasional pruning—that are straightforward and fairly easy to accomplish if you plan and organize in advance. Most of that work comes in the first few years, with much fewer tasks required once your garden becomes established. Being sure about what you want to do and always approaching a task positively can bring enjoyment as well as a sense of satisfaction.

Don't be afraid to let nature take the upper hand—a little untidiness goes a long way in providing for wildlife that can't thrive in manicured spaces. Let native plants do their thing; if you tend to be a neatnik, try to reserve it for the veggie beds and areas very close to the house. Fall "cleanups" should only involve sweeping up leaves from hard surfaces and any lawn, weeding, and removing any annual vegetable crops to prevent disease—not removing all the dying plant material that can provide cover and protection for wild ones during the harsh winter months. If you need to tidy up in spring, do it as late in the season as possible to cause the least disturbance.

### Weeding

Although many plants that we don't want or that are growing in what we consider the wrong place in our yards might be difficult to eradicate and cause a headache, plants really are not good or evil (unlike some methods of plant control that I can think of). Enthusiastic, hardy native plants that we call *pioneer species*, whose job it is to colonize disturbed, inhospitable landscapes and make way for later succession, are not weeds. In fact, many are suitable for the garden, including native asters, bleeding heart, and alders.

But some nonnative plants, as previously mentioned, can become so widespread that native flora and fauna are devastated. We can't blame plants that have had the misfortune of being accidentally or, more commonly, intentionally brought to our area. Unfortunately, such plants compete for essential nutrients, light, and water, and may inhibit or even cause the death of less vigorous plants that belong here. So when I use the term "weed" in this chapter,

it's to describe a nonnative plant that has the ability to spread vigorously and outcompete useful plants, and possibly escape to natural areas and inflict heavy damage.

For example, garlic mustard (*Alliaria petiolata*) produces chemicals that suppress beneficial mycorrhizal fungi that most plants, including trees in native forests, require for optimum growth. These sci-fi chemicals don't affect the fungi in garlic mustard's native soil, which is one reason why this plant belongs in that soil and not here. Weeds can also act as hosts for pests or diseases that may in turn affect your desired plants. So you will need to eradicate them, particularly during the first couple of years, while your new plants are getting established, but keep an eye out for weeds that might sneak in from neighboring yards in the future, too.

Weeds can be *annuals*, *biennials*, or *perennials*. An annual completes its life cycle and goes to seed in a single growing season, while a biennial grows vegetatively the first year and produces flowers and seeds its second (and last) year. Perennials live longer than two growing seasons and produce seeds each year. The best time to weed is before plants go to flower (since some seem to produce seeds in a heartbeat), so you won't have to pull out their offspring the following year. Annuals that pop up in late summer or fall, when the rains start, might die over the winter (but don't count on it!).

No weed control method should harm or compete with other plants or animals, trigger or exacerbate soil erosion or compaction,

LEFT Some plants need more moisture than others. Seeing them in their natural settings will help determine if they are a good fit for your site.

or reduce the soil's organic matter content. Weeding in late winter and spring can disturb ground-nesting bees and other insects, so try to do it after they are out and about. Simply pull weeds or use a hand fork for small spaces; hoeing is an option but it may damage desirable plants that have shallow roots. In large areas, weeds can also be cut or mowed to the ground—this method causes the least disruption to soil of the sort that might set the stage for even more weed seed germination and moisture loss. Keep paths weeded too, so there's less chance of spread from pathways.

A well-maintained garden needs less weeding than you might think, and it can be a relaxing, even therapeutic, task. A friend of mine likes to get together periodically with two friends for "gardening parties" where they take turns weeding each other's yards. Others prefer a more constant approach, weeding for fifteen minutes or so every few days or when weather allows. I find this method easiest on my back, and it tends to get weeds before they grow so large that they are harder and more disruptive to pull out. Remember that many weeds thrive in disturbed ground, so minimizing cultivation, adding mulch (except in areas where bees might nest), and growing ground cover that shades and outcompetes weeds will help minimize them.

## Watering

Water is precious, and luckily a great many Pacific Northwest native plants are tolerant of our warm, dry summers. However, the plants we set in the ground—particularly in the spring—will not make it without supplemental water during the period when their roots are becoming established (generally two to five years). Even plants described as drought tolerant need adequate moisture until they are established. "Adequate" means whatever will sustain a plant. Needs will vary—*Corydalis* spp., for example, needs much more moisture than *Ceanothus* spp.

Some plants, when placed at the upper edge of their tolerance for sun, may need more frequent watering, especially before they are established. My shade-loving deer ferns (*Blechnum spicant*) will gladly take as much moisture as I can dole out, especially those that have to take a bit of sun. Other species are even more sensitive to drought, such as western maidenhair fern (*Adiantum aleuticum*), which is often found basking in waterfall mist and probably won't make it without supplemental water past the establishment phase (unless you are lucky enough to have a stream on your property).

Then there are those, like bleeding heart (*Dicentra formosa*), that naturally go dormant during the dry period but usually stay alive due to fleshy roots that sustain them until winter rains. With summer irrigation, bleeding heart will stay green and possibly even bloom again during late summer or fall.

At the opposite extreme are the diehards that can really take drought. Those plants, such as many trees and shrubs, and perennials like yarrow (*Achillea millefolium* var. *occidentalis*) and some penstemons, will survive nicely without regular summer water once established. Some even *need* drought conditions and may react negatively to summer watering, so once they appear to be established, leave them alone unless they become dangerously dehydrated during the active growth phase or periods of excessive heat.

Other site conditions, like soil type, wind exposure, and topography, may also create watering issues. Fortunately, there are ways of simplifying complications and minimizing water use.

Because your planting plan groups plants with similar needs together, you are halfway to providing adequate moisture conditions; fall planting will also help get your plants off to a good start. For plants that need summer irrigation beyond the first two to five years, it will be much easier and less wasteful and time consuming to water them all in one place, rather than here and there all over the yard. To save time on watering, soaker hoses can be snaked through beds and borders, or drip systems can be used with T-joints that allow tubes to be attached for individual drip heads (even for containers). These two systems provide a gradual but steady flow of water that penetrates deeply into the soil with minimal leaching and evaporation, particularly when watering is done in the early morning. You can program the area that needs the most moisture to be watered perhaps twice a week during the hottest part of the summer, and have other low-water areas watered less often. Plants that have self-sown tend to be more tolerant of drought than those grown in pots, in my experience.

Whether you hand water or use a system, for best results water *deeply and infrequently*, allowing the water to *slowly* penetrate the roots, rather than shallowly and often and with great force. The former promotes stronger, deeper roots, while the latter will do the opposite. Watering slowly, deeply, and infrequently also conserves water that is easy to take for granted. The best time to water is in the morning, and the earlier the better. If you must water in the evening, try to keep leaves dry to cut down on waterborne diseases like powdery mildew. Other problems can result from getting foliage and flowers wet in full sunlight, including a scorched appearance, so avoid sprinklers.

There are several other ways to conserve soil moisture. One is to avoid cultivating the soil during the warm months. As the top of the soil dries, it insulates the soil below from quick moisture loss. But when you dig or pull weeds, causing moist soil to be exposed to the air, it quickly dries out.

In addition, maintaining well-structured soil, as mentioned in Chapter 4, is paramount. As soil becomes more fertile, its water-holding capacity will increase. Adding organic matter not only creates a spongelike effect, increasing water absorption, but it also retains it for later use. Strive to prevent compaction too, which can prevent absorption and cause water to puddle or run off. Adding a layer of insulating mulch in late spring will further limit water loss, as well as keep down weeds that can rob the soil of moisture.

## Mulching

Applying mulch is a great means of weed control, but it has many other very useful functions. Mulch helps protect roots from temperature extremes, greatly assisting new growth in the spring, and conserves moisture in two ways: by shading the soil surface and by slowing down evaporation from the soil. Organic mulch also provides nutrients to plants, feeds soil microbes, improves soil structure, and cushions the impact of rainfall, preventing erosion that may reduce nutrients available to plants.

Fallen leaves are the perfect mulch to protect soil and to help beneficial bugs like ground beetles and syrphid fly larvae overwinter.

The best mulch may be live mulch—ground cover plants such as coast strawberry (*frageria chiloensis*) or kinnikinnick (*Arctostaphylos uva-ursi*) for sun or partial shade, and sorrel (*Oxalis* spp.), wild ginger (*Asarum caudatum*), and mosses for shade. Until ground covers have spread and taller plants have filled in, you'll need to do their job.

Autumn is the ideal time to spread a 2- to 3-inch-deep mulch (finer material should be less thick) such as compost or fallen leaves out to plants' drip lines (the areas directly under the outer edges of their branches), although it can also be applied in the spring after the soil warms up. Finely ground bark and wood chips are less desirable because they break down quickly and can use up nitrogen in the process.

Whenever you mulch and whatever with, be sure to keep mulch 4 to 6 inches away from tree trunks, and don't smother smaller plants.

And moderation is key: Don't cover every square inch of your yard with mulch. Leave some bare soil where ground-nesting bees can raise

## keeping your garden healthy: the basics

- Leave most of your garden untidy, so beneficial insects and spiders can overwinter and birds can find food and shelter. Allow seed heads to remain for seed eaters in fall and winter. Studies show that perennials left uncut result in 100 times the number of beneficial visitors that manicured plants get.
- Don't rake up or blow away fallen leaves on bare soil. Leaf cover protects and enriches the soil and greatly benefits ground-nesting insects and their predators.
- Take care when digging near the roots of trees and shrubs, which may be quite shallow.
- In edible gardens, allow beneficial predators to move in and tackle any pests first. Letting some pests remain encourages the natural predator-prey cycle to continue and provides better control over time.
- A diverse garden that attracts pollinators will also attract beneficial insects, so major pest outbreaks in vegetable gardens should be rare. If not, use alternatives to pesticides, such as floating row covers, pheromone traps, and pest-resistant plant varieties. Even commonly used insecticidal soap kills insects, the majority of which are beneficial.

- Eschew all poisons in your yard. Aside from causing a slow and cruel death to the intended victim, poisons go beyond the target species. In addition, birds of prey or mammals may eat poisoned rodents, causing secondary poisoning.
- Allow trees and shrubs to assume their natural shapes whenever possible; don't shear or trim shrubs into topiary shapes that diminish cover for birds, and never "top" trees. If shrubs grow beyond imposed boundaries, obtain a good pruning book to carefully size them back so they still look natural, or remove them and replant with something more appropriate.
- Refrain from using products like compost that contain peat, which is mined from ancient wetlands that regulate surface-water purity and flow and are home to many rare plants and animals. Harvesting peat involves draining a bog of most of its moisture, permanently destroying it and compromising surrounding bogs, while large amounts of valuable wildlife habitat are ruined.
- For fences, arbors, and the like, allow minimal contact between wood and soil, to cut down on the speed of decay and give a longer life to your wood. For example, use concrete footings with metal brackets for fence posts and stand wooden

their young (natural leaf litter is OK). Such bees usually nest in sparsely vegetated areas, often on well-drained slopes. Heavy mulching can increase the number of garden slugs and snails, so don't mulch heavily around plants that are slug favorites, like larkspurs (*Delphinium* spp.)

Organic mulches are better than inorganic ones because they eventually break down and enrich the soil. Bagged mulches are available, but you can save money and make your garden more sustainable by simply mulching with fallen leaves—nature's acclaimed mulch—from your trees. If you need to buy mulch, avoid products made from endangered species such as cypress trees. Avoid products labeled just "wood" or "hardwood mulch." And don't use rock mulch or gravel, except in rock garden situations.

benches on bricks or similar material that keeps wood above soggy soil.

- Avoid using unnecessary plastic in the garden. Made from fossil fuels, plastics may take thousands of years to break down. When improperly disposed of, they create pollution that can kill or maim wildlife. Plastics are most acceptable when they will have a long useful life, can definitely be recycled, and/or are made of recycled plastics themselves.

- Walk on paths or stepping-stones when traversing planted areas—plants don't grow well in compacted soil, and roots will avoid it.

- Refrain from working soil when it's saturated, or even walking on it when possible. Stand on a plank if you need to work during the wet winter months.

- Disinfect tools, especially if disease is present in a section of your garden, before moving on to another section. Clean them again when you're done, and lightly oil them before storing.

- Keep a garden log to track plantings, record plant names, and remind you when to perform seasonal tasks—and anything else you don't want to forget.

## Feeding

Plants are continually taking nutrients from the soil, but unlike most cultivated fruiting plants (like garden-variety vegetables), native plants are generally not voracious feeders. Some natives, such as giant chain fern (*Woodwardia fimbriata*), may even be damaged by the addition of fertilizer. Amending soil with organic matter—which slowly supplies small amounts of nutrients to soil organisms, which in turn make important nutrients available to plants—is usually all that's needed for native species.

Fallen leaves, which break down fairly quickly and offer high nutrient amounts—up to fifteen times more nitrogen than woody debris provides—are the best way to "feed" native plants. However, if your site has been under concrete or the soil has been heavily mulched with wood chips, it may be best to add an organic, slow-release fertilizer before you plant. If you do, choose renewable products over synthetic or mined products. Not only are they safer for the environment, they supply additional micronutrients that many synthetic fertilizers do not, and they last much longer.

The difference between organic and synthetic fertilizers is the impact they have on

soil life. Synthetic fertilizers are basically salts that, studies show, can destroy soil structure, burn plant roots, and kill essential soil life. That teaspoon of lively soil that can hold up to a billion helpful bacteria turns nearly lifeless when chemically treated, hosting as few as 100. Organic matter such as compost and green manures, on the other hand, contains little salt and doesn't release its nutrients immediately. Instead, it is decomposed by microflora and -fauna that live in the root zone and is turned into a mineralized form available to roots. This very slow release of nutrients prevents injury to roots, while still-decomposing plant residues maintain a reserve of nutrients in the soil.

To determine whether you need to add any supplemental nutrients and, if so, which ones you should add, have your soil tested by a lab (see Resources) and use single-nutrient fertilizers instead of complete fertilizer whenever appropriate. A word of caution: Even organic fertilizers can burn roots and pollute if improperly used. To reduce risk of runoff, avoid applying fertilizers near streams or drainage areas.

## Pruning

Native gardens have no more tendency to turn into jungles than any other type of garden. "Overgrown" gardens are the result of poor planning and inappropriate plant choices, not the fact that they contain plants native to our region. If you choose plants that when mature will fit in your space and not overwhelm it, there should be little need to prune, except for cutting out unwanted suckers and the occasional dead branch, and annually pruning any cultivated fruit trees you may have. Allowing plants to attain their natural shape maximizes the habitat needed by wildlife; shearing and other drastic pruning does just the opposite.

If you need to prune, do it in late winter, before March, while plants are dormant and before breeding season begins (usually in March). Use sharp, appropriately sized tools and make clean cuts close to branches or trunks, but not flush: Cut just outside the "collar" (the slightly swollen area where a branch attaches to a larger branch or trunk), making the smallest wound possible. For long or thick branches, shorten them first to reduce their weight and the potential for ripped bark. Using a saw, make your first cut a short way into the underside of the branch and then cut through the remainder from the top to meet the first cut.

When in doubt about how to approach a pruning project, obtain a good pruning book, or consult a reputable and certified arborist or a group like Seattle-based Plant Amnesty. After pruning, you may have a large amount of branches and twigs, which are perfect for creating brush or log piles on the ground that small animals may use for shelter or perching.

LEFT The best mulch is usually a green one.

# CHAPTER 6
## *multiplication by division, and other propagation methods*

"Though I do not believe that a plant will spring up where no seed has been, I have great faith in a seed. Convince me that you have a seed there, and I am prepared to expect wonders."
—Henry David Thoreau

**I'VE ALWAYS BEEN INTRIGUED BY THE REFRESHING** process of creating new plants. As a child, I remember being amazed at the itty-bitty plants my father grew from seed in the basement under lights for our summer vegetable garden. I knew they were special and never touched his prodigies. I still get a little excited when I see a seed germinating or something taking root. I do my own propagation whenever time allows, when I can't find a certain plant for sale, or when I want to save some cash. It takes just a little effort and makes me feel like I've accomplished something.

There are many ways to propagate plants, but this chapter will focus on what I think are the easiest methods: seed, cuttings, division, and layering. Though the majority of the plants in this book should be fairly easy to find at native plant nurseries, plant sales, or possibly even urban garden stores, if you need a large number of plants, such as for an extensive meadow garden, seeding will be the easiest and least expensive method. Most of the plants in this book can be propagated

Ripe seeds of nodding onion (*Allium cernuum*) up close, ready for sowing

Broad-leaved penstemon (*Penstemon ovatus*), grown from seed, is ready for the garden.

can also harvest very small amounts of seed from locally abundant and healthy wild populations nearby, but never harvest from plants that are rare or seem to be struggling in their habitat, and never dig up or divide wild plants. Cuttings may be OK, but to be sure you collect legally and sustainably, read the Garry Oak Ecosystems Recovery Team's "Ethical Guidelines for the Collection and Use of Native Plants" (see Appendix C).

## Growing from Seed

Propagation by seed is the most ecologically beneficial way to multiply plants, because seed, or sexual, reproduction nurtures genetic variation better than vegetative methods such as division, layering, and cuttings. The greater the diversity in a plant population, the higher the likelihood that some may adapt and succeed in a slowly changing environment. Sexual reproduction, then, allows species to evolve and adapt to changes in the environment, where those that are best suited to survive are better able to pass their genetic information onto the next generation. Although this may not be of utmost importance if you are only propagating a few plants, it is reassuring to know that you are doing your part to protect native plants' genetic integrity.

If you've never grown plants from seed or have only grown annual seedlings for your vegetable garden, you may logically think that the best time to start native seeds is spring, but that is generally not the case. Again, we need to follow what nature would do and sow native seeds just after they ripen in summer or fall, before the onset of winter (although a few species may also germinate if sown in the spring).

from seed, which helps preserve genetic diversity; to find other techniques, check on a given plant's listing page, where the optimal method or methods for that species is noted.

Seeds may be located through seed exchanges, nurseries that specialize in natives, friends with native plant gardens, and rescue situations. Whenever possible, obtain seeds from plants that originated near your area. You

Willows (*Salix* spp.) are easy to propagate by hardwood cuttings, root sucker transplantation, or seed.

After seeds ripen, they need to go through a period of dormancy, an adaptation that ensures that they germinate only when temperature and moisture conditions become optimal. To emerge from dormancy, most require exposure to cold temperatures and moist conditions, known as *stratification*. Every winter, as I pile on layers of fleece and don those fluffy slippers that the cats try to nap on, I have to remind myself that rainy, cold weather does have at least one purpose: Stratification serves to soften tough seed coats, activate enzymes, and convert starch into sugars that seed embryos need to develop.

The simplest way to accomplish cold stratification is to sow the seeds directly into or onto the soil in late summer or fall, to allow natural exposure to cold and moisture. Most seeds within fleshy fruits, such as serviceberry and madrone, benefit from fresh sowing but should be separated from their pulp beforehand (but not in the way that fruit-eating birds do!), to reduce chances of molding and to speed germination. Seeds may also be sown in trays or pots, moistened, and placed outdoors out of direct sunlight—either partially buried in moist soil, gravel, or sand and covered with glass or plastic sheeting to keep out seed stealers and excessive winter rain, or in a cold frame. This not only makes transplantation easier, it is also best for seeds that may take more than a year to germinate.

Whether directly in the ground or in pots, the outdoor method is favorable for most seeds that germinate best when planted fresh after harvest and not allowed to dry out. It is essential for seeds that *must* be planted soon after harvest, such as fawn lilies and tiger lilies. You can also mimic nature by tucking seeds into a dampened paper towel and placing the towel in a sealed plastic bag. Store the bag in your refrigerator for three to four months, then remove the seeds and pot them up or sow them outside. For seeds that don't need to be planted right after harvest and that you prefer not to plant right away, you can prepare them for storage by air-drying them for a couple of weeks and separating the seeds from the remains of any fruit.

The seeds of some plant species, like lupine, have very tough seed coats that can be impervious to water and gases and thus prevent or delay germination. You can alter and weaken such a covering with a process called *scarification*, which mimics the natural microbial processes that occur over long periods outdoors and results in permeability of tough seed coats. Seed coats can be mechanically scarified by nicking with a knife (avoiding the little spot where the first root will emerge from), rubbing with sandpaper, or shaking seeds within a jar filled halfway with coarse sand. Then, soak the seeds in hot tap water until they absorb water and sink (usually several hours). Scarified seeds don't store well, so plant them as soon as possible after treatment.

*Seed sowing techniques:* To propagate seeds in pots or flats, use a growing medium (preferably without peat) that will nurture germinating seeds and grow healthy seedlings. It should hold moisture without getting soggy, but also drain quickly.

Fill a flat or pot with your soil mix, and tamp it gently to remove large air spaces. Since many native seeds have been shown to germinate most quickly and thoroughly when uncovered (providing they are kept moist), gently press all but large seeds into the soil surface. For seeds that need darkness to germinate, cover them with a very thin layer of finely textured cover like screened, weed-free leaf mold. Inorganic materials such as coarse sand or grit work well as coverings for potted seeds because they decrease the possibility of fungus, algae, or moss growth.

For seeds with unknown light needs, press them into the soil or cover them with only a very light dusting of soil—if you have enough seeds, shift into science project mode and sow some with covering and some without. Soil coverings can be helpful during dry periods when frequent mistings aren't possible, and for any known to be hindered by light. Sow larger seeds to a depth of twice their smallest diameter (unless they require light). Keep in mind that native plant propagation isn't an exact science. Success comes down to how we can best mimic natural, optimal conditions for germination; the best planting technique may simply be whatever works the best for you.

For seeds grown indoors in pots or flats, I like to water from the bottom, that is, immersing the underside of the pots in standing water in a sink or container, until water is drawn up from beneath to the surface. This way the entire growing medium is moistened and the seeds on top are not disturbed. To slow down evaporation before germination, loosely cover pots or flats with clear plastic bags, venting them once or twice a day. Very small seeds typically sprout best when regularly misted from above, but as soon as they sprout, begin watering from beneath. Remove all coverings immediately after germination, to help prevent fungal disease that can kill seedlings. After seedlings grow their second set of leaves, water again from above. When handling small seedlings, pick them up by their expendable seed leaves, rather than their very delicate stems, and support their roots with a spoon or trowel.

To sow seeds directly into or onto garden soil, proceed in a similar way, using leaf mold to cover seeds if necessary. If sowing in the fall, let nature handle the watering.

Here's an example of the sowing process for Oregon grape (*Mahonia* spp.): Oregon grape is easily grown from seeds removed from a ripe berry's pulp in autumn. Either dry the whole fruit out of direct sunlight for several weeks and separate the seeds from the dried pulp (gently crushing the dried fruit on white paper usually releases the seeds), or crush the fresh fruit, remove the seeds, rinse them, and dry them out of direct sunlight. Sow the seeds ¼ inch deep directly into the ground outdoors, in a cool spot, and cover them with a very thin layer of mulch. They should germinate the following spring as the seed coat is pushed aside by the growing shoot, but some may take two winters.

## seed storage

How long seeds can be stored and remain viable generally depends on their characteristics, whether or not they were fully mature when harvested, how carefully they were handled, and the amount of desiccation a particular type can tolerate. Some seeds, like tiger lily (*Lilium columbianum*), will germinate only if planted soon after harvest, while others may be long-lived in optimal storage conditions. I was able to germinate some ten-year-old *Penstemon ovatus* seeds, and one researcher reported finding viable *Ceanothus velutinus* seeds that were determined to be over 200 years old. (Most will not last that long!)

When storing seeds, keep in mind that optimal storage basically requires the opposite of conditions for germinating them: Instead of moist, warm, and light, think dry, cool, and dark. Seeds should be fully dried before storage, but never at temps higher than around 95°F. One exception: The seeds of legumes like beans and peas should not be dried as completely as other seeds. Native legumes include lupines, beach peas, and vetches.

Place the dried seeds in paper packets (great way to reuse envelopes), not plastic bags, label them, and store in an airtight container in your refrigerator or another dark place, like a cool, dry basement. Toss some silica desiccant packets (those "Do not eat" packets that come with products that need to be kept dry) or rice grains into the container (not the envelopes) to help keep humidity down.

# making potting medium

I started making my own potting soil mixtures after I learned about the environmental destruction associated with peat extraction. The mining of ancient, nonrenewable peat bogs is a highly pernicious operation that destroys habitat for many rare species. In addition, peat bogs are major carbon sinks that hold four times as much carbon as forests do, so when peat is extracted from the bogs, enormous amounts of carbon dioxide are released into the atmosphere.

It also dawned on me that somehow, some way, my parents and grandparents managed to grow plants without modern packaged mixes that contain peat, perlite, and vermiculite (the latter two of which are also mined and nonrenewable) and became popular about thirty years ago. If you want nothing to do with ripping up ancient peat bogs and other destructive mining operations, you can make your own potting medium. Like everything you make from scratch, it's usually better than packaged items, since you know exactly what's going into it. I've used coir, a by-product of the coconut industry—it holds moisture well so is a good substitute for peat and vermiculite. But it's more exotic than a palm tree in Puyallup, so it's not perfect due to the extensive shipping involved. For that reason, I've moved on to using a mixture of screened homemade leaf mold, aged compost or worm castings, and coarse sand. All planting medium should be light in texture and retain moisture, but drain well.

You can also grow them in pots with potting medium that is kept moist (but not wet) in a shaded, protected place outdoors.

## Ferns

Ferns have complex life cycles and are very different from flowering plants that produce seeds, but the propagation technique is somewhat similar. Most can also be divided, but it can be difficult and potentially harmful to the plants. Instead, do what nature does and grow them from spores, which are produced by those little dots, called *sori*, that you will find on the underside of a leaf or along the edge of a leaf. When dispersed, spores germinate on moist soil. After a series of sexual interactions (probably not interesting enough to keep you up at night), baby ferns result, and the species lives on.

My favorite way to propagate ferns is by just letting them do their magic in the privacy of the garden, all by themselves. Then, when the young ferns are a few inches tall, I gently relocate them, on a cool, cloudy day, to the chosen area. But if you want a little more control, here's how to propagate ferns indoors:

1. Gather some leaves with plump ripe sori (if you can shake some spores onto a piece of white paper, they're ready).
2. If the spores don't fall out easily, wait a few days or weeks, or put the leaves into an envelope and let it sit for a week in a dry place at room temperature, after which the sori should release their spores.

RIGHT Ripe sori of a western sword fern (*Polystichum munitum*)

Sometimes common names are descriptive, like piggy-back plant (*Tolmeia menziesii*), whose leaves sprout juvenile plants on their top side.

3. Prepare a pot or flat with moist potting soil.
4. Sprinkle the spores thinly and evenly onto the soil, and place a clear plastic bag over the pot.
5. Place the covered pot on a bright windowsill but out of direct sunlight, or under grow lights at 65°–75°F.

6. Mist the soil regularly so it doesn't dry out.
7. Remove the covering when tiny ferns start growing, but keep the soil moist.
8. Transplant baby ferns after they have several fronds, usually a few months after sowing.

## Division

The quickest way to propagate a plant is by division or separation, so if you like immediate gratification, this one's for you. Although many species can't be divided, with those that spread laterally by modified stems called rhizomes, like *Iris tenax*, it's a breeze—as long as it's done carefully and at the right time of the year, when the plant is in or near dormancy. Others may spread laterally by new shoots, or by the growth of new bulbs, both of which may be separated from the parent plant or bulb.

The rule of thumb is to divide your spring-blooming plants in the fall, and fall-blooming plants in the early spring. For those that bloom during summer, it's probably safest to do it in the fall, so they will have the entire winter to recover. Many perennials do best when they are divided every few years, flowering more profusely and adding to the beauty and benefits already in place.

Do your divisions or separations on a cool, cloudy day, especially if the plant is growing in the sun—this will cut down on the shock and stress the plant may experience. Like other types of surgery, it's best done cleanly, quickly, and painlessly (please be careful with sharp tools). Here's how:

With a spade, dig up the whole plant, cutting its roots with a pair of pruning shears or a sharp knife if necessary (which is much less stressful for the plant than ripping it from the ground). Rhizomes can be divided by cutting them, with a clean knife, into pieces that each have buds and roots. Replant them so that the buds are facing upward and the roots are at a level similar to those of the parent plant.

To divide plants with tightly bound fibrous roots, you will have to cut sections apart with a knife; those with looser roots should allow you to just tease them apart. Generally, it's best to end up with fewer sections that have a fair amount of viable root left and at least one vegetative bud, rather than tiny pieces with very little root mass. Keep the roots moist and out of sunlight until you can place them in their new homes (preferably on a cool, cloudy day) or pot them up to give away. After planting, all divisions should be kept somewhat moist, but not soggy.

Bulbs like camas can be dug up and gently pulled apart in early fall and replanted soon afterward. Lily bulbs may be divided by breaking off scales from dormant bulbs, which should then be planted with tips upward and just below the surface in pots kept moist and out of hot sunlight.

## The Cutting Edge

Most woody plants can be propagated by stem cutting, which is a good way to grow species that are difficult by seed. *Hardwood cuttings* utilize the previous season's growth and are collected during dormancy in winter. *Semi-hardwood cuttings*, on the other hand, are taken during the growing season, but not when plants are growing quickly. The application of a rooting hormone (which can be purchased at gardening stores) to cut ends helps promote root formation, but is not necessary for plants that root easily, like red-twig dogwood

and willows. *Softwood cuttings* are also taken from the new growth of woody plants, are most successful if there are no flower buds on the cutting, and may be treated with root hormone. *Root cuttings* may also be taken on dormant plants that produce suckers, although this is not commonly done.

Regardless of the stage at which you take cuttings, they should always be made with clean, very sharp pruning shears or a razor blade, in early morning on cool, cloudy days to cut down on water loss. Plants should be hydrated and cuttings should be used soon after collection. Prepare pots that are at least 4 inches deep with a potting mixture of compost and coarse sand. Moisten the soil, and with a thin stick make 3-inch-deep vertical holes about 6 inches apart. Cut 6- to 8-inch stem pieces diagonally, and remove buds and leaves from the bottom 3 inches. Place the cuttings in the holes. Firm up the soil around the cuttings and moisten again. Keep them under clear plastic, to create a mini-greenhouse, and out of direct sun. Transplant rooted cuttings at the end of the growing season, when they are dormant.

## The Flexibility of Layering

A sometimes slower, but easy and low-stress, way of propagating is to use a technique called *ground layering*. Like division and cuttings, it's an asexual method, so all new plants will have exactly the same flower, fruit, and leaf characteristics as the parent. Nature often uses this method, when the droopy branches of a flexible shrub or vine touch the ground, stay there, and develop roots. The section touching soil is still attached to the main plant and receives nutrients and water from it, but the new roots that

form on the underside will allow it to grow into another plant. My two golden currant plants (*Ribes aureum* var. *aureum*) are still young, but in a few years an arching branch may bend over and take root (as long as the branch stays in contact with the soil). I can then either leave the new plant where it wants to be, or, once it has grown an ample amount of roots, cut it free of the mommy plant and either replant it elsewhere or pot it up and give it away.

You can layer on purpose, as well. In spring or late summer, bend a flexible side shoot or branch until it touches the ground, or, if you're short of ground space or just want to efficiently get it into a pot, bend it so it touches a pot of soil. Whatever potting soil you use should drain well but be kept moist. A little wounding can help the piece take root: With sandpaper, gently scrape a little of the stem or branch's outer covering on the side that will touch the soil, or with a sharp knife make a very shallow cut into the stem (don't cut all the way through). Rooting hormone may be applied after the wounding, but is often not necessary.

Bury the wounded branch slightly, and gently insert an inverted-U-shaped metal stake to keep the stem in place; a rock may also work. To keep the part aboveground somewhat upright, tie it loosely to a small stake. Keep the area moist, and roots should form within a few months. Cut the new plant from the mother plant with sharp pruning shears, close to the new plant. Dig up the new plant, preserving as many roots as possible, and replant it in a new location.

Besides golden currant, most plants that have a somewhat droopy habit or tend to trail on the ground take well to ground layering: rhododendron, red-twig dogwood, honeysuckle, clematis, and thimbleberry, to name a few.

Some plants, like strawberries, create specialized structures that facilitate propagation by layering of a different type. *Stolons*, also called runners, produce new shoots and plantlets where they touch the soil. The plantlets then take root while still attached to the parent plant, and the stolon eventually breaks down. New plants may be detached from the parent plant once small roots have developed and grown elsewhere. Some grass species also produce stolons, and fawn lily (*Erythronium* spp.) produces white stolons that grow horizontally from the bulb, either underground or near the surface of the soil under fallen leaves.

Whether propagating plants to save money or to creatively increase the cover in your garden, you can't go wrong. You can also give plants you've grown to other native plant enthusiasts or donate them to fundraiser plant sales. At-home propagation is also a great way to teach children about the ways that plants reproduce.

LEFT Golden currant (*Ribes aureum* var. *aureum*) is easy to propagate by ground layering.

# 100 native plants for the garden

"I knew, of course, that trees and plants had roots, stems, bark,
branches and foliage that reached up toward the light. But I was coming
to realize that the real magician was light itself."
—Edward Steichen

**THIS SECTION SPOTLIGHTS SOME OF THE BEST PACIFIC** Northwest plants for supporting biodiversity at home. Among them you will find choice evergreen and deciduous trees and shrubs, a couple of meandering vines, and a variety of evergreen and deciduous perennials in myriad sizes, textures, and forms. The plants are listed alphabetically by botanical name and are grouped according to their light requirements, since the amount of sunlight (or lack of it) that your site has is one of the most important considerations when determining what to grow.

The plants in this portion of the book are certainly not your only choices; any plants native to your specific area or other areas will likely work, as long as you make sure their needs will be met in the conditions you have. There were additional plants I wanted to include, but some had to be pruned out: alder, fritillary, juncus, and juniper are just a few of the worthy species that just didn't fit into these limited pages.

Oregon iris (*Iris tenax*), threeleaf foamflower (*Tiarella trifoliata* var. *trifoliata*), one-leaf onion (*Allium unifolium*), wood sorrel (*Oxalis oregana*)

I give all 100 of these plants five stars due to their ecological benefits. The flowering perennials are perfect for pollinators, the woody plants provide excellent wildlife cover and food, and dozens of others are overachievers that also stabilize or enrich soil. Many are used in restoration projects, and most (though not all) are long-lived, with a few, sadly, rare or endangered in the wild.

But I also treasure all 100 because they are wonderful garden plants. The majority are easy to grow (as long they fit in your conditions), not terribly difficult to locate at plant nurseries, and fairly simple to propagate should you be prone to DIY. Many are suitable for small gardens, but entries for those that are not will have a notation to that effect. Incidentally, nearly half of them are growing and thriving in my own yard. All of them are beauty queens, some year round, and I dare you not to fall madly in love with at least a few.

Love can be a bit blind though, so beware: If you have young children who are at that stage where nearly everything ends up in their mouth, or dogs who like to broaden their culinary horizons, consider that a few of these plants may be toxic when nibbled on. However, most are not (unless humongous amounts are consumed) and in fact were used extensively by Native Americans either medicinally or for food. If there is concern, either avoid or keep the following native plants where children and other cherished members of your family can't tangle with or ingest them: Milkweed (*Asclepias* spp.) is essential for monarch butterflies but may be toxic if large quantities are ingested; the seeds of honeysuckle (*Lonicera* spp.) may be toxic, as are all parts of larkspurs (*Delphinium* spp.), native or not. And then there's natural latex:

About 10 percent of flowering plants worldwide create the milky cocktail of toxic chemicals, a fluid the plants use to poison insects or heal their wounds. I've never had any reactions to the native plants in my yard, but I've learned to armor myself against the fluid of *Euphorbia* plants, which makes me intensely itchy wherever it touches my skin. For several weeks following a pruning session with our fig trees when the sap was running, my husband looked as though I had beaten him up. Keep in mind that any plant could cause an allergic reaction for some people. When in doubt, wear gardening gloves and other protective clothing.

## Lighting the Way

One of the major factors that determine plant survival is light. Essential for photosynthesis, it also triggers the blooming period of many plants. While the majority of nonnative, horticultural species require full sunlight for optimal growth, many regional natives have evolved to survive in a wide range of light conditions, increasing opportunities in our gardens. You will notice that the majority fall under the partial-shade category, with fewer in the sun and shade sections.

But there are no fixed divisions—many could also have been placed in another section due to their versatility, so be sure to check more than one section. If you have a mostly shady yard, for example, also take a look at the plants in the partial-shade section, since some of them, such as vine maple (*Acer circinatum*) and Oregon boxwood (*Paxistima myrsinites*), are quite versatile. Whether a plant can handle a wide range of conditions or a narrower one, you will find detailed information on each of the listing pages.

Map 2. Hardiness Zones

### Average Annual Extreme Minimum Temperature

| Temp (F) | Zone | Temp (C) |
|---|---|---|
| -40 to -35 | 3a | -40 to 37.2 |
| -35 to -30 | 3b | -37.2 to -34.4 |
| -30 to -25 | 4a | -34.4 to -31.7 |
| -25 to -20 | 4b | -31.7 to -28.9 |
| -20 to -15 | 5a | -28.9 to -26.1 |
| -15 to -10 | 5b | -26.1 to -23.3 |
| -10 to -5 | 6a | -23.3 to -20.6 |
| -5 to 0 | 6b | -20.6 to -17.8 |
| 0 to 5 | 7a | -17.8 to -15 |
| 5 to 10 | 7b | -15 to -12.2 |
| 10 to 15 | 8a | -12.2 to -9.4 |
| 15 to 20 | 8b | -9.4 to -6.7 |
| 20 to 25 | 9a | -6.7 to -3.9 |

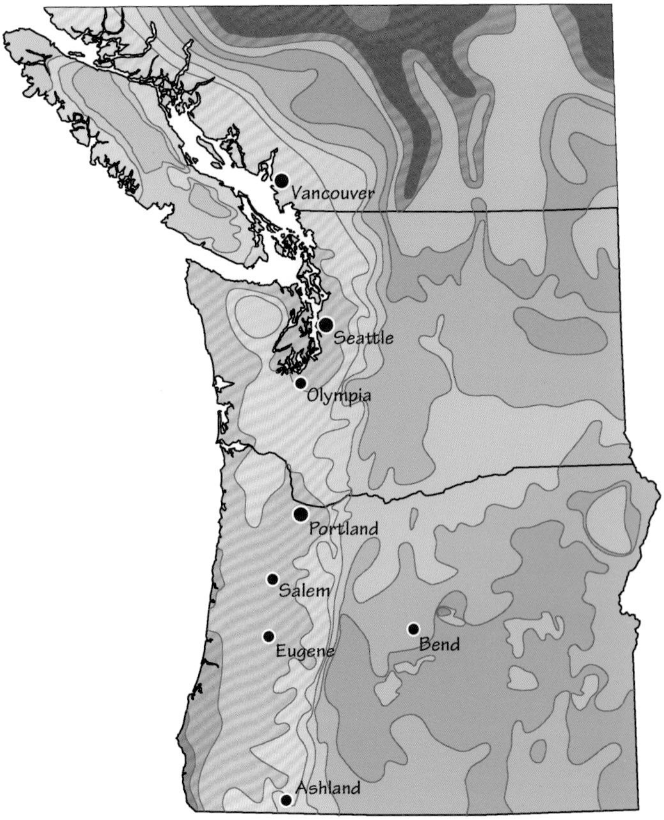

Adapted from the United States Department of Agriculture and Agriculture and Agri-Food Canada.

Besides light, you will find other factors on each species' page to consider as you make your choices, beginning with a few brief facts about each plant, followed by information in the following categories:

→ **Hardiness zones:** Plant hardiness zones are based on the average annual minimum winter temperature. Essentially, the higher the zone's number, the milder the winter climate. Growing plants from a colder hardiness zone than yours should be fine, as long as other conditions are compatible. Plants that belong in a hardiness zone warmer than yours may not survive,

however; if you want to try growing them, be sure to mulch in fall to prevent frost penetration during the winter.

→ **How big:** Every plant needs elbow room, and the distance at which you should set plants away from other plants, buildings, or fences depends on their size at maturity. Take note of the estimated mature size of each plant—width as well as height. Your goal is to choose plants that will eventually fill the space you have and not require much (if any) pruning to keep them in bounds—besides being demanding, frequent pruning can be detrimental to plants and prevents them from attaining their natural and most attractive size and form. Also keep in mind that the form or size a plant takes may change with light conditions: Plants grown in shade often become leggier than they would in sun. This is typical of evergreen huckleberry (*Vaccinium ovatum*), which ranges in size from 4 feet tall in sun to up to 12 feet tall in shade. Some plants may also grow larger in rich soil or just have an inherent vigor that others may not. If you have a very small yard, not all plants will be suitable— some will either become so large and gangly that they would take over a small lot, have a tendency to develop into thickets that only a tiny bird or snake can penetrate, or spread very quickly. Such plants are generally best left to larger gardens, and this is noted in their descriptions.

→ **Bloom traits:** If your aim is to provide for pollinators, you can't go wrong with the choices on these lists (except for ferns, which are beneficial in other ways). Flowers on some plants appear as early as late winter; others bloom in spring and/ or summer, with a few into fall. Note the "Benefits to wildlife" sections if you want to attract certain species to nectar- or pollen-rich plants.

→ **Sun and soil:** With a few exceptions, most of these species do not have very specific soil needs. However, some plants, such as rhododendrons, ferns, huckleberries, and bunchberry, like their roots in acidic soil (pH 4–6); group plants with similar pH needs in the same area. All plants will benefit from the addition of organic matter to the soil, but some, especially those that

hang with a woodsy crowd, as in ferns and tall bugbane (*Cimicifuga elata*), require extra rich soil, which should point you in the direction of your compost bin. Except for a few species that naturally grow in bogs and other wetlands, all will do best in soil that drains well. Species that are drought tolerant after establishment are noted, as are those that need especially fast-draining soil, such as most *Penstemon* and all *Lewisia* species; it's important that their growing space be amended with coarse sand, gravel, or pumice if they are not grown in a rock garden setting.

→ **Where it grows:** This provides a general idea of the type of terrain and elevation the species occurs in naturally, to help you decide whether you've got what it takes. For example, plants that grow in coniferous forests at low to middle elevations (known for their acidic soils, which come from the accumulation of conifer needles and other plant debris on the topsoil, as well as the growth of mosses) will likely prefer slightly acidic soil. If plants typically grow on rocky slopes or outcrops, they will need well-drained soil and perhaps be good candidates for a rock garden. Species' native ranges are mentioned when possible, especially if a species occurs only in a limited area within the region.

→ **How to space it:** A good rule of thumb is to space most plants the width of a mature plant apart, or slightly closer. A perennial that grows to about 3 feet wide, for example, would be placed roughly 3 feet from another, measured from center to center. Plant generously, as nature does, so that branches overlap a bit, especially those that don't like full sun, such as western redcedar trees.

→ **Help it thrive:** Because natives are so trouble-free when properly sited, the suggested maintenance tasks are mostly limited to irrigation recommendations and an occasional tip about pruning or division.

→ **Associates:** This tells you which other plants might be found growing alongside the described species in the wild. These lists are roughly organized from large to small, but they are far from exhaustive. Because some species grow in several different plant communities, it's difficult to list each and every plant that may be associated with them. For example, in British Columbia, Pacific dogwood (*Cornus nuttallii*) is a common subcanopy tree in Douglas-fir (*Pseudotsuga menziesii*) and western hemlock (*Tsuga heterophylla*) forests; in Washington, it is common in Douglas-fir, western hemlock, and Pacific silver fir (*Abies amabilis*) mixed forests. Other vegetation growing with Pacific dogwood may include grand fir (*A. grandis*), noble fir (*A. procera*), Pacific yew (*Taxus brevifolia*), western redcedar (*Thuja plicata*), bigleaf maple (*Acer macrophyllum*), vine maple (*A. circinatum*), low Oregon grape (*Mahonia repens*), and salal (*Gaultheria shallon*). However, at low elevations in Oregon's Willamette Valley it occurs in a different community, with Garry oak (*Quercus garryana*), bigleaf maple (*Acer macrophyllum*), Oregon ash (*Fraxinus latifolia*), incense cedar (*Calocedrus decurrens*), and madrone (*Arbutus menziesii*). If you would like more detailed information about associated plants, the USDA's Forest Service operates a website (www.fs.fed.us/data base/feis/plants/) that lists most native plants' general distribution, habitat types, and plant communities, which should help determine more precisely which plants naturally grow together in your area.

→ **Benefits to wildlife:** All species will provide for native insects, which are essential to other wildlife. Additional benefits listed are fairly general, but examples are usually included. Your yard, depending on its location, may attract fewer species or other species than those listed. Benefits to threatened or endangered wildlife are noted whenever possible.

→ **Substitute for:** The nonnative species listed here are those that have either proven to be invasive in natural areas, are difficult to eradicate once established in gardens, or are simply common, horticultural species that offer little or no ecological benefit. They often have a similar habit or appearance, or may even be related to the described native species.

→ **How to propagate:** Methods of propagation are listed for each species. (For basic instructions, see Chapter 6.)

→ **Related species:** One to three related species are mentioned at the end of each listing. Since these country cousins may grow to different sizes or shapes or have differing moisture needs, one of them may actually fit your setting better than the main attraction on the page—so be sure to read all the way to the bottom. With a few exceptions, the related species' light needs are the same, but those species may be more difficult to find in nurseries or may naturally occur in a limited area within the region.

# plants for full sun or mostly sun

**THE PLANTS IN THIS SECTION NEED AT LEAST** half a day of sun during the growing season. Some can tolerate all-day sun, particularly those labeled "*full* sun to light shade," but most will do fine with anything between all day and half a day. If you live in an area that gets very hot during the summer months, or the site you are planting is a south-facing slope, be sure to choose only plants that can tolerate considerable sun. Plants grown in cooler areas generally can handle more direct sun.

Narrowleaf milkweed (*Asclepias fascicularis*)

*Abies grandis*
# Grand fir

| | |
|---|---|
| PLANT TYPE: | Tall coniferous tree |
| SIZE: | 70–120 feet x 30 feet |
| LIGHT REQUIREMENTS: | Sun to partial shade |
| WATER REQUIREMENTS: | Low to medium |
| HARDINESS ZONES: | 3b to 9b |

One of many firs native to the Northwest, this tall, handsome long-lived conifer has a pyramidal habit. Flattened needles are deep green and arranged in two rows. Female cones are pale green and upright on branches, while male cones hang below. This is a valuable evergreen tree popular with birds, although it will be healthiest in larger gardens located away from urban air pollution.

**How big:** 70–120 feet tall x 30 feet wide.

**Bloom traits:** Male cones are pendant on low branches and bear pollen in late spring. Pale-green upright cones develop higher on the tree, ripen in late summer, and shatter when they mature.

**Sun and soil:** Full sun to partial shade. Moist, well-drained, deep soil.

**Where it grows:** Moist coniferous forests, at low to middle elevations.

**How to space it:** 20–30 feet apart.

**Help it thrive:** Drought tolerant when mature, but some supplemental summer water, especially when young, is beneficial.

**Associates:** Douglas-fir, western redcedar, Pacific silver fir, Sitka spruce, Pacific dogwood, shiny-leaf ceanothus, huckleberries, Oregon boxwood, thimbleberry, vanilla leaf, and others.

**Benefits to wildlife:** Provides food and nesting and roosting sites for many birds, including owls, swifts, and woodpeckers, as well as tree-dwelling mammals such as squirrels. Host species for pine white butterfly larvae. Provides thermal and hiding cover for many wild species.

**Substitute for:** English holly (*Ilex aquifolium*).

**How to propagate:** From seed sown outdoors, covered with a thin layer of mulch and protected from strong sunlight. Cones should be collected in fall and stored in a dry place for a month before seeds are extracted.

**Related species: Noble fir** (*Abies procera*) is also stately but grows taller and wider and has stiff branches. Intolerant of shade, it grows at middle elevations and is used as a Christmas tree. **Pacific silver fir** (*A. amabilis*) grows smaller and narrower in garden situations, to about 60 feet tall and 15 feet wide. It is shade tolerant, occurs at middle elevations, and needs moist, well-drained soil.

*Achillea millefolium* var. *occidentalis*
# Yarrow

| | |
|---|---|
| PLANT TYPE: Deciduous perennial | |
| SIZE: 1–3 feet x 1–3 feet | |
| LIGHT REQUIREMENTS: Sun to partial shade | |
| WATER REQUIREMENTS: Low | |
| HARDINESS ZONES: 3b to 11 | |

This sun-loving, upright perennial blooms throughout summer and is a favorite of pollinators. Finely dissected grayish-green leaves are aromatic. Large, flat-topped clusters of whitish flowers sway in the breeze. A long-lived addition to meadow or pollinator gardens, it may even be used as a lawn substitute with infrequent mowing. Yarrow is sometimes added to native seed mixtures for protecting soil and rehabilitating disturbed sites such as rangelands, mined lands, and park and restoration areas. Considered a good companion plant that attracts beneficial insects while repelling pests. Not to be confused with the introduced Eurasian variety, *Achillea millefolium* var. *millefolium*.

**How big:** 1–3 feet tall x 1–3 feet wide.

**Bloom traits:** Clusters of 10–30 tiny white, cream, or pale-pink flowers bloom from mid- to late spring until late summer and serve as nectar and pollen-rich landing pads for beneficial insects. Fruits are small achenes that contain one seed.

**Sun and soil:** Full sun to partial shade. Well-drained soil, moist or dry. Spreads very slowly by rhizomes.

**Where it grows:** Dry to moist open forests, grasslands, roadsides, and rocky hillsides, at low to high elevations.

**How to space it:** 2–3 feet apart.

**Help it thrive:** Summer water until established (2–5 years). Thrives in drought conditions once established.

**Associates:** Ceanothus, Idaho fescue, meadow checkermallow, penstemon, goldenrod, and others.

**Benefits to wildlife:** Flowers provide for many pollinators, including syrphid flies, bees, and numerous butterflies including swallowtails, hairstreaks, mourning cloaks, and the endangered Oregon silverspot. Host plant for painted lady butterfly larvae. Some cavity-nesting birds use yarrow to line their nests. Provides forage for many species, including deer and upland birds.

**Substitute for:** Nonnative yarrow.

**How to propagate:** From seed dried and sown in midspring or fall, or by division.

**Related species:** Many varieties, including *Achillea millefolium* 'Salmon Beauty,' 'Paprika,' and 'Lavender Beauty.'

*Allium cernuum*
## Nodding onion

PLANT TYPE: Perennial bulb

SIZE: 6–18 inches x 6–12 inches

LIGHT REQUIREMENTS: Sun to partial shade

WATER REQUIREMENTS: Low

HARDINESS ZONES: 3b to 9b

A charming little onion with downturned pink flowers, which grows from a bulb. Leaves are basal, green, and grasslike. Looks best grown in clumps or drifts at the front of perennial beds, in rock gardens or meadow gardens, on green roofs, or tucked into stone walls or along steps where the flowers can be viewed from below. The bulbs are edible in small amounts.

**How big:** 6–18 inches tall × 6–12 inches wide.
**Bloom traits:** Pink, or occasionally white, flowers bloom in umbrella-shaped clusters at ends of shoots in late spring to midsummer. Fruit is a 3-lobed capsule with black seeds.
**Sun and soil:** Full sun to partial shade. Moist to somewhat dry, well-drained soil.
**Where it grows:** Open woodlands, coastal bluffs, and moist meadows or slopes, at low elevations.
**How to space it:** 12–18 inches apart.
**Help it thrive:** Drought tolerant once established, but does best with occasional summer water. To prevent seeds from self-sowing, cut flower stalks at the base before capsules ripen.
**Associates:** Douglas-fir, Garry oak, Oregon iris, Menzies' delphinium, dodecatheon, and others.
**Benefits to wildlife:** Nectar attracts bees, hummingbirds, and gray hairstreak butterflies.

**Substitute for:** Spanish bluebells (*Hyacinthoides hispanica*), nonnative allium.
**How to propagate:** From seed collected from ripened capsules in late summer and sown outdoors, or division of cultivated bulbs in spring.
**Related species:** Taper-tip onion (*Allium acuminatum*) has bright rose to purple upright flowers and occurs in open, rocky areas.

*Arbutus menziesii*
## Pacific madrone

| | |
|---|---|
| PLANT TYPE: Deciduous perennial |
| SIZE: 30–50 feet x 20–40 feet |
| LIGHT REQUIREMENTS: Sun to partial shade |
| WATER REQUIREMENTS: Very low |
| HARDINESS ZONES: 7b to 9b |

A broad-leaved evergreen and textural wonder, madrone may be either single or multitrunked. Bronzy, peeling bark reveals a smooth, pale-olive trunk and branches that mature to a deep copper-mahogany. Fragrant, small white flowers are densely arranged at the tips of twisting branches in spring. Bright orange to reddish berries ripen in early fall. Grow this endearing, spectacular wildlife magnet as a specimen tree, or in drifts in sunny, dry areas, including slopes, where it will control erosion.

**How big:** 30–50 feet tall × 20–40 feet wide.

**Bloom traits:** Sprays of urn-shaped, white flowers bloom mid- to late spring. Fall-ripening fruits are edible (though not tasty) reddish, pea-sized berries that may persist into winter.

**Sun and soil:** Full sun to light shade. Slightly acidic, sharp-draining soil is essential, as madrone is susceptible to several fungal diseases. May be difficult to establish, so choose site carefully. Small plants (less than 2 feet tall) are much more likely to survive than large ones; plant them in fall just before winter rains, and let nature take its course.

**Where it grows:** Open forests, rocky bluffs near the coast, south-facing slopes, and other dry or well-drained sites, at low to middle elevations.

**How to space it:** 20–30 feet apart.

**Help it thrive:** Occasional summer water the first year, followed by little to no supplemental water in subsequent years. Drought and salt-spray tolerant.

**Associates:** Douglas-fir, Garry oak, salal, ceanothus, oceanspray, manzanita, native grasses, licorice fern, and others.

**Benefits to wildlife:** Provides habitat for many species, especially cavity-nesting and open-nesting birds, mammals, and other wildlife. Flowers provide for bees, spring azure butterflies, and other insects. Fruit attracts myriad bird species, as well as small mammals and deer. Leaves are a major food source for deer and elk, as well as for larvae of the ceanothus silkmoth, Mendocino saturnia moth, and echo blue and brown elfin butterflies.

**Substitute for:** English holly (*Ilex aquifolium*).

**How to propagate:** From seed collected from ripe fruit, removed from pulp, and planted in fall. Grow in pots if relocation is necessary, and plant at a very young age.

**Related species:** No other *Arbutus* species occur in the Pacific Northwest.

plants for full sun or mostly sun

*Arctostaphylos columbiana*
## Hairy manzanita

| | |
|---|---|
| PLANT TYPE: | Evergreen shrub |
| SIZE: | 5–10 feet x 5–10 feet |
| LIGHT REQUIREMENTS: | Sun to light shade |
| WATER REQUIREMENTS: | Low |
| HARDINESS ZONES: | 7a to 9b |

Among the largest of the manzanitas, this slow-growing, upright, evergreen shrub has a wonderful architectural habit and outstanding texture. Grayish-green, thick, hairy leaves adorn the tips of gray, hairy branches. With age, branches become smooth and mahogany-brown, with bark that peels. Excellent at providing nectar for early foraging pollinators and other species later in the year. This is a striking shrub for a sunny, well-drained site such as a spacious rock garden. Useful for erosion control.

**How big:** 5–10 feet tall × 5–10 feet wide.

**Bloom traits:** Clusters of urn-shaped white to pale-pink flowers bloom in late winter to spring. Small reddish fruits known as drupes resemble little apples and may persist into winter.

**Sun and soil:** Full sun to light shade; intolerant of full shade or extreme heat. Prefers slightly acidic, loose, well-draining soil, but tolerates very acidic soils.

**Where it grows:** Coastal areas, rocky, dry slopes, and coniferous forest clearings, at low to middle elevations.

**How to space it:** 6–8 feet apart.

**Help it thrive:** Summer water until established (2–5 years). Prune only to remove dead wood so natural shape is retained.

**Associates:** Grand fir, shore pine, madrone, vine maple, salal, Oregon grape, snowbrush, beargrass, Oregon stonecrop, and others.

**Benefits to wildlife:** Flowers provide late winter to early spring nectar for bees and hummingbirds. Fruit supplies food for many bird species, as well as mammals such as deer, raccoons, foxes, chipmunks, and coyotes. Larval host species for echo blue and brown elfin butterfly, and ceanothus silkmoth.

**Substitute for:** Privet (*Ligustrum vulgare*), cotoneaster (*Cotoneaster* spp.).

**How to propagate:** From seed removed from pulp, treated with hot water, and planted outdoors in fall; may be difficult. Stem cuttings in early spring.

**Related species:** Hairy manzanita and the ground-hugging kinnikinnick hybridize to form **media manzanita** (*Arctostaphylos × media*), a 2-foot-tall shrub with slightly hairy leaves. **Hoary manzanita** (*A. canescens*) matures at about 6 feet tall and naturally occurs only in southwestern Oregon and California.

## *Arctostaphylos uva-ursi*
## Kinnikinnick or bearberry

PLANT TYPE: Evergreen low shrub

SIZE: 4–8 inches x 2–10 feet

LIGHT REQUIREMENTS: Sun to light shade

WATER REQUIREMENTS: Low

HARDINESS ZONES: 3b to 9b

An evergreen, low ground cover with small, thick, glossy, paddle-shaped leaves on flexible reddish stems that root where they touch the ground. Urn-shaped blossoms become brilliant red berries in late summer. A tough but very attractive and well-mannered mat-forming shrub that spreads slowly in rock or pollinator gardens or slopes; looks wonderful cascading down walls. Controls erosion and tolerates salt spray.

**How big:** 4–8 inches tall x 2–10 feet wide.

**Bloom traits:** Clusters of pendant, urn-shaped white to pale-pink flowers bloom in spring. Fruits are bright red berries that persist into winter.

**Sun and soil:** Full sun to dappled shade; tolerates all but deep shade or extreme heat. Prefers slightly acidic, moist to dry, well-drained soil but can tolerate somewhat heavy soils.

**Where it grows:** Rocky, dry slopes and coniferous forest openings, at low to high elevations.

**How to space it:** 5–8 feet apart.

**Help it thrive:** Summer water until established (2–5 years). May be slow to establish.

**Associates:** Garry oak, paper birch, Douglas-fir, aspen, fescue, coastal strawberry, and others.

**Benefits to wildlife:** Flowers provide nectar for bees and hummingbirds. Fruit supplies food for songbirds and many ground-feeding birds, as well as foxes, bears, deer, and a variety of small mammals. Host plant for brown elfin and hoary elfin butterfly larvae. Browse species for deer.

**Substitute for:** English ivy (*Hedera helix*), common St. John's wort (*Hypericum perforatum*), cotoneaster (*Cotoneaster procumbens*, *C.* 'Tom Thumb,' and other low cotoneasters).

**How to propagate:** From seed removed from pulp, treated with hot water, and planted outdoors in fall. Easier is vegetatively, by stem cuttings taken in late fall to winter or spring, or by layering technique.

**Related species: Media manzanita** (*Arctostaphylos × media*) is a hybrid between kinnikinnick and hairy manzanita. It grows to about 2 feet tall and naturally occurs near the coast. **Pinemat manzanita** (*A. nevadensis*) is similar to kinnikinnick but with stiffer branches.

*Asclepias speciosa*
# Showy milkweed

| | |
|---|---|
| PLANT TYPE: Deciduous perennial | |
| SIZE: 2–3 feet x 2–3 feet | |
| LIGHT REQUIREMENTS: Sun to light shade | |
| WATER REQUIREMENTS: Low to medium | |
| HARDINESS ZONES: 4a to 9b | |

As the common name says, this perennial is very ornamental in flower, with large clusters of fragrant, dusty-rose colored flowers that bloom for a long period and 4- to 8-inch pale, fuzzy green leaves. Highly appealing to pollinators, especially when grown in large swaths such as within a meadow or pollinator garden, or sunny border. May be toxic if ingested; sap is a skin irritant.

**How big:** 2–3 feet tall × 2–3 feet wide; spreads slowly by rhizomes.

**Bloom traits:** Rounded clusters of about 20 small rosy pink to purplish flowers bloom from late spring to midsummer. Fruit is a 4-inch-long seedpod that splits open to release flattened seeds attached to silky strands that are distributed by wind.

**Sun and soil:** Sun to light shade. Minimal nutrient requirements, but cannot handle root disturbance. Moist, well-drained soil is best, but can tolerate minimal drought. Tolerates sandy soils.

**Where it grows:** Open, moist to dry areas, including grasslands, meadows, roadside ditches, and near streams, at low to middle elevations.

**How to space it:** 2–3 feet apart.

**Help it thrive:** Low to moderate summer water. Though often labeled weedy because it likes to travel within the garden, unwanted plants are easy to pull out.

**Associates:** Ponderosa pine, Garry oak, aster, lupine, camas, goldenrod, and others.

**Benefits to wildlife:** Flowers provide nectar for bees, hummingbirds, and butterflies such as pale swallowtail and painted lady. Primary host plant for monarch butterfly larvae and host plant for field crescent butterfly larvae. Milkweed beetles eat the seeds. Ladybugs and birds such as bushtits eat aphids sometimes attracted to the plants (but the aphids do not spread to other plants).

**Substitute for:** Purple loosestrife (*Lythrum salicaria*); tropical milkweed or bloodflower (*Asclepias curassavica*).

**How to propagate:** From seed collected in fall and planted in spring, rhizome cutting in spring, or division of large plants in spring.

**Related species: Narrowleaf milkweed** (*Asclepias fascicularis*) also grows to 2–3 feet tall but has very narrow leaves and smaller flower clusters. **Purple milkweed** (*A. cordifolia*) has deep pink to purple flowers and naturally occurs in southwestern Oregon.

*Betula papyrifera*
## Paper birch

| | |
|---|---|
| PLANT TYPE: Deciduous tree | |
| SIZE: 40–80 feet x 20–30 feet | |
| LIGHT REQUIREMENTS: Sun to partial shade | |
| WATER REQUIREMENTS: Medium | |
| HARDINESS ZONES: 3b to 9a | |

A medium-sized single or multitrunked tree with white papery bark that peels horizontally with age. Young trees often have deeper, reddish-copper colored bark. Pointed oval leaves turn a rich golden yellow in fall. Looks lovely planted with a backdrop of tall, dark conifers, which set off its interesting bark. May attract aphids, so site it away from patios and driveways. Relatively short-lived, to about 60 or 70 years.

**How big:** 40–80 feet tall x 20–30 feet wide.
**Bloom traits:** Male and female catkins bloom in early to late spring as leaves develop. Fruits are winged nutlets of female catkins that are dispersed by wind.
**Sun and soil:** Sun, but with shade from hot afternoon sun. Intolerant of heat and deep shade. Its shallow roots need to be cool and prefer soil rich in organic matter, but will grow on a variety of well-drained, slightly acidic (pH 5.0–6.5), moist soils.
**Where it grows:** Cool, moist slopes and forested wetlands, at low to high elevations.
**How to space it:** 20 feet apart.
**Help it thrive:** Moderate summer water.
**Associates:** Douglas-fir, hazelnut, Scouler willow, highbush cranberry, elderberries, blackberries, huckleberries, gooseberries, and others.
**Benefits to wildlife:** Many birds and small mammals eat paper birch seeds, including siskins, finches, and chickadees, and voles and shrews. Insects attracted to birch provide food for birds such as warblers, nuthatches, and woodpeckers. Host species for mourning cloak, green comma, western tiger swallowtail, and pale swallowtail butterfly larvae. Browse species for deer, elk, beavers, hares, and chipmunks. Ruffed grouse eat catkins and buds, and woodpeckers create holes in the bark to feed on sap, which hummingbirds may also consume. Provides cover for many species, and cavities in older trees are used by birds and mammals to nest and roost. Bark provides nesting material.
**Substitute for:** Cutleaf birch (*Betula pendula*).
**How to propagate:** From seed collected in late summer or fall, before they drop from catkins, and planted outdoors in fall.
**Related species:** Water birch (*Betula occidentalis*) has dark reddish-brown bark that doesn't peel. It grows in nutrient-rich soils of wetlands and moist forests, where it provides habitat for many wild animals.

*Calocedrus decurrens*
## Incense cedar

| | |
|---|---|
| PLANT TYPE: Coniferous tree | |
| SIZE: 50–100 feet x 10–15 feet | |
| LIGHT REQUIREMENTS: Sun to light shade | |
| WATER REQUIREMENTS: Low | |
| HARDINESS ZONES: 5a to 9b | |

Tall, aromatic, and handsome, this pyramidal conifer has a straight, tapering trunk and a narrow form in landscape settings that make it worthy of more garden cultivation. Flat sprays of foliage are shiny and bright green, while the exfoliating bark is a dark reddish-brown. Not a true cedar, this is a versatile, very long-lived tree that is more heat and drought tolerant than the distantly related western redcedar. Grow it in groups, as an evergreen screen, or as a specimen tree in large or small gardens. Useful for erosion control.

**How big:** 50–100 feet tall x 10–15 feet wide, usually shorter in garden situations.
**Bloom traits:** Cones are 1 inch long and light brown.
**Sun and soil:** Full sun to light shade. Moist to dry, slightly acidic soil. Heat tolerant once established.
**Where it grows:** Mixed conifer forests and open, dry woodlands at low to high elevations in Oregon.
**How to space it:** 10–15 feet apart.
**Help it thrive:** Summer water until established (2–5 years).
**Associates:** Douglas-fir, western hemlock, Garry oak, salal, serviceberry, Cascade Oregon grape, and others.

**Benefits to wildlife:** Many insectivorous birds use this tree, especially woodpeckers, red-breasted nuthatches, and golden-crowned kinglets. Provides cover for raptors, including owls and bald eagles that roost and/or nest in large trees, as well as for other animals, particularly in winter.
**Substitute for:** English holly (*Ilex aquifolium*).
**How to propagate:** From seed collected from cones and planted outdoors in fall or early spring, and grown in light shade.
**Related species:** No other *Calocedrus* species occur in North America.

*Camassia leichtlinii*
# Great camas or wild hyacinth

| | |
|---|---|
| PLANT TYPE: | Perennial bulb |
| SIZE: | 2-3 feet x 1 foot |
| LIGHT REQUIREMENTS: | Sun |
| WATER REQUIREMENTS: | Low |
| HARDINESS ZONES: | 7a to 9b |

Camas are related to lilies and produce captivating, starlike flowers on tall spikes in midspring that attract pollinators. Leaves are long and linear. Plant bulbs in autumn in a sunny spot where spring bulbs would be welcome, such as beneath deciduous trees that don't leaf out too early, in rock gardens or meadow gardens, and in perennial borders. May also be grown in pots.

**How big:** 2–3 feet tall x 1 foot wide.

**Bloom traits:** Flowers range from pale yellow to pale lavender, violet-blue, or deep purple and have 6 petallike tepals and 6 yellow stamens, in perfect symmetry. Fruit is a capsule with numerous black seeds.

**Sun and soil:** Full sun to light shade. Prefers moist soil in winter and spring but needs to dry out in summer, so grow them in areas that aren't frequently irrigated in summer. Prefers soil rich in organic matter, but tolerates heavy clay soils.

**Where it grows:** Moist meadows, slopes, and grasslands, at low to middle elevations.

**How to space it:** 1 foot apart.

**Help it thrive:** Allow leaves to remain after flowering, to gather energy for the following year. Don't keep moist in summer. Cut back spent flowers to prevent self-sowing, if desired.

**Associates:** Garry oak, oceanspray, red-twig dogwood, tufted hairgrass, monkeyflower, graceful cinquefoil, and others.

**Benefits to wildlife:** Provides nectar for bees, hummingbirds, and butterflies such as the endangered Fender's blue butterfly. Deer and elk browse leaves.

**Substitute for:** Garden-variety hyacinth, Spanish bluebells (*Hyacinthoides hispanica*).

**How to propagate:** From seed collected in summer and planted in fall outdoors, or by separation of mature bulbs in fall.

**Related species: Common camas** or **wild hyacinth** (*Camassia quamash*) grows 1–2 feet tall and can tolerate colder winters (3b to 9b). *Camassia l.* subsp. *leichtlinii* has pale-yellow flowers, while *Camassia l.* subsp. *suksdorfii* is deep violet-blue.

*Campanula rotundifolia*
## Common harebell or **Scotch bluebell**

PLANT TYPE: Deciduous perennial

SIZE: 1–2 feet x 1–2 feet

LIGHT REQUIREMENTS: Sun to light shade

WATER REQUIREMENTS: Low to medium

HARDINESS ZONES: 3b to 9b

Charming little bell-shaped, blue-violet flowers adorn this tough and versatile yet delicate-looking perennial through most of the summer. Leafy, slender stems grow about 2 feet tall and are often bent over by the blossoms. Grow this wildflower with other sun-loving perennials along paths, tucked into rock gardens, or within meadow gardens. Leaves may be eaten raw in salads.

**How big:** 1–2 feet tall × 1–2 feet wide; may spread slowly by rhizomes.

**Bloom traits:** Nodding, 5-petaled blue-violet or sometimes white flowers bloom in late spring to late summer. Fruits are small capsules with multiple tiny, flat brown seeds.

**Sun and soil:** Full sun to light shade. Moist to somewhat dry, gravelly, well-drained soil. This plant will grow with enthusiasm in fertile soil, but it can be toned down in leaner, nutrient-poor soils.

**Where it grows:** Sunny cliffs and rock outcrops, along streams, and in grassy meadows, at low to high elevations.

**How to space it:** 12–18 inches apart.

**Help it thrive:** Drought tolerant once established, but some supplemental summer water is beneficial, especially in hot areas.

**Associates:** Aster, penstemon, potentilla, yarrow, goldenrod, and others.

**Benefits to wildlife:** Flowers attract native bumble-bees, hummingbirds, and swallowtail butterflies. Seeds are eaten by birds such as finches.

**Substitute for:** Creeping bellflower (*Campanula rapunculoides*), policeman's helmet (*Impatiens glandulifera*).

**How to propagate:** From seed collected in fall and planted, uncovered, in fall or spring, or by division of rhizomes in spring or fall; will self-sow.

**Related species:** The uncommon **Scouler's bellflower** (*Campanula scouleri*) is usually shorter and has pale-blue to white, bell-shaped flowers with petals that flare backward.

*Ceanothus prostratus*

## Prostrate ceanothus or squaw carpet

| | |
|---|---|
| PLANT TYPE: Low evergreen shrub | |
| SIZE: 2–3 inches x 4–8 feet | |
| LIGHT REQUIREMENTS: Sun to partial shade | |
| WATER REQUIREMENTS: Low | |
| HARDINESS ZONES: 4b to 9b | |

A very low evergreen shrub that forms a mat with rooting branches. Leaves are thick, toothed, and glossy. Fragrant pale- to bright-blue flower clusters lead to clusters of small red fruits. This is a fast-growing, pollinator-attractive ground cover for a rock garden or sunny slope. Good for erosion control.

**How big:** 2–3 inches tall × 4–8 feet wide.

**Bloom traits:** Tight, flat-topped clusters of light-blue flowers bloom from late spring to early summer. Fruit is a capsule with 3 little "horns."

**Sun and soil:** Full sun to partial shade (preferably only in the afternoon) and quick-draining gritty or rocky soil.

**Where it grows:** Dry, conifer forests and open plateaus at low to middle elevations.

**How to space it:** 4–8 feet apart.

**Help it thrive:** Occasional summer water until established (2–5 years). Very tolerant of drought once established.

**Associates:** Garry oak, Douglas-fir, snowbrush, yarrow, lupine, and others.

**Benefits to wildlife:** Flowers attract bees, hummingbirds, and butterflies, including pale swallowtail, hedgerow hairstreak, and brown elfin. Ceanothus is the *only* host plant for California tortoiseshell butterfly larvae and the primary one for pale swallowtail; it also provides for brown elfin and hedgerow hairstreak larvae. Browse species for deer and elk. Provides year-round cover for birds and small mammals.

**Substitute for:** Common St. John's wort (*Hypericum perforatum*), English ivy (*Hedera helix*).

**How to propagate:** From seed collected in late summer or fall, treated with hot water, and sown outdoors; hardwood cuttings taken in late winter; semihardwood cuttings taken during summer; or ground layering.

**Related species:** Siskiyou mat (*Ceanothus pumilus*) is similar but has smaller leaves and occurs in rocky, serpentine soil in southwestern Oregon and northwestern California.

## Ceanothus velutinus
## **Snowbrush** or **mountain balm**

| | |
|---|---|
| PLANT TYPE: | Evergreen shrub |
| SIZE: | 6–12 feet x 6–12 feet |
| LIGHT REQUIREMENTS: | Sun to light shade |
| WATER REQUIREMENTS: | Low |
| HARDINESS ZONES: | 6b to 9b |

This fast-growing, evergreen shrub has aromatic, glossy, deep green leaves and rounded panicles of white blossoms. Use this hardy and attractive butterfly shrub in a mostly sunny situation, as a wide hedge, screen, or specimen plant, or grow it en masse on a sunny slope. Reportedly not long-lived, but this may be exacerbated by overwatering.

**How big:** 6–12 feet tall × 6–12 feet wide.

**Bloom traits:** Dense pyramidal clusters of fragrant, tiny white flowers bloom for a long period, from midspring into summer. Fruit is a capsule that encloses a single seed.

**Sun and soil:** Full sun to light shade (preferably only in the afternoon); intolerant of full shade. Endures poor soil, since it is capable of fixing nitrogen, although organic matter is appreciated. Tolerates drought and heat due to its deep roots.

**Where it grows:** Open woodlands and sunny hillsides, at low to high elevations.

**How to space it:** 6–12 feet apart.

**Help it thrive:** Occasional summer water until established (2–5 years). Very tolerant of drought once established. Old stems may be thinned out to encourage new growth.

**Associates:** Western hemlock, Douglas-fir, western redcedar, Pacific silver fir, ninebark, vine maple, tall Oregon grape, Cascade Oregon grape, Oregon boxwood, and others.

**Benefits to wildlife:** Flowers attract bees, hummingbirds, and butterflies, including pale swallowtail, hedgerow hairstreak, and brown elfin. Ceanothus is the *only* host plant for California tortoiseshell butterfly larvae and the primary one for pale swallowtail; snowbrush also provides for brown elfin, echo blue, Lorquin's admiral, and hedgerow hairstreak butterfly larvae and ceanothus silkmoth larvae. Browse species for deer and elk. Provides year-round cover for birds and small mammals.

**Substitute for:** Privet (*Ligustrum vulgare*), butterfly bush (*Buddleja davidii* and hybrids).

**How to propagate:** From seed collected in late summer or fall, treated with hot water, and sown outdoors; hardwood cuttings taken in late winter; semihardwood cuttings taken in summer; or by ground layering.

**Related species:** California lilac (*Ceanothus thyrsiflorus*) is a larger shrub, popular in gardens due to its beautiful pale- to deep-blue blossoms. It hybridizes easily, so there are many cultivars.

*Crataegus douglasii*

## Black hawthorn or Douglas hawthorn

| | |
|---|---|
| PLANT TYPE: | Deciduous tree |
| SIZE: | 12–30 feet x 12–20 feet |
| LIGHT REQUIREMENTS: | Sun to partial shade |
| WATER REQUIREMENTS: | Low to medium |
| HARDINESS ZONES: | 3b to 9b |

A deciduous, slow-growing, multistemmed large shrub or small tree with a rounded, compact crown. Thick, lustrous, dark green leaves offer red fall color. Bark is rough and scaly, and branches are thorny and extremely strong. Fragrant white flowers appear in spring, followed by dark reddish-purple berries in late summer. Grow this excellent wildlife plant in a sunny area, or as part of a large hedgerow. Will eventually form a thicket.

**How big:** 12–30 feet tall x 12–20 feet wide.

**Bloom traits:** Clusters of scented, 5-petaled white flowers bloom in late spring. Fruits are edible pomes that become almost black when ripe.

**Sun and soil:** Full sun to light shade. Thrives in fine-textured, fertile, moist soil but is fairly drought tolerant.

**Where it grows:** Moist, open forests or edges, along streams or lakeshores, at low to high elevations.

**How to space it:** 15–20 feet apart.

**Help it thrive:** Some summer water is beneficial once established, especially in hot areas.

Suckers may be removed during winter when plants are dormant.

**Associates:** Black cottonwood and quaking aspen, or, in drier habitats, ponderosa pine, chokecherry, and others.

**Benefits to wildlife:** Flowers attract bees and other insects, and hummingbirds. Host plant for pale swallowtail and mourning cloak butterfly larvae. Fruit provides for many birds, including thrushes, robins, waxwings, woodpeckers, and band-tailed pigeons, as well as mammals such as coyotes and foxes. Thorny thicket provides cover for many wildlife species, including nesting and brooding cover for birds.

**Substitute for:** English hawthorn (*Crataegus monogyna*).

**How to propagate:** From seed collected when ripe, cleaned of pulp, and planted outdoors.

**Related species:** Suksdorf's hawthorn (*Crataegus douglasii* var. *suksdorfii*) has slightly different flowers and longer leaves, and is less common.

*Deschampsia cespitosa*
# Tufted hairgrass

| | |
|---|---|
| PLANT TYPE: | Perennial grass |
| SIZE: | 2–4 feet x 1–3 feet |
| LIGHT REQUIREMENTS: | Sun to partial shade |
| WATER REQUIREMENTS: | Low to medium |
| HARDINESS ZONES: | 3b to 9b |

An ornamental, fine-textured, cool-season bunchgrass that forms tussocks of basal leaves with tall, loose, frothy spikes. Leaves are a shiny bright green when not drought stricken. Grow it in mostly sunny, moist meadow gardens, where it will complement other flowering plants, near ponds, in rain gardens, and other moist places. Useful in restoration projects and preventing erosion. May be grown in containers.

**How big:** 2–4 feet tall x 1–3 feet wide.

**Bloom traits:** Tiny flowers are grouped into silky panicles on upright stems in spring and remain until the following spring.

**Sun and soil:** Full sun to partial shade. Tolerates salt water and a variety of soils and pH levels, although it prefers slightly acidic soil. It can tolerate summer drought but thrives with some summer water.

**Where it grows:** Moist areas along shores, bogs, marshes, grasslands, and ditches, and on moderately dry slopes, at low to high elevations.

**How to space it:** 1–3 feet apart.

**Help it thrive:** Summer water until established (2–5 years). Drought tolerant afterward, but looks and grows best with water during hot periods.

**Associates:** Garry oak, Oregon ash, black hawthorn, Douglas spirea, western columbine, Oregon iris, yarrow, sedges, checker mallow, and others.

**Benefits to wildlife:** Provides fall and winter seeds for birds like towhees, juncos, sparrows, and goldfinches, and perches for them. Host plant for juba skipper butterfly larvae. Mature plants provide winter cover and dense nest sites for ground-nesting birds and small mammals.

**Substitute for:** Orchard grass (*Dactylis glomerata*), jubata grass (*Cortaderia jubata*), tall oat grass (*Arrhenatherum elatius*), cheatgrass (*Bromus tectorum*), and other invasive grasses.

**How to propagate:** From seed collected in late summer or early fall and sown outdoors.

**Related species:** Wavy hairgrass (*Deschampsia flexuosa*) occurs in British Columbia and does well in dry, shady gardens or woodland settings.

*Festuca idahoensis*

# Idaho fescue

PLANT TYPE: Perennial grass

SIZE: 10–36 inches x 10–18 inches

LIGHT REQUIREMENTS: Sun to partial shade

WATER REQUIREMENTS: Low

HARDINESS ZONES: 3b to 9b

An attractive, long-lived bunchgrass with dense tufts of narrow, green to bluish-green blades that are overshadowed by flowering spikes as tall as 3 feet. Will self-sow to create a wonderful drought-tolerant ground cover, or use it to complement or even highlight other flowering plants. Useful for controlling erosion.

**How big:** 10–36 inches tall x 10–18 inches wide.

**Bloom traits:** Spikelets are made up of 6 florets and bloom from late spring to midsummer. Fruit is a grain.

**Sun and soil:** Full sun to partial shade. Grows on a wide variety of well-drained soils, from moist to dry, but does not need very fertile soil.

**Where it grows:** Rocky slopes, canyons, hillsides, and open, dry grasslands, at low to high elevations.

**How to space it:** 1–2 feet apart.

**Help it thrive:** Occasional summer water until established (2–5 years). Flower spikes may be cut back in spring.

**Associates:** Douglas-fir, white fir, western hemlock, Garry oak, bitter cherry, ceanothus, and others.

**Benefits to wildlife:** Seeds are eaten by many birds, including sparrows and towhees, and small mammals like rabbits. Host plant for butterfly larvae, including the Sonora skipper, mardon skipper, and clouded sulphur. Browse species for deer and elk. Provides shelter for small creatures.

**Substitute for:** Bermuda grass (*Cynodon dactylon*).

**How to propagate:** From seed collected in summer, removed from covering, and planted outdoors in fall.

**Related species:** Red fescue (*Festuca rubra*) is more loosely tufted and needs more moisture; it can take periodic mowing. **California fescue** (*F. californica*), native to Oregon and California, is drought tolerant and has graceful, 4-foot-tall stems.

*Fraxinus latifolia*
# Oregon ash

| | |
|---|---|
| PLANT TYPE: Deciduous tree | |
| SIZE: 40–60 feet x 30–40 feet | |
| LIGHT REQUIREMENTS: Sun to partial shade | |
| WATER REQUIREMENTS: Low to medium | |
| HARDINESS ZONES: 6a to 9b | |

The region's only native ash, this tall, upright deciduous tree has gray bark and compound leaves that turn bright gold in autumn. Leaves usually appear after the spring-blooming flower panicles on female trees. With a lifespan of 250 years, this ash grows quickly for its first 50 years, then slows down. An excellent choice to add shade in large, moist landscapes, especially near wetlands or areas prone to flooding.

**How big:** 40–60 feet tall x 30–40 feet wide.

**Bloom traits:** Panicles of yellowish-green flowers bloom on female trees in early to late spring. Fruits are clusters of 2-inch-long winged samaras with a single seed.

**Sun and soil:** Full sun to partial shade; does not tolerate full shade. Moist to seasonally wet soil.

**Where it grows:** Moist to wet areas near wetlands, floodplains, and along streams, at low elevations in Washington and Oregon.

**How to space it:** 25–30 feet apart.

**Help it thrive:** Low to moderate summer water. A fungus may attack and disfigure leaves, but without harm to the tree.

**Associates:** Red alder, bigleaf maple, Garry oak, and willows in moist habitats; in drier habitats, Douglas-fir and grand fir. In southwestern Oregon, California laurel, white alder, California black oak, Garry oak, ponderosa pine, and others.

**Benefits to wildlife:** Birds including grosbeaks, finches, and grouse eat the seeds. Host plant for western tiger swallowtail larvae. Provides cover for various wildlife, as well as nest sites for many cavity-nesting birds. Browse species for deer and elk.

**Substitute for:** Black locust (*Robinia pseudoacacia*), Norway maple (*Acer platanoides*).

**How to propagate:** From seed collected when winged fruits ripen in fall, and sown outdoors.

**Related species:** None naturally occur in the Pacific Northwest.

*Holodiscus discolor*

# Oceanspray

PLANT TYPE: Deciduous shrub

SIZE: 8–16 feet x 8–12 feet

LIGHT REQUIREMENTS: Sun to partial shade

WATER REQUIREMENTS: Low

HARDINESS ZONES: 4b to 9b

A versatile, multistemmed, deciduous shrub that blooms for a long period and is especially important for butterflies. Twiggy, upright, arching branches are often weighed down by lavish, frothy plumes of tiny, creamy-white flowers that will stop you in your tracks. Oval, textured leaves are deep green and sustain many butterfly species. This is a fabulous shrub for large hedgerows, slopes, and open woodland gardens. Good for stabilizing slopes and preventing erosion.

**How big:** 8–16 feet tall x 8–12 feet wide.

**Bloom traits:** Large, feathery panicles with a woodsy scent are composed of hundreds of tiny 5-petaled flowers that bloom profusely in midsummer and remain, slightly browned, until winter. Fruits are dry capsules that enclose the seeds.

**Sun and soil:** Mostly sun to partial shade; does not thrive in deep shade. Moist to dry soil; tolerates low nutrients and drought.

**Where it grows:** Mixed conifer forests, rocky shrublands, high floodplains, and near streams, at low to middle elevations.

**How to space it:** 8–12 feet apart.

**Help it thrive:** Summer water until established (2–5 years).

**Associates:** Douglas-fir, western hemlock, Garry oak, madrone, vine maple, salal, hairy honeysuckle, and others.

**Benefits to wildlife:** Flowers support bees and butterflies. Insects attracted to plants provide winter and spring food for birds such as bushtits. Seeds are eaten by songbirds. Host plant for echo blue, brown elfin, pale swallowtail, and Lorquin's admiral butterfly larvae. Browse species for deer and elk. Provides nesting habitat and cover for many birds and mammals, as well as amphibians in the Coast Range.

**Substitute for:** Tamarisk (*Tamarix ramosissima*), butterfly bush (*Buddleja davidii*).

**How to propagate:** From seed collected and planted in fall outdoors, or hardwood cuttings taken in late fall or winter.

**Related species:** Desert oceanspray (*Holodiscus dumosus*) is a smaller species that occurs east of the Cascades in southern Oregon.

## *Iris tenax*
## Oregon iris or **toughleaf iris**

| | |
|---|---|
| PLANT TYPE: | Deciduous perennial |
| SIZE: | 8–18 inches x 10–20 inches |
| LIGHT REQUIREMENTS: | Sun to partial shade |
| WATER REQUIREMENTS: | Low to medium |
| HARDINESS ZONES: | 6b to 9b |

All of the region's irises are undemanding and beautiful garden plants, and this one is a gem. An uncommon, low-growing, deciduous perennial with tough, light-green grasslike leaves, it grows in compact clumps. Flowers are usually soft lavender to deep purple and seem to float above the arched foliage. Use this lovely iris in meadow and rock gardens, in the foreground of perennial borders, or at the edges of woodland gardens.

**How big:** 8–18 inches tall × 10–20 inches wide.

**Bloom traits:** Purple, lavender, or sometimes yellow to creamy white flowers bloom in late spring to early summer on erect stems. Fruit is a large capsule with many seeds.

**Sun and soil:** Full sun to partial shade. Moist to dry soil.

**Where it grows:** Open woodlands, meadows, and roadsides, at low to middle elevations, in Washington and Oregon.

**How to space it:** 1–2 feet apart.

**Help it thrive:** Can tolerate drought once established, but some summer water is beneficial.

**Associates:** Douglas-fir, Garry oak, ponderosa pine, large-leaf lupine, delphinium, camas, blue-eyed grass, heuchera, nodding onion, and others.

**Benefits to wildlife:** Provides nectar for bees and the endangered Fender's blue butterfly, and cover for small birds and other wildlife.

**Substitute for:** Yellow flag iris (*Iris pseudacorus*),

BOTTOM PHOTO Related species *Iris innominata*

garden-variety bearded iris.

**How to propagate:** From seed collected in late summer or fall and planted outdoors soon afterward, or by rhizome division in early spring.

**Related species:** Douglas iris (*Iris douglasiana*) has 2-foot-long evergreen leaves and flowers that range from the palest lavender to deep purple. Often a vigorous grower, it tolerates poor or sandy soil, wind, and full sun. **Golden iris** (*I. innominata*) has narrow, evergreen leaves and lovely gold (or occasionally purple) flowers and needs some shade. Both naturally occur in southwestern Oregon.

*Lewisia columbiana*
## Columbia lewisia or **bitterroot**

| | |
|---|---|
| PLANT TYPE: Perennial | |
| SIZE: 10–12 inches x 6–12 inches | |
| LIGHT REQUIREMENTS: Sun to light shade | |
| WATER REQUIREMENTS: Low | |
| HARDINESS ZONES: 5a to 9a | |

Rock gardeners covet this evergreen, succulent taprooted perennial that is often long-lived and spectacular when in flower. Fleshy, narrow, spoon-shaped leaves grow up to several inches long, while upright stems support sprays of inch-wide flowers in late spring to summer. This is a wonderful perennial for fast-draining rocky or gravelly sites. May also be grown in unglazed clay (or other porous) containers, where it will be easiest to keep roots from rotting. *Lewisia c.* var. *columbiana* is a species of special concern in British Columbia and is listed as imperiled in Oregon. *Lewisia c.* var. *rupicola* is listed as imperiled in Oregon. Lewisias should *never* be collected from the wild.

**How big:** 10–12 inches tall × 6–12 inches wide.
**Bloom traits:** Flowers are conspicuous, varying from white with deep-pink stripes to pale lavender or magenta, and bloom from late spring to midsummer. Fruit is a round capsule that holds the seeds.
**Sun and soil:** At least 4 hours of sun, with some afternoon shade in hot areas. Slightly acidic soil (pH 5.5–6.5) must be fast-draining and not too rich.
**Where it grows:** Rocky slopes, gravelly outcrops, and crevices, at middle to high elevations.
**How to space it:** 1 foot apart.
**Help it thrive:** During dormant periods (after flowering) try to keep soil somewhat dry; resume watering when growth resumes. If container-grown, place in a sheltered location when dormant, such as under eaves. Raised rocky or scree beds, composed of 2 parts sand, 2 parts crushed rock or pea-sized gravel, and 1 part compost, with the plant's crown placed slightly higher than the surroundings, work well.
**Associates:** Ponderosa pine, scarlet gilia, sedum, penstemon, dodecatheon, sulphur-flower buckwheat, and others.
**Benefits to wildlife:** Flowers provide for bees, syrphid flies, and butterflies. Seeds may be eaten by some birds, such as finches.
**Substitute for:** Common succulents, such as *Sempervivum* spp. (hens and chicks).
**How to propagate:** From seed collected in late summer or fall and sown outdoors in well-draining soil.
**Related species:** Siskiyou lewisia (*Lewisia cotyledon*) may be the easiest to grow. It has wider evergreen, spoon-shaped leaves and numerous whitish flowers, typically in early summer. Cultivated plants often have intensely and brightly colored flowers—from peach to hot pink. *L. cotyledon* var. *howellii* is listed as rare in Oregon.

*Lupinus polyphyllus*
## Large-leaved lupine or bigleaf lupine

| | |
|---|---|
| PLANT TYPE: Deciduous perennial | |
| SIZE: 2–4 feet x 2–4 feet | |
| LIGHT REQUIREMENTS: Sun to partial shade | |
| WATER REQUIREMENTS: Low to medium | |
| HARDINESS ZONES: 3b to 9b | |

An ornamental perennial with old-fashioned charm, from which many hybrid lupines have been developed. Palmately divided bright-green leaves arise from hollow stems. Dense spikes of purplish, sweet pea–like flowers bloom during summer. An important pollinator plant, this lupine is a treasure planted in moist meadow or cottage gardens, perennial borders, or near sunny ponds. Often used in prairie and wetland restoration projects and for erosion control.

**How big:** 2–4 feet tall x 2–4 feet wide.

**Bloom traits:** Tall spikes of lightly fragrant, bluish-purple (sometimes pink or yellow) flowers bloom in profusion from late spring to midsummer. Fruit is a pod with hard-coated seeds.

**Sun and soil:** Full sun to partial shade. Moist soil preferred, but will tolerate dry periods if not prolonged.

**Where it grows:** Open forests, meadows, and coastal valleys, at low to middle elevations.

**How to space it:** 2–4 feet apart.

**Help it thrive:** Slightly drought tolerant once established, but since it prefers cool conditions, moderate summer water, especially during hot periods, is beneficial. Lupines are legumes that improve soil by "fixing" atmospheric nitrogen into a form useful to plants, so do not use nitrogen fertilizers. Not long-lived in rich, heavy soils.

**Associates:** Garry oak, Oregon ash, black hawthorn, Douglas spirea, snowberry, western columbine, iris, yarrow, sedges, checker mallow, and others.

**Benefits to wildlife:** Flowers provide pollen for native bumblebees. Host plant for silvery blue, painted lady, and orange sulfur butterfly larvae. Aphids attracted to plants are preyed upon by syrphid fly larvae. Seeds are eaten by birds such as sparrows and finches, as well as small mammals.

**Substitute for:** Mullein (*Verbascum thapsus*), garden-variety lupines, purple loosetrife (*Lythrum salicaria*).

**How to propagate:** From seed collected in summer or fall and planted outdoors. Seeds require scarification first.

**Related species:** Seashore lupine (*Lupinus littoralis*) has smaller, slightly silvery leaves and is shorter in stature. It occurs naturally near the coast in sandy soil, although it is tolerant of other soil types. A much more drought-tolerant type is **silky lupine** (*L. sericeus*), which grows to 2 feet tall and has hairy, silvery leaves and flowers that range from lavender to purple or, rarely, creamy yellow to white. **Bicolor lupine** (*L. bicolor*) is a 16-inch annual native to dry, sunny meadows and prairies. Hybrids of *L. polyphyllus*, such as **Russell hybrid lupines** (*L. polyphyllus* subsp. *polyphyllus*), can become weedy or invasive outside their native range.

*Mimulus guttatus*
## Yellow monkeyflower

| | |
|---|---|
| PLANT TYPE: | Deciduous perennial or annual |
| SIZE: | 2–3 feet x 1–2 feet |
| LIGHT REQUIREMENTS: | Sun to partial shade |
| WATER REQUIREMENTS: | Low to medium |
| HARDINESS ZONES: | 4a to 9b |

A deciduous perennial or annual with a highly variable form, from upright to recumbent. Rounded leaves are smooth. Large, trumpet-shaped bright-yellow flowers put on a show from spring to fall and benefit pollinators. This sunny wildflower may be a bit assertive in small gardens; other *Mimulus* species described below are less vigorous. Use it in moist meadow gardens, near ponds and wetlands, or in containers.

**How big:** 2–3 feet tall x 1–2 feet wide; perennial form spreads by rhizomes.

**Bloom traits:** Bright-yellow flowers, which bloom on racemes during summer, have 5 lobes; the lower 3 often have reddish-brown spots. Fruit is a papery capsule containing tiny seeds.

**Sun and soil:** Sun to partial shade. Moist soil is best; will be smaller in dry conditions.

**Where it grows:** Along streams and seeps, on wet cliffs, and in moist meadows, at low to middle elevations nearly everywhere in the region.

**How to space it:** 2–3 feet apart.

**Help it thrive:** Moderate summer water, especially during droughts, is beneficial.

**Associates:** Showy fleabane, camas, milkweed, sedges, Oregon iris, and others.

**Benefits to wildlife:** Flowers attract native bees and hummingbirds. Host plant for Mylitta crescent and snowberry checkerspot butterfly larvae.

**Substitute for:** Purple loosestrife (*Lythrum salicaria*), creeping jenny (*Lysimachia nummularia*).

**How to propagate:** From seed collected in summer or fall and pressed onto surface of soil (needs light to germinate) in fall or spring.

**Related species:** Coastal monkeyflower (*Mimulus dentata*) has hairy, veined leaves and similar yellow flowers and grows mainly near the coast. Shrubby monkeyflower (*M. aurantiacus*) has thick, pointed leaves and yellowish-orange flowers. It is drought tolerant but not cold tolerant (zones 8a to 9b), so mulch it or grow it in containers that can be moved indoors in winter.

*Penstemon cardwellii*
## Cardwell's penstemon or beardtongue

| | |
|---|---|
| PLANT TYPE: Evergreen low shrub | |
| SIZE: 6–12 inches x 2–3 feet | |
| LIGHT REQUIREMENTS: Sun to partial shade | |
| WATER REQUIREMENTS: Low | |
| HARDINESS ZONES: 5b to 9b | |

A low, evergreen shrublet with thick, oval, bright-green leaves. Dazzling lavender to purple tubular flowers bloom on 4- to 8-inch stalks in late spring and into summer. Add this gorgeous, compact, mat-forming small shrub to rock gardens and gentle slopes, or grow it with other low plants in mostly sunny spots.

**How big:** 6–12 inches tall × 2–3 feet wide.

**Bloom traits:** Large lavender to rosy purple tubular flowers are grouped along short stems, from late spring to early or midsummer. Fruit is a capsule that contains the seeds.

**Sun and soil:** Full sun to light shade. Dry to moist soil that is quick draining and not too rich. Tolerates heat and drought.

**Where it grows:** Forest edges and openings, and rocky slopes, at low to middle elevations.

**How to space it:** 2–3 feet apart.

**Help it thrive:** Drought tolerant once established, but some summer water may be beneficial.

**Associates:** Sitka alder, currants, gooseberries, yarrow, scarlet paintbrush, pearly everlasting, sedum, fescue, and others.

**Benefits to wildlife:** Flowers attract a variety of pollinators, including hummingbirds, bumblebees, wasps, bee flies, moths, and several species of butterfly, including swallowtail and Lorquin's admiral. Provides cover for overwintering insects.

**Substitute for:** Common St. John's wort (*Hypericum perforatum*), English ivy (*Hedera helix*).

**How to propagate:** From seed collected in late summer and planted outdoors in fall or early spring, ground layering in spring, or stem cuttings in late summer.

**Related species:** There is a penstemon for nearly every situation. **Barrett's penstemon** (*Penstemon barrettiae*) grows to about 16 inches tall in dry, rocky places, blooms in springtime, and has similar flowers. It is endemic only to the Columbia River Gorge and is at high risk of extinction, listed as a threatened species in Oregon and Washington. **Broad-leaved penstemon** (*P. ovatus*) is usually deciduous, has bluish-purple blossoms, and grows 2–3 feet tall in damp, well-drained soil; it can handle regular summer water. **Cascade penstemon** (*P. serrulatus*) is deciduous and grows to 2 feet, with bright-purple flowers that bloom in whorls during summer; it likes regular water with good drainage.

*Pinus contorta* subsp. *latifolia*

## Shore pine

| | |
|---|---|
| PLANT TYPE: Evergreen tree |
| SIZE: 25–50 feet x 20–40 feet |
| LIGHT REQUIREMENTS: Sun to light shade |
| WATER REQUIREMENTS: Low to medium |
| HARDINESS ZONES: 7a to 9b |

This attractive, evergreen conifer is adaptable and fast growing, with a rounded and compact habit when young. Intricately branched, it has 2-inch-long deep-green needles, dark-brown bark, and small cones. A valuable pine for smaller yards, used as an evergreen screen, in rock gardens, or any sunny spot where wildlife can enjoy its many assets. Tolerates salt spray and wind.

**How big:** 25–50 feet tall × 20–40 feet wide; usually larger in open areas, smaller in gardens.

**Bloom traits:** Small, numerous cones may persist on branches for many years.

**Sun and soil:** Full sun to light shade; does not tolerate shade. Thrives in moist, acidic soil, but tolerates nutrient-poor or fairly dry soil once established.

**Where it grows:** Rocky slopes, coastal dunes, seaside bluffs, and wetland edges near the coast and its inlets, at low elevations.

**How to space it:** 20–25 feet apart.

**Help it thrive:** Moderately drought tolerant once established; may benefit from summer water.

**Associates:** Western hemlock, redwood, mountain hemlock, western redcedar, huckleberries, Labrador tea, sedges, sword fern, bunchberry, and others.

**Benefits to wildlife:** Seeds are eaten by many birds, including siskins, jays, nuthatches, grosbeaks, finches, and crossbills, as well as mammals such as chipmunks and squirrels. Insectivorous birds like woodpeckers, chickadees, and bushtits feed on bark and cones. Host plant for pine white and western pine elfin butterfly larvae. Provides thermal and hiding cover for myriad wild species, and nest sites for many birds. Mature trees offer nesting and roosting cavities.

**Substitute for:** Nonnative pines.

**How to propagate:** From seed collected in fall when seeds are ripe, and planted outdoors.

**Related species:** The magnificent **ponderosa pine** (*Pinus ponderosa*) has long, lustrous needles and cinnamon-colored bark when mature. It grows taller, needs good drainage, and can be found on sunny, dry, open sites, mostly in the Willamette Valley and interior southwestern Oregon. **Lodgepole pine** (*P. contorta* var. *latifolia*) is tall and narrow and occurs in the Cascades east of the Puget Trough. **Western white pine** (*P. monticola*) grows large and symmetrical, with bluish-green needles and pale bark. It requires well-drained soil and can handle moist to dry conditions and partial shade.

*Populus tremuloides*
## Quaking aspen

| | |
|---|---|
| PLANT TYPE: Deciduous tree | |
| SIZE: 25–60 feet x 15–30 feet | |
| LIGHT REQUIREMENTS: Sun | |
| WATER REQUIREMENTS: Medium | |
| HARDINESS ZONES: 3b to 9a | |

In sharp decline in the West, groupings of this ornamental, narrow, fast-growing deciduous tree create biological hotspots of great importance to wildlife. Triangular to heart-shaped bluish-green leaves quiver audibly with the slightest breeze, and turn a clear gold in autumn. Young bark is smooth, white to pale gray that eventually darkens on older trees. Grow this elegant tree in groups in the foreground of dark conifers for a glowing effect, near streams, or within moist meadow or prairie gardens. Tolerates windy conditions. **Important note:** Quaking aspen is often not suitable for very small yards in urban areas. Due to intrusive roots, keep it away from pipes, sewers, and foundations. If in doubt, check with your local nursery.

**How big:** 25–60 feet tall x 15–30 feet wide; usually stays smaller in gardens.

**Bloom traits:** Trees are either male or female. Female catkins grow to 4 inches long, while males are 1–2 inches. Fruit is an oval capsule.

**Sun and soil:** Full sun to light shade; intolerant of full shade. Grows in a variety of soils, but well-drained, slightly acidic soil rich in organic matter is best.

**Where it grows:** Moist montane forest openings, woodland edges, valley slopes, along watercourses, and, less commonly, in lowland clearings. Occurs in parts of the Willamette Valley.

**How to space it:** 5–20 feet apart.

**Help it thrive:** Moderately drought tolerant once established, but will do best with some supplemental summer water. Roots will produce suckers many feet away, but these are easily snipped away.

**Associates:** Garry oak, black hawthorn, woodland strawberry, aster, lupine, and others.

**Benefits to wildlife:** Herbivorous insects attract many insectivorous birds and bats. Winter buds are eaten by birds like finches, and many other species eat the catkins, including siskins, chickadees, and migratory birds. Leaves, twigs and bark are consumed by mammals such as deer, porcupine, and rodents and rabbits, which in turn attract raptors and coyotes. Host species for western tiger swallowtail, mourning cloak, Lorquin's admiral, and propertius duskywing butterfly larvae. Mature trees provide nest sites for cavity-nesting bats and birds such as owls, woodpeckers, and chickadees. Provides refuge and thermal cover for myriad species.

**Substitute for:** White poplar (*Populus alba*).

**How to propagate:** From seed collected in early summer and planted outdoors soon afterward and kept moist, hardwood cuttings taken during winter, or by transplanting suckers in late winter.

**Related species:** The cultivar *Populus tremuloides* 'Pendula' has weeping branches. **Black cottonwood's** (*P. trichocarpa*) fast growth is valuable for habitat restoration in wet areas such as floodplains, but is appropriate only for large sites.

*Potentilla gracilis*
# Graceful cinquefoil

| | |
|---|---|
| PLANT TYPE: | Deciduous perennial |
| SIZE: | 1-2 feet x 1-2 feet |
| LIGHT REQUIREMENTS: | Sun to partial shade |
| WATER REQUIREMENTS: | Medium |
| HARDINESS ZONES: | 3b to 9b |

A member of the rose family, this perennial wildflower grows from a multibranched woody crown. Deeply divided leaves are green above, silvery underneath, have toothed edges, and turn yellow and orange in fall. Bright-yellow flowers bloom in clusters throughout the summer months. Makes a lovely addition to perennial beds, meadow gardens, or the sunny edges of woodland sites. May be grown in containers. Blue-listed (of special concern) in British Columbia.

**How big:** 1–2 feet tall × 1–2 feet wide.

**Bloom traits:** Clusters of showy, yellow, 5-petaled flowers bloom from early to late summer. Fruit is a small achene.

**Sun and soil:** Full sun to partial shade; intolerant of deep shade. Moist to somewhat dry well-drained soil rich in organic matter.

**Where it grows:** Open, moist forests and meadows at low to high elevations.

**How to space it:** 2 feet apart.

**Help it thrive:** Moderately drought tolerant once established, but will benefit from supplemental summer water.

**Associates:** Cascara, Oregon ash, Douglas spirea, lupine, camas, checker mallow, Oregon iris, and others.

**Benefits to wildlife:** Flowers are valuable to bees, butterflies, and other beneficial insects. Host plant for the two-banded checkered skipper, and possibly other butterfly larvae. Deer resistant.

**Substitute for:** Sulfur cinquefoil (*Potentilla recta*), creeping buttercup (*Ranunculus repens*).

**How to propagate:** From seed collected in late summer and sown outdoors in fall, lightly covered, or by careful clump division in spring.

**Related species:** Sticky cinquefoil (*Potentilla glandulosa*) has pale-yellow flowers. **Beautiful cinquefoil** (*P. pulcherrima*) is similar and grows in montane regions.

*Pseudotsuga menziesii*
# Douglas-fir

| | |
|---|---|
| PLANT TYPE: | Evergreen large tree |
| SIZE: | 70–125 feet x 20–25 feet |
| LIGHT REQUIREMENTS: | Sun to partial shade |
| WATER REQUIREMENTS: | Low |
| HARDINESS ZONES: | 3b to 9b |

Although not a true fir, this quintessentially Northwest conifer is a major component of western North American forests. Giant yet graceful, evergreen and fast growing, it is long lived and an excellent provider for wildlife. Densely leaved branches have flattened "needles" that are soft and bright green in springtime. Three-pronged pendulous cones fall when mature. Bark is thick, dark reddish-brown and corky on mature trees. The state tree of Oregon, this magnificent tree creates shaded conditions for woodland plants and is useful for adding privacy.

**How big:** 70–125 feet tall × 20–25 feet wide in garden settings; can grow to 300 feet tall in natural areas.
**Bloom traits:** Cones grow to 4 inches in length and turn brown and bristly at maturity.
**Sun and soil:** Full sun to partial shade. Moist to rather dry, well-drained soil.
**Where it grows:** Moist to dry woods at low to subalpine elevations throughout the region.
**How to space it:** 15–25 feet apart.
**Help it thrive:** Summer water until established (2–5 years).
**Associates:** Pacific silver fir, Sitka spruce, western hemlock, incense cedar, vine maple, Sitka alder, sword fern, and others.
**Benefits to wildlife:** Seeds are extremely important for small mammals and many species of birds. Host plant for pine white butterfly larvae. Native squirrels and other animals eat new foliage, inner bark, and pollen cones. Browse species for deer and elk. Provides thermal and hiding cover and nest sites for myriad species. Snags supply cavity-nesting habitat for forest birds.
**Substitute for:** English holly (*Ilex aquifolium*).
**How to propagate:** From seed collected and planted in fall; may self-sow.
**Related species:** East of the Cascades and to the Rocky Mountains is a bluish form (*Pseudotsuga m.* var. *glauca*) that may not grow as tall. Cultivars also exist that are dwarf versions or have pendulous branches.

*Quercus garryana*

## Garry oak or Oregon white oak

| | |
|---|---|
| PLANT TYPE: | Deciduous, rounded, large tree |
| SIZE: | 40–80 feet x 30–50 feet |
| LIGHT REQUIREMENTS: | Full sun to partial shade |
| WATER REQUIREMENTS: | Low |
| HARDINESS ZONES: | 5b to 9b |

The only oak native to British Columbia and Washington, and the predominant one in Oregon, this majestic, slow-growing, long-lived deciduous tree has unlimited wildlife appeal. Inconspicuous flowers bloom as rounded, deeply lobed, lustrous leaves appear in spring. Large acorns mature the following year. Bark is deeply furrowed on mature trees that develop craggy branching patterns. Grow this awe-inspiring oak in sunny spots where space allows. The decline of Garry oak habitat has been severe.

**How big:** 40–80 feet tall × 30–50 feet wide, usually smaller and shrublike on dry, rocky sites.

**Bloom traits:** Small, inconspicuous catkins (male) or flower clusters (female) in late spring. Fruit is an edible acorn.

**Sun and soil:** Full sun to partial shade. Moist to dry, well-drained soil.

**Where it grows:** Rocky slopes and bluffs, as well as the richer, well-drained soil of inland valleys at low elevations. Occurs east of the Coast Ranges to the Cascades, throughout the Columbia River Gorge, and in the southeasternmost parts of Vancouver Island as well as nearby islands.

**How to space it:** 20–40 feet apart.

**Help it thrive:** Summer water until established (2–5 years). Drought tolerant thereafter, but occasional water is beneficial during long droughts. Less moisture will stunt its growth.

**Associates:** Douglas-fir, Oregon ash, madrone, hazelnut, Indian plum, serviceberry, snowberry, oceanspray, tall Oregon grape, camas, sword fern, Idaho fescue, and others.

**Benefits to wildlife:** Flowers attract native bees. Host plant for gray hairstreak, California sister, and propertius duskywing butterfly larvae. Acorns sustain populations of many mammals and birds. Provides cover, perching, and nesting habitat for birds such as woodpeckers, nuthatches, and vireos, and rodents such as ground squirrels. Studies show that oaks support more insect herbivores than any other plant genus.

**Substitute for:** Norway maple (*Acer platanoides*), horse chestnut (*Aesculus hippocastanum*).

**How to propagate:** From seed planted after harvest.

**Related species:** California black oak (*Quercus kelloggii*) is another spectacular oak. Native from the southern half of Oregon to California from low to high elevations, it is also drought tolerant and valuable to wildlife.

*Ribes aureum* var. *aureum*
# Golden currant

| | |
|---|---|
| PLANT TYPE: | Deciduous shrub |
| SIZE: | 3–6 feet x 3–6 feet |
| LIGHT REQUIREMENTS: | Full sun to partial shade |
| WATER REQUIREMENTS: | Low |
| HARDINESS ZONES: | 3b to 9b |

This small to medium-sized thornless, deciduous, long-lived shrub has an upright, arching habit that may be trained into various shapes. Although mostly endemic east of the Cascades, it has a tolerance for a variety of conditions that makes it suitable for some westside gardens. Small, light-green lobed leaves are complemented by clusters of conspicuous, golden-yellow fragrant flowers in early to late spring. Translucent gold to reddish berries ripen in late summer. Leaves turn red in autumn. Will eventually spread, so allow enough space or prune shoots to control growth. Useful for erosion control.

**How big:** 3–6 feet tall x 3–6 feet wide; spreads slowly by rhizomes or stems that touch the soil.

**Bloom traits:** Clusters of numerous, tubular, deep-yellow flowers bloom along stems in early to late spring. Fruit is a flavorful berry that ripens in late summer.

**Sun and soil:** Full sun to partial shade. Prefers fertile, well-drained moist to dry soil.

**Where it grows:** Forest edges, grasslands or other open areas near streams, at low to high elevations.

**How to space it:** 6–8 feet apart.

**Help it thrive:** Drought tolerant once established, but occasional summer water, especially in hot areas, is beneficial. Winter pruning of older stems stimulates new growth.

**Associates:** Ponderosa pine, Douglas-fir, quaking aspen, ceanothus, serviceberry, fescue, and others.

**Benefits to wildlife:** Flowers provide nectar for hummingbirds and bees. Foliage and fruit used by many animals, including fruit-eating birds, ground squirrels, beavers, and coyotes. Host plant for hoary comma butterfly larvae. Insects on plants provide food for birds.

**Substitute for:** Scotch broom (*Cytisus scoparius*), gorse (*Ulex europaeus*).

**How to propagate:** From seed planted in fall, semihardwood or hardwood cuttings in summer or fall, or ground layering in spring or summer.

**Related species:** Blue currant or stink currant (*Ribes bracteosum*) is usually taller and grows in wetter, shadier conditions. Flowers are white to greenish and berries are black and waxy; flavor is variable.

*Salix scouleriana*
## Scouler willow

PLANT TYPE: Deciduous shrub or small tree

SIZE: 20–30 feet x 10–15 feet

LIGHT REQUIREMENTS: Full sun to partial shade

WATER REQUIREMENTS: Low to medium

HARDINESS ZONES: 3b to 9b

A robust, fast-growing, deciduous tall multi-stemmed shrub or small tree with a rounded crown. Bark is thin and gray, and leaves are dark green and lance shaped. Male flower clusters are soft catkins composed of many flowers, larger than horticultural pussy willows. Male and female flowers are on different plants, so grow both for seed production. May be best in larger gardens or as part of a substantial hedgerow. Protects soil from erosion.

**How big:** 20–30 feet tall × 10–15 feet wide.

**Bloom traits:** Catkins appear before leaves, in early to midspring. Fruit is a reddish-brown, pointed capsule that releases a fluffy substance that carries the tiny seeds, which ripen in late spring.

**Sun and soil:** Full sun to partial shade; does not tolerate full shade. Prefers moist soil but requires less water than many other willows.

**Where it grows:** Deciduous or conifer forest openings and edges, along streams, and in wetlands, at low to middle elevations.

**How to space it:** 10–20 feet apart; eventually forms thickets.

**Help it thrive:** Can tolerate short periods of drought, but does best with some summer water.

**Associates:** Douglas-fir, grand fir, ponderosa pine, quaking aspen, cascara, red-twig dogwood, ninebark, twinberry, white spirea, western coneflower, monkeyflower, blue-eyed grass, rushes, and others.

**Benefits to wildlife:** Flowers provide pollen and nectar for bees in early spring. Small and large mammals feed on buds, leaves, and seeds. Host plant for western tiger swallowtail, great comma, dreamy duskywing, and mourning cloak butterfly larvae. Important browse species for deer and elk. Provides cover for many mammals and birds.

**Substitute for:** Russian olive (*Elaeagnus angustifolia*).

**How to propagate:** From seed planted soon after collection in late summer or fall on top of soil or, more simply, by freshly cut pieces of hardwood partially buried in moist soil between November and March.

**Related species:** Sitka willow (*Salix sitchensis*) grows up to 25 feet tall, with 2–3 inch catkins and bright-green leaves. Shining willow (*S. lucida*) tolerates flooding and can grow to 40 feet tall with 5-inch-long female catkins.

*Sidalcea campestris*
## Meadow checkermallow

PLANT TYPE: Deciduous perennial

SIZE: 3–5 feet x 1–2 feet

LIGHT REQUIREMENTS: Full sun to partial shade

WATER REQUIREMENTS: Low to medium

HARDINESS ZONES: 5b to 9b

A tall, easy-to-grow perennial wildflower arising from a taproot and stout rhizomes. Lower leaves are round, deeply divided, and dark green; upper leaves are smaller and share the hairy stem with lovely pale-pink or lavender flowers. This pollinator-attracting plant does well in sunny perennial borders and meadowlike sites. Increasingly uncommon in nature due to habitat loss and invasive species, it is a species of concern in Oregon.

**How big:** 3–5 feet tall × 1–2 feet wide.

**Bloom traits:** Tall raceme composed of pale flowers up to 2 inches in diameter, which bloom from late spring to midsummer. Seeds ripen in late summer or early fall.

**Sun and soil:** Full sun to partial shade. Not fussy about soil, but prefers soil rich in organic matter. Drought tolerant once established but will benefit from summer water, especially in hot areas.

**Where it grows:** Dry to moist remnants of prairies and wetlands, along streams, roadsides, on slopes, and woodland edges, at low elevations, mainly in the Willamette Valley.

**How to space it:** 2 feet apart.

**Help it thrive:** Drought tolerant, but does best with some summer water.

**Associates:** Garry oak, Oregon ash, black hawthorn, Douglas spirea, snowberry, large-leaved lupine, tiger lily, tufted hairgrass, sedges, rushes, yarrow, western columbine, and others.

**Benefits to wildlife:** Flowers provide for an array of bumblebees, solitary bees, wasps, beetles, flies, and butterflies, including Oregon's endangered Fender's blue butterfly. Host plant for West Coast lady, common checkered skipper, painted lady, gray hairstreak, and American lady butterfly larvae.

**Substitute for:** Foxglove (*Digitalis purpurea*), mullein (*Verbascum thapsus*).

**How to propagate:** From seed planted outdoors soon after collection in fall, or by division of mature woody rhizomes into pieces with several buds and planted at ground level; may self-sow.

**Related species:** Henderson's checkermallow (*Sidalcea hendersonii*) has deep-pink flowers and needs moist to wet soil. It grows naturally along the coast, to 5 feet tall; it is endangered in Oregon, uncommon in Washington, and a species of concern in British Columbia. **Cusick's checkermallow** (*S. cusickii*) is very rare, restricted to native prairie remnants in western Oregon where it is a species of concern; it has deep-pink flowers, grows to 3 feet tall, and tolerates heavy soils. **Nelson's checkermallow** (*S. nelsoniana*) grows to 3 feet tall with lavender-pink flowers. It is an endangered species in Washington and threatened in Oregon.

## *Sisyrinchium idahoense*
# Blue-eyed grass

| | |
|---|---|
| PLANT TYPE: Deciduous perennial |
| SIZE: 8–16 inches x 4–12 inches |
| LIGHT REQUIREMENTS: Full sun to partial shade |
| WATER REQUIREMENTS: Low to medium |
| HARDINESS ZONES: 4a to 9b |

This dainty iris relative has tufts of bluish-green grasslike leaves, and taller flowering stems that support flower clusters of 1 to 5 blossoms. Allow it to naturalize for a showy display at pond edges and boggy places, or with other small moisture-loving plants at the front of a perennial bed or rock garden. Good rain garden plant.

**How big:** 8–16 inches tall × 4–12 inches wide.

**Bloom traits:** Flowers, up to 1 inch in diameter, consist of 6 rounded petals with a sharp point and are usually a deep bluish-purple with a yellow "eye" in the center. Blooms from midspring to midsummer. Black seeds ripen in globe-shaped capsules, in late summer or early fall.

**Sun and soil:** Full sun to partial shade. Thrives in moist to wet conditions but can tolerate some summer dryness.

**Where it grows:** Moist areas such as wetland edges, grassy meadows, ditches, and along streams, at low to middle elevations.

**How to space it:** 12 inches apart.

**Help it thrive:** Some summer water is beneficial, especially in hot areas.

**Associates:** Western hemlock, Sitka spruce, quaking aspen, twinberry, red-twig dogwood, cinquefoil, monkeyflower, large-leaved lupine, rushes, sedges, and others.

**Benefits to wildlife:** Provides nectar for pollinators like bees, and seeds for birds such as song sparrows.

**Substitute for:** Sweet vernal grass (*Anthoxanthum odoratum*).

**How to propagate:** From seed planted in spring or outdoors soon after collection in late summer, or careful division of mature clumps; may self-sow.

**Related species: Western blue-eyed grass** (*Sisyrinchium bellum*) is similar but occurs only from Oregon to California in our region. Mainly coastal **golden-eyed grass** (*S. californicum*) has bright-yellow flowers and might sub for weedy tall buttercup (*Ranunculus acris*). **Grasswidow** (*S. douglasii*) has larger, reddish-purple flowers, blooms earlier, and is quite drought tolerant.

*Solidago canadensis*
# Canadian goldenrod

PLANT TYPE: Deciduous perennial

SIZE: 2–5 feet x 2–3 feet

LIGHT REQUIREMENTS: Sun to partial shade

WATER REQUIREMENTS: Low to medium

HARDINESS ZONES: 3b to 9b

Late-blooming plumes of bright golden yellow, fragrant flowers top this tough, leafy perennial. Plant this pollinator magnet in meadow and wildflower gardens, near ponds, in drainage ditches, or other open, mostly sunny situations. Holds its own against aggressive competitors.

**How big:** 2–5 feet tall x 2–3 feet wide; spreads by rhizomes.

**Bloom traits:** Hundreds of tiny, fragrant flower heads bloom on symmetrical, arching flower stalks from midsummer to midfall. Frequently mistaken for sneeze-inducing ragweed. Fruit is a small achene.

**Sun and soil:** Full sun to partial shade; does not tolerate shade. Tolerates a wide range of soils, textures, and moisture conditions but prefers moist soils. To minimize spreading, keep soil dry and not too rich.

**Where it grows:** Wet to dryish meadows, fields, open woodlands, and roadside ditches, at low to middle elevations.

**How to space it:** 2–3 feet apart.

**Help it thrive:** Drought tolerant once established, but some summer water is beneficial.

**Associates:** Garry oak, milkweed, tufted hairgrass, camas, common harebell, and others.

**Benefits to wildlife:** Important nectar source for native bees and butterflies, such as the checkered skipper, clouded sulphur, gray hairstreak, monarch, and the endangered Oregon silverspot.

**Substitute for:** Tansy ragwort (*Senecio jacobaea*), yellow glandweed (*Parentucellia viscosa*).

**How to propagate:** From seed collected in fall and sown outdoors in fall or spring, or by division of rhizomes in spring or late summer.

**Related species:** Giant goldenrod (*Solidago gigantea*) is less common, has hairless stems, and grows slightly taller. **Northern goldenrod** (*S. multiradiata*) can be found in British Columbia and Washington and is a more compact plant.

*Symphyotrichum subspicatum*
## Douglas aster

| |
|---|
| PLANT TYPE: Deciduous perennial |
| SIZE: 3 feet x 3 feet |
| LIGHT REQUIREMENTS: Sun to partial shade |
| WATER REQUIREMENTS: Medium |
| HARDINESS ZONES: 6a to 9b |

In midsummer to midfall, this multistemmed perennial is studded with pale lavender-blue, daisylike flowers. Leaves are narrowly oblong. This pollinator plant looks wonderful growing in drifts with other similarly sized perennials or shrubs, in moist meadow or wildflower gardens, or toward the back of a low perennial border. Also known as *Aster subspicatus*.

**How big:** 2–3 feet tall × 2–3 feet wide; spreads slowly by rhizomes.

**Bloom traits:** The yellow center of the flowering head is made up of many tiny disk florets; the colorful outer "petals" are known as ray florets. Fruit is an achene, often hairy.

**Sun and soil:** Full sun to partial shade. Moist soil rich in organic matter.

**Where it grows:** Moist woodlands, coastal areas, and along streams, at low to middle elevations.

**How to space it:** 3 feet apart.

**Help it thrive:** Somewhat drought tolerant once established, but does best with summer water, especially in hot areas.

**Associates:** Garry oak, quaking aspen, lupine, pearly everlasting, Oregon iris, checker mallow, and others.

**Benefits to wildlife:** Attractive to many insects, it provides nectar and pollen for bees and nectar for many butterfly species, including woodland skipper, pine white, painted lady, red admiral, mourning cloak, and the endangered Oregon silverspot. Host plant for field crescent and other butterfly larvae.

**Substitute for:** Tall verbena (*Verbena bonariensis*), chicory (*Cichorium intybus*).

**How to propagate:** From seed collected in fall and sowed after harvest or in spring, or by rhizome division in early spring; may self-sow.

**Related species: Leafy aster** (*Symphyotrichum foliaceus*) also prefers moist soil and grows 1–2 feet tall. **California aster** (*S. chilensis*) is less widespread in our region and occurs in open, drier habitats.

# *plants for partial shade*

**THE PLANTS IN THIS CATEGORY CLEARLY DEMONSTRATE** that many natives are quite versatile when it comes to light needs, and most of them deserve bonus points for being likely to adapt well when your yard's shade increases over the years due to tree and shrub growth. A few listed here, like red-twig dogwood, are so accomplished at making do that they could also be placed in both the sun and shade categories. Plants that can tolerate either quite a bit of sun or mostly shade are noted. The majority in this section, though, fall somewhere in the middle and will not be able to tolerate all-day sun or deep shade—for those you will need to refer to the previous or next section.

Tiger lily (*Lilium columbianum*)

*Acer circinatum*
# Vine maple

| | |
|---|---|
| PLANT TYPE: | Deciduous small tree |
| SIZE: | 10–25 feet x 10–15 feet |
| LIGHT REQUIREMENTS: | Partial shade |
| WATER REQUIREMENTS: | Low to moderate |
| HARDINESS ZONES: | 5b to 9b |

A small, typically multitrunked deciduous tree or large shrub with year-round appeal. Graceful, horizontally tiered branches support rounded, lobed leaves—bright green in springtime, turning stunning shades of gold, orange, and red in autumn. Burgundy and white flowers appear in spring, just before leaf growth begins, followed by winged samaras propelled by breezes. A colorful, long-lived addition to smaller gardens, as part of a hedgerow, or planted en masse beneath taller trees in larger spaces. Controls erosion on moist hillsides.

**How big:** 10–25 feet tall × 10–15 feet wide.

**Bloom traits:** Clusters of small, showy burgundy and white flowers bloom in early to late spring. Fruit is a winged samara that turns reddish as it ripens.

**Sun and soil:** Part sun to light shade. The more sunlight, the more upright and compact it will be, but it is best suited to light shade, or even mostly shade, which results in its signature broad, somewhat vinelike habit. Moist, well-drained soil is best, but will tolerate some drought.

**Where it grows:** Moist forests, clearings, and along streams, at low to middle elevations.

**How to space it:** 10–20 feet apart.

**Help it thrive:** Some supplemental summer water is beneficial.

**Associates:** Douglas-fir, western hemlock, western redcedar, Sitka spruce, western sword fern, deer fern, fairy bells, bleeding heart, foamflower, woodland strawberry, and others.

**Benefits to wildlife:** Flowers attract bees and other insects. Host plant for western tiger swallowtail and mourning cloak butterfly larvae. Seeds are eaten by many birds, including grosbeaks, finches, and woodpeckers, as well as mammals such as chipmunks. Browse species for deer and elk. Provides cover for many species.

**Substitute for:** Amur maple (*Acer tataricum* var. *ginnala*), Japanese maples (*A. palmatum* and *A. japonica*).

**How to propagate:** From seed collected as they ripen and immediately sown outdoors, or by ground layering.

**Related species: Douglas maple** (*A. glabrum* var. *douglasii*) is similar in size, coloring, and year-round interest, but takes drier conditions. **Bigleaf maple** (*A. macrophyllum*) is a much more massive tree with large leaves. Mature trees provide excellent wildlife habitat and shade, and are often lushly adorned with moss and ferns.

*Amelanchier alnifolia*
## Serviceberry or juneberry

PLANT TYPE: Deciduous shrub

SIZE: 8–18 feet x 6–10 feet

LIGHT REQUIREMENTS: Sun to partial shade

WATER REQUIREMENTS: Low

HARDINESS ZONES: 3b to 9b

One of about 20 species worldwide, this deciduous, multibranched shrub or small tree has unlimited appeal. Oval, bluish-green leaves turn yellow to red in autumn. Feathery white, fragrant flowers bloom in profusion during springtime and are followed by deliciously sweet, blueberrylike fruit, favored by both wildlife and people. Dr. Art Kruckeberg, author and professor emeritus of botany at University of Washington, wrote, "There is scarcely a habitat in the Pacific Northwest that does not support stands of serviceberry"—as part of a hedgerow, within a shrub border, on a hillside, or as a screen, windbreak, or specimen plant.

**How big:** 8–18 feet tall x 6–10 feet wide.

**Bloom traits:** Clusters of white, 5-petaled flowers bloom in early to late spring. Edible, pea-sized fruits known as pomes ripen to purple in mid- to late summer.

**Sun and soil:** Part sun to light shade, but will tolerate full sun in cool areas. Moist to dry, well-drained soil. Tolerates most soil types, but is not adaptable to very heavy clay soils without organic matter, or poorly drained sites. Keep closely competing plants away from its roots. May be slow to establish.

**Where it grows:** Open woodlands, slopes, coastal bluffs, prairies, and meadows, at low to high elevations.

**How to space it:** 6–10 feet apart.

**Help it thrive:** Summer water until established (2–5 years). Little orange fungal spots on leaves will not harm the plant but could spread spores to nearby junipers.

**Associates:** Garry oak, Douglas-fir, shore pine, Cascade Oregon grape, white spirea, and others.

**Benefits to wildlife:** Flowers supply pollen and nectar for large numbers of bees, as well as hummingbirds and spring azure butterflies. Fruit is relished by many bird species, including waxwings, chickadees, woodpeckers, and tanagers, as well as mammals such as raccoons, ground squirrels, foxes, and bears. Host plant for pale swallowtail, brown elfin, Lorquin's admiral, and California hairstreak butterfly larvae. Provides dense cover for birds and small mammals. Browse plant for deer and elk.

**Substitute for:** Burning bush (*Euonymus alatus*).

**How to propagate:** From seed separated from pulp, dried, and planted outdoors in fall, or softwood cuttings taken in early summer.

**Related species:** Dwarf serviceberry (*Amelanchier a.* var. *pumila*) is a smaller shrub but may be difficult to locate.

*Aquilegia formosa*
# Western columbine

| | |
|---|---|
| PLANT TYPE: | Deciduous perennial |
| SIZE: | 1–3 feet x 1–2 feet |
| LIGHT REQUIREMENTS: | Partial shade |
| WATER REQUIREMENTS: | Low to moderate |
| HARDINESS ZONES: | 3b to 9b |

A common but quintessential and graceful perennial, with delicate soft-green foliage and upright, thin stems that bear multiple, brightly colored nodding flowers. Versatile and charming, it belongs in almost every garden, where it will be at home under trees at the front of borders, or within partly shaded meadow or pollinator gardens. *Formosa* means "beautiful" in Latin.

**How big:** 1–3 feet tall × 1–2 feet wide.

**Bloom traits:** Tubular, orangish-red and yellow flowers that bloom from spring through summer have 5 spurs that contain nectar very attractive to pollinators. Flower stems may be cut back for a second round of flowers, but leave some of the small black seeds that are formed in follicles for the birds and for self-sowing.

**Sun and soil:** Partial shade to light sun; can tolerate mostly sun with extra moisture. Soil rich in organic matter is best, but will grow in lean soils. Drought tolerant once established, but does better with supplemental summer water.

**Where it grows:** Open to partly shaded moist, rocky or forested sites, along streams and seeps, and in mountain meadows, at low to high elevations.

**How to space it:** 12–18 inches apart. May be short-lived but will self-sow.

**Help it thrive:** Does best with some summer water.

**Associates:** Douglas-fir, western hemlock, western hazelnut, alumroot, tiger lily, Oregon iris, and others.

**Benefits to wildlife:** A magnet for hummingbirds and bees (bumblebees may make holes in the spurs to obtain nectar), flowers also attract pale and tiger swallowtail butterflies and sphinx moths. Various birds eat the seeds, including finches, song sparrows, and juncos, and insectivorous birds consume herbivorous insects on the plants.

**Substitute for:** Garden-variety columbines.

**How to propagate:** From seed collected in summer and sown in fall or spring. Transplant young plants while small, so taproot is not disturbed.

**Related species:** Yellow columbine (*Aquilegia flavescens*) occurs in moist alpine areas of the Cascades.

*Carex obnupta*
## Slough sedge

| | |
|---|---|
| PLANT TYPE: | Evergreen perennial |
| SIZE: | 2–3 feet |
| LIGHT REQUIREMENTS: | Sun to partial shade |
| WATER REQUIREMENTS: | Medium to high |
| HARDINESS ZONES: | 7b to 9b |

Over 500 species of sedge are native to North America, and many occur in our region. Perennial, tuft-forming, and grasslike, they have stiff, coarse, flat leaves and are fast growing. Some like it dry and some like it wet; slough sedge needs moisture. It has inconspicuous flowers on tall, graceful spikes, and thick rhizomes, and is evergreen in mild winters. Perfect for rain gardens or grown along the edges of ponds or other wet places; it is often used in wetland restoration projects. This sedge is useful for stabilizing stream banks, controlling erosion, competing with nonnative species, and removing pollution and sediments from storm water.

**How big:** 2–3 feet tall; spreads by rhizomes.

**Bloom traits:** Tall spikes (up to 5 feet) produce attractive male and female flowers that bloom from midspring to midsummer. Fruit is a disk-shaped small achene that contains a single seed.

**Sun and soil:** Partial sun to light shade, and moist to wet soil. Can handle standing water, as well as some summer drought.

**Where it grows:** Near lakes, rivers, swamps, marshes, and wet meadows, at low elevations.

**How to space it:** 2 feet apart.

**Help it thrive:** Moderate summer water.

**Associates:** Grand fir, red alder, Oregon ash, western redcedar, red-twig dogwood, black hawthorn, twinberry, Indian plum, ninebark, Nootka rose, Sitka and Scouler willows, red huckleberry, Douglas' spirea, snowberry, tufted hairgrass, taper-tipped rush, common rush, monkeyflower, cinquefoil, and others.

**Benefits to wildlife:** Provides seeds for many types of birds, including waterbirds and songbirds like finches, towhees, and sparrows. Leaves are used as nesting material, and entire plants provide shelter for many small animals, such as turtles. Frogs and salamanders may attach their eggs to the base of stems.

**Substitute for:** Pendant sedge (*Carex pendula*).

**How to propagate:** From seed collected and scattered outdoors after harvest, or by division of rhizomes. Planting should always be done in the fall.

**Related species: Sawbeak sedge** (*Carex stipata*) has shorter flowering spikes. **Golden sedge** (*C. aurea*) has yellow bracts that surround the fruit. **Greensheath sedge** (*C. feta*) lacks rhizomes and has a tufted appearance.

## Clematis ligusticifolia
## Western clematis or virgin's bower vine

| | |
|---|---|
| PLANT TYPE: Deciduous vine | |
| SIZE: 25–35 feet | |
| LIGHT REQUIREMENTS: Sun to partial shade | |
| WATER REQUIREMENTS: Low | |
| HARDINESS ZONES: 4a to 9b | |

A vigorous, deciduous, semiwoody climbing vine with gorgeous summer blossoms that mature into eyecatching, fluffy seed heads. Tough, adaptable, and undemanding, although it needs a strong support, such as a lengthy fence or hedgerow it can twine through.

**How big:** 25–35 feet.

**Bloom traits:** Multiple fragrant white flowers bloom in close clusters during summer. Fruits called achenes mature in feathery, showy seed heads in late summer and into fall.

**Sun and soil:** Sun to partial shade. Situate so the root area is shaded but stems are in the sun, or at least partial sun. In hot areas, provide afternoon shade. Likes moist, nonacidic soil amended with organic matter, but is quite drought tolerant once established.

**Where it grows:** Moist, coniferous forests, wooded foothills, and along streams, at low to middle elevations.

**How to space it:** 20–30 feet apart.

**Help it thrive:** Summer water until established (2–5 years). May be rejuvenated every few years by cutting back above growing points 1–2 feet aboveground.

**Associates:** Ponderosa pine, alder, juniper, black hawthorn, chokecherry, red-twig dogwood, Idaho fescue, and others.

**Benefits to wildlife:** Provides nectar for hummingbirds, bees, butterflies, and other insects. Birds and other small animals use it for cover. Browse species for deer and elk.

**Substitute for:** Traveler's joy (*Clematis vitalba*), Japanese honeysuckle (*Lonicera japonica*).

**How to propagate:** From seed collected in late summer or fall and sown soon afterward outdoors (may be slow to germinate), semihardwood cuttings in late spring, or ground layering in spring.

**Related species:** Rock clematis (*Clematis columbiana*), with its delicate but showy bluish-purple pendant flowers, grows to 6–8 feet and can be left to scramble among shrubs or rocks, or trained up a trellis. Native to areas east of the Cascades. May not be easy to find in nurseries.

*Cornus nuttallii*
# Pacific dogwood

| | |
|---|---|
| PLANT TYPE: Deciduous tree | |
| SIZE: 30–50 feet x 20–25 feet | |
| LIGHT REQUIREMENTS: Partial shade | |
| WATER REQUIREMENTS: Low | |
| HARDINESS ZONES: 5b to 9b | |

This deciduous, flowering rounded tree has angular branches and exquisite creamy-white blossoms in springtime and sometimes in fall. Leaves turn shades of yellow, pink, and red in autumn. Makes an elegant specimen tree, especially when placed in the foreground of dark conifers.

**How big:** 30–50 feet tall x 20–25 feet wide.

**Bloom traits:** Tiny flowers bloom in clusters at the center of 4 to 7 white petallike bracts. Fruits are clusters of bright-red drupes that ripen in late summer.

**Sun and soil:** Partial shade to light sun; leaves and trunk may burn in full sun. Moderately tolerant of shade but needs good air circulation. Soil needs to be well drained, and moist to somewhat dry in summer. Give it plenty of space and air circulation to prevent fungal disease, to which it is susceptible. Thrives with natural water, such as near streams, not sprinklers.

**Where it grows:** Mixed conifer forests or more open areas near streams, at low to middle elevations.

**How to space it:** 20–25 feet apart.

**Help it thrive:** Little or no summer water once established. Prune only to remove dead or rubbing branches so distinctive branching pattern is preserved.

**Associates:** Douglas-fir, western hemlock, Pacific silver fir, grand fir, noble fir, Pacific yew, western redcedar, bigleaf maple, Garry oak, Oregon ash, incense cedar, madrone, vine maple, Pacific rhododendron, red huckleberry, salal, low Oregon grape, and others.

**Benefits to wildlife:** Flowers attract bees and other insects. Fruit provides food for birds such as woodpeckers, thrushes, tree swallows, band-tailed pigeons, grosbeaks, sparrows, and jays. Host plant for spring azure butterfly larvae.

**Substitute for:** Princess tree (*Paulownia tomentosa*).

**How to propagate:** From seed collected in fall and sown outdoors.

**Related species:** A cross between *Cornus nuttallii* and *C. florida,* **Eddie's White Wonder** is less susceptible to fungal disease and may be a better choice in areas that receive supplemental summer water.

*Cornus sericea*

# Red-twig dogwood

| | |
|---|---|
| PLANT TYPE: Deciduous shrub | |
| SIZE: 6–15 feet tall x 8–10 feet wide | |
| LIGHT REQUIREMENTS: Sun to partial shade | |
| WATER REQUIREMENTS: Medium | |
| HARDINESS ZONES: 3b to 9b | |

A multistemmed, ornamental, fast-growing shrub that eventually forms a thicket. Fragrant white flower clusters are followed by fruits that mature to a pale blue or pearly white. Characteristic red to purplish spreading branches are especially attractive in winter, after brilliant fall leaf color. Older branches are typically grayish-green. Use it in somewhat moist spots where it can show off its year-round attributes—as part of a hedgerow, under tall trees, along a stream, or in other moist places such as a rain garden. Useful for erosion control.

**How big:** 6–15 feet tall x 8–10 feet wide.
**Bloom traits:** Flat, 2- to 3-inch-wide clusters of small 4-petaled white flowers bloom in late spring to early summer. The fruit ripens in late summer and is available through fall or possibly the winter months.
**Sun and soil:** Sun to full shade; it is most colorful when it receives some sun. Does best in moist, well-drained soil rich in organic matter, but is somewhat tolerant of drought.
**Where it grows:** Moist woodlands, floodplains, and along streams and other wet places, at low elevations.
**How to space it:** 8–10 feet apart.
**Help it thrive:** Moderate summer water is beneficial. Branches may be cut to base to stimulate new branching.

**Associates:** Douglas-fir, western hemlock, western redcedar, black hawthorn, vine maple, willows, alders, cottonwood, aspen, birch, gooseberries, and others.
**Benefits to wildlife:** Flowers are valuable to bees, orange sulfur butterflies, and other insects. Fruits are consumed by many birds, including flickers, grosbeaks, crows, thrushes, waxwings, and tree swallows. Some birds, such as band-tailed pigeons and wild turkeys, eat both fruit and buds. Mammals that eat the fruit, twigs, and foliage include deer, elk, rabbits, black bears, and beavers. Host species for echo blue butterfly larvae. Provides cover and nesting habitat for songbirds.
**Substitute for:** Portugal laurel (*Prunus lusitanica*).
**How to propagate:** From seed collected in fall and planted outdoors, softwood cuttings taken in late summer, hardwood cuttings taken in winter, ground layering, or sprouts collected from suckering underground stems.
**Related species:** Yellow-twig dogwood (*Cornus sericea* 'Flaviramea') is similar but has yellow branches and twigs.

*Corylus cornuta* var. *californica*

# California hazelnut

PLANT TYPE: Deciduous shrub or small tree

SIZE: 10–20 feet x 10–20 feet

LIGHT REQUIREMENTS: Sun to shade

WATER REQUIREMENTS: Low to medium

HARDINESS ZONES: 3b to 9b

A deciduous, ornamental, multistemmed large shrub or small tree with arching branches and velvety, soft-green leaves that turn pale yellow to orange in autumn. Begins cheerfully blooming very early—often in January—with dangly male catkins and clusters of inconspicuous reddish female flowers. Though plants have both male and female flowers, they will produce more of their delicious nuts when another plant is nearby. A beautiful woodland plant that offers texture and wildlife appeal, it will eventually sucker to form a thicket.

**How big:** 10–20 feet tall × 10–20 feet wide.

**Bloom traits:** Male catkins hang in profusion on bare branches in mid- to late winter, female flowers are wind pollinated and much less noticeable tiny, feathery clusters of bright-red stigmas. Fruit is a hard-shelled, edible nut with a short, beaklike point.

**Sun and soil:** Can tolerate full sun or mostly shade. Though it prefers moist, well-drained soil rich in organic matter, it has some tolerance of drought once established and of clay soils if not completely saturated.

**Where it grows:** Understory of mixed or hardwood forests, moist rocky slopes, or along streams, at low to middle elevations.

**How to space it:** 10–20 feet apart.

**Help it thrive:** Drought tolerant once established, but some summer water is beneficial, especially in sunny situations. Suckers may be removed during winter while plants are dormant. May be trained into a small tree.

**Associates:** Garry oak, serviceberry, Douglas-fir, western hemlock, red alder, vine maple, serviceberry, salal, thimbleberry, western sword fern, woodland strawberry, and others.

**Benefits to wildlife:** A variety of species eat and disperse the nuts, including chipmunks, squirrels, and jays. Rabbits and deer eat leaves and sprouts. Provides cover for mammals and birds.

**Substitute for:** English hawthorn (*Crataegus monogyna*), common hazelnut (*Corylus avellana*).

**How to propagate:** From seed collected in late summer or early fall (while husks are still a little green) and planted outdoors, or ground layering, or semihardwood cuttings in fall, or transplantation of suckers in early spring.

**Related species:** Beaked hazelnut (*Corylus cornuta* var. *cornuta*) is found east of the Cascades and has a longer "beak." Agricultural filberts are mostly cultivars of European species, which may hybridize with California hazelnut.

*Delphinium nudicaule*

## Canyon delphinium or red larkspur

PLANT TYPE: Deciduous perennial

SIZE: 1–2 feet x 1–2 feet

LIGHT REQUIREMENTS: Partial shade

WATER REQUIREMENTS: Low

HARDINESS ZONES: 7a to 9b

This striking plant is one of hummingbirds' springtime favorites. Flaming scarlet flowers top delicate stems with deeply divided leaves. Grow this stunning perennial in partly shaded perennial borders, rock gardens, and meadow gardens. Though native to just the southwestern Oregon coastal mountains in our region, it is included due to its value to hummingbirds and its early bloom, and its status of "imperiled" in the state. Toxic if ingested.

**How big:** 1–2 feet tall x 1–2 feet wide.

**Bloom traits:** Flowers consist of 5 scarlet to reddish-orange sepals, the uppermost prominently spurred, and 4 smaller red-and-yellow petals that, positioned to the side of the larger spur, assist hummingbirds in obtaining nectar. Bloom period is from early to late spring. Fruit is a follicle that contains many small black seeds.

**Sun and soil:** Partial shade, although it will thrive in full sun with extra summer water. Well-drained, moist to dry soil. Tolerates heavy soil.

**Where it grows:** Open woodlands, canyons, moist rocky slopes and cliff faces, and along streams, at low to middle elevations in southwestern Oregon and into California.

**How to space it:** 1–2 feet apart.

**Help it thrive:** Drought tolerant once established, but some summer water is beneficial.

**Associates:** Redwood, Garry oak, Douglas-fir, silk tassel bush, snowberry, bitter cherry, goldenrod, yarrow, and others.

**Benefits to wildlife:** Pollinated mostly by hummingbirds. Birds such as finches may eat the seeds. Host plant for clodius parnassian butterfly larvae.

**Substitute for:** Purple and garden loosestrife (*Lythrum salicaria* and *Lysimachia vulgaris*), scarlet sage (*Salvia splendens*), garden-variety delphiniums.

**How to propagate:** From seed collected when follicles dry and planted outdoors in fall; protect from slugs. May hybridize with other delphiniums. Stems are very fragile, so use care when transplanting.

**Related species:** *Delphinium nudicaule* 'Laurin,' a selected cultivar, is especially brilliant in color. **Menzies' larkspur** (*D. menziesii*), with blue flowers, likes sun or partial shade and moist soil.

*Dodecatheon hendersonii*
## Henderson's shooting star

| | |
|---|---|
| PLANT TYPE: Perennial deciduous bulb | |
| SIZE: 6–14 inches x 6–8 inches | |
| LIGHT REQUIREMENTS: Partial shade | |
| WATER REQUIREMENTS: Low | |
| HARDINESS ZONES: 7a to 9b | |

This eye-catching little summer-deciduous wildflower will bring you to your knees in early to late spring when its little dartlike flowers put on their show. Leafless stems arise from rosettes of spoon-shaped leaves and present as many as 15 spectacular flowers that gracefully nod with backward-swept petals. Of the several species that occur in our region, this one needs to dry out in summer after it seasonally dies back, so it is perfect for drought-tolerant wildflower or meadow gardens, rock gardens, or other well-drained, partly shaded sites. Looks best when planted in drifts.

**How big:** 6–14 inches × 6–8 inches.
**Bloom traits:** Spring-blooming flowers have lavender to magenta petals that recurve, while the stigma and style protrude forward. Fruit is a rounded capsule that encloses the seeds.
**Sun and soil:** Partial shade. Moist soil in winter and spring, but drier later, during dormancy.
**Where it grows:** Open woodlands and grasslands, at low to middle elevations.
**How to space it:** 8–12 inches apart.
**Help it thrive:** Little to no summer water.
**Associates:** Garry oak, Douglas-fir, hazelnut, baldhip rose, Oregon iris, and others.
**Benefits to wildlife:** Especially valuable to native bumblebees capable of "buzz pollination," in which pollen that is firmly attached to a flower's anthers is released by vibrations from a bee's

indirect flight muscles and transferred to the stamens by its legs and mandibles.
**Substitute for:** Spanish bluebells (*Hyacinthoides hispanica*) or other garden-variety spring bulbs.
**How to propagate:** From seed collected in late summer and planted in fall or early spring, or very careful separation of bulblets just after flowering or in fall.
**Related species: Pretty shooting star** (*Dodecatheon pulchellum*) looks similar but is best for moist (or irrigated) gardens, and near streams or ponds. The uncommon **Jeffrey's shooting star** (*D. jeffreyi*) is taller, blooms in summer, and needs moist conditions.

*Erigeron glaucus*
## Seaside daisy

PLANT TYPE: Deciduous perennial

SIZE: 4–10 inches x 24 inches

LIGHT REQUIREMENTS: Partial shade to sun

WATER REQUIREMENTS: Low

HARDINESS ZONES: 8a to 9b

Among the dozens of perennial *Erigerons* native to the region, this one is short in stature but long on pollinator appeal and beauty. Oval to spoon-shaped leaves are succulent and largest at the base of the plant. Daisylike lavender-blue flowers bloom in profusion during summer. Grow this compact plant where it can slowly spread into drifts—at the edge of meadow or perennial gardens, or in rock gardens. Tolerates wind and salt spray.

**How big:** 4–10 inches tall; spreads slowly to about 24 inches wide.

**Bloom traits:** Many tiny yellow flowers make up the flowerhead, which is subtended by a lavish fringe of lavender-blue, petallike rays. Fruit is an achene.

**Sun and soil:** Partial shade to sun; provide afternoon shade in hot areas. Moist to dry, well-drained soil (tolerates sandy soil); will spread more readily in fertile, moist soil.

**Where it grows:** Coastal bluffs and near beaches, at low elevations.

**How to space it:** 1–2 feet apart.

**Help it thrive:** Drought tolerant, but is happiest with supplemental summer water in hot, sunny areas.

**Associates:** Shore pine, Port Orford cedar, hairy manzanita, kinnikinnick, sticky monkeyflower, salal, sword fern, yarrow, and others.

**Benefits to wildlife:** Flowers provide nectar for bees, bee flies, and butterflies.

**Substitute for:** Bachelor's button (*Centaurea cyanus*).

**How to propagate:** From seed collected in late summer and planted in fall or spring, or by rhizome division in early fall.

**Related species:** A bigger cousin, **showy fleabane** (*Erigeron speciosus*), is more cold tolerant and blooms nearly all summer. It grows from a taproot to about 2 feet tall and wide. **Willamette daisy** (*E. decumbens*) is listed as endangered federally and in Oregon.

*Erythronium oregonum*

# White fawn lily or **Oregon fawn lily**

| | |
|---|---|
| PLANT TYPE: Deciduous perennial bulb | |
| SIZE: 8–16 inches x 6–8 inches | |
| LIGHT REQUIREMENTS: Partial shade | |
| WATER REQUIREMENTS: Low to medium | |
| HARDINESS ZONES: 7a to 9b | |

"[W]hite, with gold in their hearts" was the way the artist Emily Carr described fawn lilies that grew in grassy fields near her childhood home of Victoria, BC. Also sometimes called dogtooth violet or trout lily, this perennial bulb will add an ethereal elegance to every garden. Deciduous, paired basal leaves, oblong, dark green and mottled with brown, are striking in themselves. In early spring, 1 to 3 nodding, captivating flowers adorn a leafless stem. Grow this lovely plant in an open woodland setting, prairie garden, or partly shaded rock garden.

**How big:** 8–16 inches tall × 6–8 inches wide.

**Bloom traits:** 1- to 2-inch, early- to late-spring-blooming flowers have soft-white, petallike tepals that curve back and usually have some yellow or orange where they converge. Fruit is an oval, 3-sided capsule that matures several months after flowering.

**Sun and soil:** Dappled to partial shade; does not tolerate very deep shade. Slightly acidic (pH 5–6.5), well-drained soil rich in organic matter. Bulbs should never be allowed to fully dry out, but do not tolerate constantly wet conditions.

**Where it grows:** Moist to dry woodlands to open, gravelly prairies at low elevations.

**How to space it:** 8 inches apart, planted in drifts.

**Help it thrive:** Slight summer water. Dormancy begins in summer, but it is best to keep soil slightly moist.

**Associates:** Oregon ash, Garry oak, oceanspray, snowberry, sword fern, camas, native grasses, and more.

**Benefits to wildlife:** Flowers provide for native bumblebees and hummingbirds.

**Substitute for:** Spanish bluebells (*Hyacinthoides hispanica*).

**How to propagate:** From seeds planted outdoors, soon after ripening. Division of bulbs after leaves have died back is possible but not recommended, due to their fragility. Will self-sow in moist soil rich in organic matter. Never collect seeds or plants from the wild.

**Related species: Pink fawn lily** (*Erythronium revolutum*) has pink-violet tepals and grows within about 60 miles of the coast in wet forests, bogs, and shaded stream banks (7b to 9b); it is a species of concern in Oregon. **Glacier lily** (*E. grandiflorum*), with yellow tepals, is generally found in alpine and subalpine meadows and clearings (3b to 8b) and will probably not do well at low elevations. **Henderson's fawn lily** (*E. hendersonii*) occurs at low to middle elevations in southwestern Oregon (7a to 9b). **Coast Range fawn lily** (*E. elegans*) is restricted to high elevations of the Coast Range in Oregon and is a threatened species.

*Fragaria vesca*
# Woodland strawberry

| | |
|---|---|
| PLANT TYPE: | Deciduous perennial |
| SIZE: | 2–5 inches x 6–8 inches |
| LIGHT REQUIREMENTS: | Partial shade |
| WATER REQUIREMENTS: | Medium |
| HARDINESS ZONES: | 3b to 9b |

A deciduous, trailing perennial with a rosette of leaves, each with 3 yellowish-green leaflets. Clusters of ½-inch flowers bloom in spring, followed by small, intensely flavored strawberries. Makes a wonderful ground cover for open, partly shaded spaces or along pathways.

**How big:** 2–5 inches tall × 6–8 inches wide; spreads politely by runners.

**Bloom traits:** Clusters of 5-petaled, white to pale-pink flowers bloom in midspring to early summer. Fruit is not technically a berry, but an aggregate accessory fruit, with numerous tiny, brown achenes (with 1 seed inside) found on the fleshy edible part of the fruit.

**Sun and soil:** Partial shade. Moist, well-drained soil, preferably rich in organic matter.

**Where it grows:** Moist open woodlands, meadows, and along streams, at low to high elevations.

**How to space it:** 1–2 feet apart.

**Help it thrive:** Moderate summer water.

**Associates:** Douglas-fir, vine maple, fairy bells, foamflower, Columbian delphinium, alumroot, bunchberry, and others.

**Benefits to wildlife:** Flowers attract bees and Sara's orange-tip butterflies. Fruit is eaten by many birds, including robins, waxwings, and towhees. Host plant for gray hairstreak and two-banded checkerspot butterfly larvae.

**Substitute for:** Cultivated garden strawberries (*Fragaria* × *ananassa*), periwinkle (*Vinca minor*).

**How to propagate:** From seed collected from a ripe fruit and sown outdoors in fall, or by removing rooting plantlets in early spring or late summer.

**Related species:** Broadpetal strawberry (*Fragaria virginiana*) is similar, but more drought tolerant and with bluish-green foliage. **Coast strawberry** (*F. chiloensis*) is evergreen with glossy leaves; it is a more assertive spreader and can usually take more sun.

*Garrya fremontii*
## Fremont's silk tassel bush
## or **bear brush**

| | |
|---|---|
| PLANT TYPE: Evergreen shrub | |
| SIZE: 8–10 feet x 8–10 feet | |
| LIGHT REQUIREMENTS: Partial shade to sun | |
| WATER REQUIREMENTS: Low | |
| HARDINESS ZONES: 6a to 9b | |

A densely leaved, attractive shrub with glossy, evergreen leaves. An extremely early bloomer, it has catkins that begin their graceful show in winter when nothing else is blooming. To produce the fruit clusters found on female plants, both male and female plants must be planted. A choice shrub for screening, as part of a hedgerow, or as a specimen shrub.

**How big:** 8–10 feet tall × 8–10 feet wide.

**Bloom traits:** Tiny flowers bloom on dangly 3- to 4-inch catkins from midwinter to midspring. Round, purple, berrylike fruit ripens in summer.

**Sun and soil:** Partial shade to sun. Moist to dry, well-drained soil.

**Where it grows:** Open woodland, slopes, foothills, and thickets, at low to middle elevations in Washington and Oregon.

**How to space it:** 8–10 feet apart.

**Help it thrive:** Summer water until established (2–5 years).

**Associates:** Garry oak, Douglas-fir, redwood, snowberry, bitter cherry, Canada goldenrod, yarrow, canyon delphinium, and others.

**Benefits to wildlife:** Fruits may be eaten by birds such as robins and towhees, and mammals such as gray foxes. Sprouts are browsed by deer. Provides evergreen cover for various birds and mammals, especially during winter.

**Substitute for:** Japanese pieris (*Pieris japonica*), cotoneaster (*Cotoneaster* spp.)

**How to propagate:** From seed collected, cleaned of pulp, and planted outdoors in fall, or hardwood cuttings taken in fall or late winter.

**Related species:** Coast or **wavyleaf silk tassel bush** (*Garrya elliptica*) is the larger and more glamorous cousin, with male catkins to 6 inches long. It has a narrower distribution (near the middle and southern Oregon coast and into California), can reach 16 feet tall and nearly as wide, and is less tolerant of drought, heat, and cold.

*Gaultheria shallon*
## Salal

| PLANT TYPE: Evergreen low shrub |
| LIGHT REQUIREMENTS: Partial shade to shade |
| SIZE: 2–5 feet x 3–8 feet |
| WATER REQUIREMENTS: Low to medium |
| HARDINESS ZONES: 6b to 9b |

This versatile, handsome evergreen low shrub is a wildlife favorite. Lustrous, thick, heart-shaped leaves are arranged alternately on reddish branches that arch gracefully. In late spring and summer, rounded, bell-like flowers appear, followed by blueberrylike fruit that ripens in late summer. Plants form dense, deep-rooted clumps that are useful under shade trees, on slopes, as rustic hedges, or even in large pots. Often relegated to parking lot plantings, it is at its best under large trees in areas that can accommodate its spread, although stems may be cut back to keep clumps within bounds.

**How big:** 2–5 feet tall x 3–8 feet wide; grows taller and more lush in shade.

**Bloom traits:** Pendant white- to pink-tinged flowers bloom at branch tips from midspring to early summer. Dark blue to purple berrylike fruits are edible, though not especially tasty.

**Sun and soil:** Partial shade to shade. Burns in full sun. Moist to dry acidic soil, rich in organic matter. Sensitive to transplantation, it may be slow to establish.

**Where it grows:** Coniferous forests, rocky slopes, and clearings, at low to middle elevations.

**How to space it:** 3–6 feet apart.

**Help it thrive:** Drought tolerant once established, but moderate summer water is beneficial. Selected stems may be cut nearly to the ground to renew the plant.

**Associates:** Douglas-fir, western redcedar, redwood, western hemlock, Sitka spruce, madrone, vine maple, rhododendron, evergreen and red huckleberry, hazelnut, sword fern, foamflower, and others.

**Benefits to wildlife:** Flowers provide for hummingbirds, butterflies, bees, and other insects. Host plant for brown elfin butterfly larvae. Berries are eaten by many birds, including towhees, robins, grouse, and band-tailed pigeons, and mammals such as squirrels, chipmunks, foxes, deer, and black bears. Browse species for deer. Provides year-round shelter for birds and small mammals.

**Substitute for:** English ivy (*Hedera helix*), spurge laurel (*Daphne laureola*).

**How to propagate:** From seed collected and cleaned of pulp in fall and planted outdoors, ground layering in spring, or semihardwood cuttings in summer; may self-sow.

**Related species:** Wintergreen (*Gaultheria ovatifolia*) is a gorgeous evergreen plant that grows to about 6 inches tall in bogs and moist forests at middle to high elevations. Unfortunately, it is difficult to establish in gardens.

plants for partial shade

*Heuchera micrantha*

## Small-flowered alumroot or crevice alumroot

| | |
|---|---|
| PLANT TYPE: Deciduous perennial | |
| SIZE: 8–12 inches x 12–16 inches | |
| LIGHT REQUIREMENTS: Partial shade | |
| WATER REQUIREMENTS: Medium | |
| HARDINESS ZONES: 5a to 9b | |

Sometimes evergreen, this low woodland perennial is at home in a variety of moist places. Leaves are about 3 inches wide, usually heart-shaped, and grow from branched rosettes. One- to 2-foot tall sprays of tiny white flowers bloom prolifically on thin reddish stems for several months. Tuck this charmer into shaded rock gardens, rock walls, or pots, or within meadow gardens, along swales, near ponds, or at the edge of woodland gardens.

**How big:** 8–12 inches tall × 12–16 inches wide.
**Bloom traits:** Dainty, small white flowers bloom in misty, open displays from late spring to midsummer. Fruit is a very small 2-part capsule with many seeds.
**Sun and soil:** Partial shade; needs more shade in hot areas. Moist, well-drained soil rich in organic matter.
**Where it grows:** Mixed or coniferous forests near shaded streams and in rocky crevices, at low to high elevations.
**How to space it:** 1–2 feet apart.
**Help it thrive:** Moderate summer water.
**Associates:** Cascade Oregon grape, woodland strawberry, sedum, deer fern, and others.
**Benefits to wildlife:** Flowers attract bees and hummingbirds. Host plant for *Greya politella* moth larvae. Foliage also provides cover for very small creatures.

**Substitute for:** Hybridized, garden-variety heucheras; yellow archangel (*Lamiastrum galeobdolon*).
**How to propagate:** From seed collected in summer or fall when ripe and sown outdoors soon afterward or in spring, or by rhizome division in late spring; may self-sow.
**Related species:** Smooth alumroot (*Heuchera glabra*) is very similar. **Roundleaf alumroot** (*H. cylindrica*) and **meadow alumroot** (*H. chlorantha*) both have narrow, spikey, pale greenish-yellow flower clusters up to 3 feet tall.

*Lilium columbianum*

## Tiger lily or Columbia lily

| | |
|---|---|
| PLANT TYPE: | Perennial bulb |
| SIZE: | 2–3 feet x 10–18 inches |
| LIGHT REQUIREMENTS: | Sun to partial shade |
| WATER REQUIREMENTS: | Medium |
| HARDINESS ZONES: | 4b to 9b |

This woodland lily is a treasure, with its numerous bright-orange-spotted flowers that dangle on tall stems from late spring to early summer. Light-green leaves are arranged in whorls around the stems. Grow it at the edges of woodland gardens, in moist meadow gardens or perennial beds, or near ponds or streams.

**How big:** 2–3 feet tall × 10–18 inches wide.
**Bloom traits:** Two-inch flowers have rolled-back, petallike tepals that are orange with red spots. Fruit is a capsule containing many flat seeds.
**Sun and soil:** Sun to partial shade. Moist to somewhat dry, well-drained soil rich in organic matter. Bulbs should not be allowed to fully dry out.
**Where it grows:** Open woodlands, meadows, and along streams, at low to middle elevations.
**How to space it:** 18 inches apart.
**Help it thrive:** Some summer water, especially in hot areas.
**Associates:** Vine maple, small-flowered alumroot, large-leaved lupine, deer fern, Western bleeding heart, and others.
**Benefits to wildlife:** Hummingbirds, bees, and butterflies such as the pale swallowtail are attracted to the flower nectar.
**Substitute for:** Garden-variety lilies.
**How to propagate:** From seed collected in mid- to late summer and planted outdoors soon afterward (sow in pots to protect from slugs), or careful separation of mature plants' bulbs in early spring.

**Related species:** The uncommon and dazzling **leopard lily** (*Lilium pardalinum* subsp. *vollmeri*) needs moist soil, grows 3 to 5 feet tall, and has larger, orange to reddish flowers in early to mid-summer; it is found in coastal southern Oregon. **Washington lily** (*L. washingtonianum*), also uncommon, grows 4 to 6 feet tall and has large, fragrant, white to pink flowers in mid- to late summer; it occurs in the Columbia River Gorge and southward into Oregon.

*Lonicera ciliosa*
## Orange honeysuckle

| | |
|---|---|
| PLANT TYPE: Deciduous vine |
| SIZE: 10–20 feet |
| LIGHT REQUIREMENTS: Partial shade |
| WATER REQUIREMENTS: Low |
| HARDINESS ZONES: 4a to 9b |

A charming, old-fashioned favorite, this deciduous vine will trail along the ground or climb up supports. Its slender, woody stems are wrapped with opposite, bluish-green leaves. Bright, trumpet-shaped flowers bejewel woodlands in early summer and are popular with hummingbirds. Wonderful in partly shaded cottage or woodland gardens, weaving through open shrubs or small trees, mingling within hedgerows, or growing up a large trellis or fence.

**How big:** 10–20 feet in length.

**Bloom traits:** Brilliant orange and yellow tubular flowers bloom in clusters in late spring to early summer. Fruits are clusters of semitransparent, orangish-red berries with many seeds that may be toxic to humans.

**Sun and soil:** Partial shade. Too much sun can lead to mildew. Moist to somewhat dry soil.

**Where it grows:** Woodland margins and forests, at low to middle elevations.

**How to space it:** 10–16 feet apart.

**Help it thrive:** Not a rampant grower, but minor pruning to direct growth and promote blossoming may be helpful. Summer water until established (2–5 years).

**Associates:** Douglas-fir, western hemlock, Garry oak, Indian plum, snowberry, Nootka rose, woodland strawberry, and others.

**Benefits to wildlife:** Flowers provide for hummingbirds, bees, and butterflies. Fruits are eaten by many birds, including robins, finches, juncos, flickers, and thrushes. Host plant for snowberry checkerspot butterfly larvae. Mature plants provide nest sites for small birds.

**Substitute for:** Japanese honeysuckle (*Lonicera japonica*), traveler's joy (*Clematis vitalba*).

**How to propagate:** From seed collected in late summer and sown, with pulp, outdoors in fall, or by hardwood cuttings in late fall.

**Related species:** Hairy honeysuckle (*Lonicera hispidula*) has fuzzy leaves and fragrant pink blossoms that bloom in midsummer; it occurs on dryish sites and has an either shrubby or vinelike habit.

*Lonicera involucrata*

# Twinberry

| | |
|---|---|
| PLANT TYPE: Deciduous shrub | |
| SIZE: 5–10 feet x 5–8 feet | |
| LIGHT REQUIREMENTS: Sun to shade | |
| WATER REQUIREMENTS: Medium | |
| HARDINESS ZONES: 3b to 9b | |

A fast-growing but long-lived deciduous shrub with deep-green oval leaves that turn yellow in fall. Small but brilliant yellow tubular flowers entice hummingbirds and bloom for several months. Lustrous black berries ripen in late summer, to the delight of fruit-eating birds. Useful as a screen, under a canopy of large trees, as part of a large hedgerow in moist conditions, or for erosion control.

**How big:** 5–10 feet tall x 5–8 feet wide.

**Bloom traits:** Paired yellow tubular flowers surrounded by colorful bracts bloom from midspring to midsummer. Fruit is a black berry (inedible for humans).

**Sun and soil:** Partial shade to nearly full sun; gets rangy in full shade. Moist soil, rich in organic matter; will need more moisture on warm, sunny sites.

**Where it grows:** Moist forests and clearings, wetlands, and along streams, at low to high elevations.

**How to space it:** 5–10 feet apart.

**Help it thrive:** Somewhat drought tolerant once established, but will do best with moderate summer water.

**Associates:** Paper birch, red-twig dogwood, yellow monkeyflower, western columbine, tufted hair grass, willows, rushes, violets, and others.

**Benefits to wildlife:** Flowers attract hummingbirds and western tiger swallowtail butterflies.

Berries are consumed by many birds, including thrushes, flickers, grosbeaks, and waxwings, small mammals, and bears. Host plant for snowberry checkerspot butterfly larvae. Provides cover for birds and mammals.

**Substitute for:** Tatarian honeysuckle (*Lonicera tatarica*); Amur honeysuckle (*Lonicera maackii*).

**How to propagate:** From seed collected in late summer and sown with or without pulp outdoors during fall, or by hardwood cuttings in late fall.

**Related species:** *Lonicera involucrata* var. *ledebourii* occurs in coastal Oregon and California.

*Mahonia aquifolium*
## Tall Oregon grape

| | |
|---|---|
| PLANT TYPE: | Evergreen shrub |
| SIZE: | 5–8 feet x 3–6 feet |
| LIGHT REQUIREMENTS: | Sun to shade |
| WATER REQUIREMENTS: | Low |
| HARDINESS ZONES: | 5a to 9b |

An icon of the Pacific Northwest and the state flower of Oregon, this is a very versatile, undemanding, and handsome evergreen shrub. With an upright growth habit, it has glossy, thick, hollylike leaves that begin coppery and mature to a deep green, with a smattering of red highlights in sunny or cold conditions. Bright golden-yellow flowers bloom in spring for a long period, and are followed by deep-blue berries that continue the colorful collage in summer. Makes a fantastic evergreen screen or barrier with its prickly leaves, but place it where it won't scratch passersby. Grow it along borders, as part of a hedgerow, or within the woodland garden.

**How big:** 5–8 feet tall × 3–6 feet wide; spreads slowly by rhizomes.

**Bloom traits:** Dense clusters of fragrant, golden-yellow flowers bloom in early to late spring at branch ends. Dusty-blue berries ripen in late summer and are edible but tart.

**Sun and soil:** Sun to mostly shade. Moist or dry soils; tolerant of acid to neutral conditions (pH 5–7). Drought tolerant, but provide some shade and more moisture in hot areas.

**Where it grows:** Open coniferous forests and edges, and rocky areas, at low to middle elevations.

**How to space it:** 4–6 feet apart.

**Help it thrive:** Summer water until established (2–5 years). May be cut back to base to renew growth. Does not transplant well.

**Associates:** Douglas-fir, western hemlock, Sitka spruce, quaking aspen, Indian plum, vine maple, oceanspray, Pacific rhododendron, serviceberry, salal, beargrass, sword fern, columbine, and many others.

**Benefits to wildlife:** Flowers attract hummingbirds, bees, and painted lady butterflies. Berries are eaten by mammals and birds such as towhees, robins, sparrows, and waxwings. Browse species for deer and elk. Provides cover for small birds, mammals, and other wildlife.

**Substitute for:** Spurge laurel (*Daphne laureola*), Scotch broom (*Cytisus scoparius*), heavenly bamboo (*Nandina domestica*).

**How to propagate:** From seed collected from fruit in late summer, cleaned of pulp, and planted outdoors.

**Related species:** Dwarf Oregon grape (*Mahonia aquifolium* 'Compacta') grows to 2 feet tall and spreads slowly to form an evergreen ground cover in part shade.

## *Oemleria cerasiformis*
## Indian plum or osoberry

PLANT TYPE: Deciduous shrub

SIZE: 12–18 feet x 10–14 feet

LIGHT REQUIREMENTS: Partial shade

WATER REQUIREMENTS: Low to medium

HARDINESS ZONES: 7a to 9b

A large, deciduous, late-winter-blooming shrub or small tree, with upright, arching branches that support oval, light-green, scented leaves. White, pendant flowers bloom prolifically and very early. Summer-ripening fruits that look like tiny plums are a favorite of many species. Although most plants are either male or female (both of which must be present to produce fruit), occasionally a plant will be both male and female. Grow this understory shrub in partly shaded conditions, such as under tall trees, in a woodland garden or partly shaded hedgerow, or as a backdrop behind smaller plants.

**How big:** 12–18 feet tall x 10–14 feet wide; smaller in sun.

**Bloom traits:** Clusters of greenish-white, scented, bell-shaped blossoms hang beneath emerging leaves in February through March. Fruits are small, colorful drupes that ripen to a deep bluish-black; they are edible when ripe, but not delicious.

**Sun and soil:** Partial shade is best; intolerant of full sun or very deep shade. Tolerates clay soil and is reasonably drought tolerant once established; cannot tolerate very wet soils.

**Where it grows:** Moist to dry woods and valleys and along streams and roads, at low elevations.

**How to space it:** 10–12 feet apart.

**Help it thrive:** Moderately drought tolerant, but will look best with some summer water. Suckers may be cut from the base.

**Associates:** Garry oak, Douglas-fir, vine maple, hazelnut, thimbleberry, deer fern, columbine, and others.

**Benefits to wildlife:** Winter flowers provide for early bumblebees and Anna's hummingbirds. Fruits are eaten by many animals, including robins, waxwings, coyotes, foxes, and deer. Provides cover for birds and other animals.

**Substitute for:** Russian olive (*Elaeagnus angustifolia*), Scotch broom (*Cytisus scoparius*).

**How to propagate:** From seed collected in early to midsummer, dried and planted outdoors, or hardwood cutting taken in late winter, or by ground layering in spring.

**Related species:** There are no other species in the genus *Oemleria*.

*Paxistima myrsinites*
## Oregon boxwood

PLANT TYPE: Evergreen low shrub

SIZE: 1–3 feet x 2–4 feet

LIGHT REQUIREMENTS: Partial shade

WATER REQUIREMENTS: Low to medium

HARDINESS ZONES: 3b to 9b

A tidy, somewhat dense, evergreen low shrub with lustrous small, paired leaves on upright, rigid stems. Diminutive fragrant reddish flowers bloom profusely for several months. Grow this mounding shrub in foundation plantings, in front of taller shrubs in woodland settings, in partly shaded rock gardens, or as a low hedge.

**How big:** 1–3 feet tall × 2–4 feet wide.

**Bloom traits:** Inconspicuous burgundy flowers with 4 petals bloom profusely from midspring to midsummer. Fruit is a capsule.

**Sun and soil:** Partial shade, although it will tolerate sun in cool areas and even the dry shade under conifers once established. Moist to dry, well drained, slightly acidic soil.

**Where it grows:** Moist to dry woodlands, or open rocky slopes, at low to high elevations.

**How to space it:** 3 feet apart.

**Help it thrive:** Summer water until established (2–5 years).

**Associates:** Douglas-fir, white fir, western and mountain hemlock, western redcedar, quaking aspen, Douglas maple, serviceberry, huckleberries, lupine, western columbine, meadow rue, bunchberry, and others.

**Benefits to wildlife:** Flowers attract bees. Browse species for deer and elk. Provides year-round cover for small birds and other wildlife.

**Substitute for:** Boxwood (*Buxus sempervirens*), Japanese holly (*Ilex crenata*).

**How to propagate:** Semihardwood cuttings or ground layering in summer.

**Related species:** None in the Pacific Northwest.

*Philadelphus lewisii*
## Mock orange

| | |
|---|---|
| PLANT TYPE: Deciduous shrub | |
| SIZE: 6–9 feet x 6–8 feet | |
| LIGHT REQUIREMENTS: Sun to partial shade | |
| WATER REQUIREMENTS: Low to medium | |
| HARDINESS ZONES: 4a to 9b | |

This ornamental, multibranched, deciduous shrub has sweetly fragrant white flowers. Versatile and fast-growing, it's a good choice near porches and patios where the fragrance will be welcome. Or grow it as a background shrub or screen, on slopes, in open woodland gardens where the glowing flowers will stand out, or as part of a large hedgerow. Useful for erosion control.

**How big:** 6–9 feet tall x 6–8 feet wide.
**Bloom traits:** Showy, 4-petaled white flowers bloom in clusters at branch tips in late spring to early summer. Fruit is a capsule that contains many tiny seeds.
**Sun and soil:** Sun to partial shade; tolerates all but very deep shade. Moist to dry soil.
**Where it grows:** Moist forest openings, along streams, or on rocky slopes and hillsides, at low to middle elevations.
**How to space it:** 6–8 feet apart.
**Help it thrive:** Summer water until established (2–5 years). Drought tolerant, although plants in full sun will benefit from summer water. Prune only as necessary to enhance shape.
**Associates:** Douglas-fir, hazelnut, oceanspray, serviceberry, Indian plum, baldhip rose, ninebark, tall Oregon grape, and others.
**Benefits to wildlife:** Provides forage for bees and butterflies, such as swallowtail and common wood nymph. Seeds are eaten by squirrels and many birds, including juncos, chickadees, grouse, and flickers. Browse species for deer and elk. Creates cover for birds and other animals.
**Substitute for:** Butterfly bush (*Buddleja davidii*), gorse (*Ulex europaeus*).
**How to propagate:** From seed collected from dry capsules in fall and sown outdoors, or semihardwood cuttings taken in summer, or hardwood cuttings taken in fall.
**Related species:** Whipplevine (*Whipplea modesta*) is a trailing distant cousin that forms a low, semiwoody groundcover for sun or shade with puffs of white flowers that bloom for many months.

*Picea sitchensis*

# Sitka spruce

| | |
|---|---|
| PLANT TYPE: | Evergreen tree |
| SIZE: | 100–200 feet x 20–40 feet |
| LIGHT REQUIREMENTS: | Sun to partial shade |
| WATER REQUIREMENTS: | Low to medium |
| HARDINESS ZONES: | 6a to 9b |

A magnificent coniferous evergreen associated with the temperate rainforest that can live over 800 years. Stiff, sharp needles grow circumferentially on branchlets, which droop gracefully on horizontal branches. Bark is thin, flakey, and reddish- to grayish brown. Best near the coast or its inlets on large properties where they can attain their natural size and form. Only remnants of Sitka spruce forests remain.

**How big:** 100–200 feet tall x 20–40 feet wide; usually smaller in cultivation.

**Bloom traits:** Male and female cones grow on separate branches of the same tree. Flowers bloom in May and cones ripen in late summer. Seeds are black and winged.

**Sun and soil:** Sun to partial shade; does not tolerate full shade. Cool settings with moist, deep, well-drained soil are best. Tolerates salt spray.

**Where it grows:** Cool, moist, well-drained sites such as river floodplains and coastal headlands, at low to middle elevations near the coast and its inlets.

**How to space it:** 25–30 feet apart.

**Help it thrive:** Moderate summer water until established.

**Associates:** Western hemlock, western redcedar, Douglas-fir, white pine, mountain hemlock, shore pine, red huckleberry, thimbleberry, salmonberry, stream violet, evergreen violet, and others.

**Benefits to wildlife:** Provides critical habitat for a large variety of mammals, birds, reptiles, and amphibians, including thermal, hiding, and migrational cover and nesting and roosting sites. Snags are particularly important for platform-nesting raptors and cavity nesters. Seeds are eaten by many bird species, and needles are eaten by blue grouse.

**Substitute for:** English holly (*Ilex aquifolium*).

**How to propagate:** From seed dried and shaken from ripe cones and planted outdoors in fall with a light layer of mulch.

**Related species:** Many cultivars, including the smaller 'Papoose,' are appropriate for small gardens.

*Polystichum munitum*
## Western sword fern

| |
|---|
| PLANT TYPE: Evergreen fern |
| SIZE: 3–4 feet x 3–4 feet |
| LIGHT REQUIREMENTS: Partial shade to shade |
| WATER REQUIREMENTS: Low |
| HARDINESS ZONES: 5a to 9b |

A familiar, versatile and adaptable workhorse, this long-lived evergreen fern has long, tough fronds that grow from woody crowns. It looks best when planted en masse in cool, shaded areas, where it is particularly drought tolerant. Place it beneath large conifers, on moist slopes, and as a backdrop for smaller woodland plants, even in partly shaded rock gardens. Useful for controlling erosion. Young fronds are edible.

**How big:** 3–4 feet tall x 3–4 feet wide.
**Sun and soil:** Partial shade to shade. Moist to somewhat dry soil, rich in organic matter. Tolerates acidic soils.
**Where it grows:** Moist, coniferous forests at mostly low elevations.
**How to space it:** 3 feet apart.
**Help it thrive:** Drought tolerant once established, but some summer water is beneficial. Brown fronds may be removed in late spring for a more tidy appearance, but leaving them provides more cover for wildlife.
**Associates:** Western redcedar, Douglas-fir, western hemlock, grand fir, bigleaf maple, vine maple, hazelnut, salal, heuchera, foamflower, deer fern, and many others.

**Benefits to wildlife:** Provides year-round cover for birds and small mammals. Browse species for deer and elk.
**Substitute for:** Bittersweet nightshade (*Solanum dulcamara*), English ivy (*Hedera helix*).
**How to propagate:** Spores propagated on moist soil; may self-sow. Large plants can be divided, but may not always survive.
**Related species:** Holly fern (*Polystichum andersonii*) is also evergreen but has lacier fronds and naturally occurs only at middle elevations. It may be difficult to locate at plant nurseries.

*Prunus emarginata* var. *mollis*

# Bitter cherry

| | |
|---|---|
| PLANT TYPE: | Deciduous tree or shrub |
| SIZE: | 15–50 feet x 10–30 feet |
| LIGHT REQUIREMENTS: | Sun to partial shade |
| WATER REQUIREMENTS: | Low |
| HARDINESS ZONES: | 4a to 9b |

An upright, sometimes multitrunked tree or deciduous shrub with lustrous reddish-brown bark. Oblong 3-inch leaves turn yellow in autumn. Clusters of white to pale pink, fragrant flowers bloom in spring and are followed by small cherries that turn dark red when ripe. Grow this attractive tree in mostly sunny woodland settings or as part of a large hedgerow.

**How big:** 15–50 feet tall x 10–30 feet wide.

**Bloom traits:** Clusters of 5 to 10 almond-scented, white or pale-pink flowers bloom from midspring to early summer. Fruit is a drupe that begins bright red and turns dark with summer ripening. Though very popular with wildlife, they are too bitter for us.

**Sun and soil:** Partial shade to sun. Moist to dryish soil.

**Where it grows:** Open conifer forests and along streams, at low to middle elevations.

**How to space it:** 15–20 feet apart.

**Help it thrive:** Moderately drought tolerant once established, but some summer water may be beneficial.

**Associates:** Douglas-fir, western hemlock, serviceberry, oceanspray, thimbleberry, Oregon boxwood, and others.

**Benefits to wildlife:** Flowers attract bees, butterflies, and other beneficial insects. Many birds eat the fruits, including tanagers, waxwings, bluebirds, towhees, and flickers. Mammals such as chipmunks, raccoons, squirrels, and black bears also favor them. Host species for swallowtail and Lorquin's admiral butterfly larvae. Browse species for deer and elk. Thickets provide cover and nesting sites for many small animals.

**Substitute for:** Sweet cherry (*Prunus avium*) and other ornamental cherry trees, Russian olive (*Elaeagnus angustifolia*).

**How to propagate:** From seed collected in summer, cleaned of pulp and sown outdoors in fall.

**Related species:** Chokecherry (*Prunus virginiana*) grows to about 12 feet tall, has longer flower clusters, and grows in similar conditions; it is more common east of the Cascades. Another bitter cherry, *P. emarginata* var. *emarginata*, is smaller and shrubbier and grows east of the Cascades.

*Rhamnus purshiana* syn. *Frangula purshiana*

# Cascara

| | |
|---|---|
| PLANT TYPE: Deciduous tree or large shrub | |
| SIZE: 30 feet x 15 feet | |
| LIGHT REQUIREMENTS: Partial shade | |
| WATER REQUIREMENTS: Low to medium | |
| HARDINESS ZONES: 4a to 9b | |

One of more than 100 *Rhamnus* species around the world, this deciduous, upright small tree or large shrub has smooth, silvery bark and glossy, bright-green, prominently veined leaves. Inconspicuous greenish flowers bloom in mid- to late spring. Dark purple berries ripen late in summer and are a favorite of many birds. This is an attractive fast grower for small, partly shady yards but may be best in rural or suburban areas due to a sensitivity to air pollution. Retains its leaves during mild winters.

**How big:** 30 feet tall × 15 feet wide.

**Bloom traits:** Small, pale-green flowers bloom at the tips of young stems in late spring to midsummer. Pea-sized fruit begins red and ripens to deep purple.

**Sun and soil:** Partial shade, in well-drained soil. Prefers moist soil with plenty of organic matter, but can tolerate dryish conditions. Tolerates mostly sunny conditions with extra summer water.

**Where it grows:** Moist to dry mixed woods and floodplains, at low to middle elevations.

**How to space it:** 10–15 feet apart. May be used as part of a hedgerow.

**Help it thrive:** Moderate summer water the first 2 to 5 years. Drought tolerant once established (especially in shade), but some occasional water is beneficial.

**Associates:** Douglas-fir, ponderosa pine, western hemlock, vine maple, red alder, and others.

**Benefits to wildlife:** Flowers provide nectar for bees and hummingbirds. Fruit attracts birds, including band-tailed pigeons. Browse species for mule deer, raccoons, foxes, and others.

**Substitute for:** English laurel (*Prunus laurocerasus*), Portugal laurel (*P. lusitanica*).

**How to propagate:** From seed collected, cleaned of pulp, and planted outdoors in fall.

**Related species: California coffeeberry** (*Rhamnus californica*) is a large evergreen shrub that grows from southwestern Oregon into California. It needs more sun than cascara.

*Ribes sanguineum*
## Red-flowering currant

| | |
|---|---|
| PLANT TYPE: | Deciduous shrub |
| SIZE: | 7–10 feet x 6–8 feet |
| LIGHT REQUIREMENTS: | Sun to partial shade |
| WATER REQUIREMENTS: | Low to medium |
| HARDINESS ZONES: | 5b to 9b |

This medium-sized, thornless deciduous shrub with an upright habit has year-round appeal. An early spring bloomer, it has striking, pendulous flower clusters that burst forth just before maple-like leaves unfold. Powdery-blue berries ripen in late summer, followed by golden autumn foliage that hangs on during mild winters. Considering its adaptability, beauty, ability to control erosion, and strong wildlife appeal, it is highly recommended for almost any garden.

**How big:** 7–10 feet tall × 6–8 feet wide; may eventually form a thicket.

**Bloom traits:** Clusters of numerous, lightly fragrant, pink tubular flowers bloom along stems in early spring. Berries are edible but not flavorful.

**Sun and soil:** Full sun to partial shade (afternoon shade is best). Needs well-drained, fertile soil. Summer water until established (2–5 years).

**Where it grows:** Shady forest edges and rocky, open, and disturbed sites, at low to middle elevations.

**How to space it:** 6–8 feet apart. Do not grow *Ribes* spp. within 1,000 feet of western white pines, to which it may transmit fungal spores.

**Help it thrive:** Moderate summer water the first 2–5 years, especially in hot areas; infrequent water thereafter (prone to root rot). Pruning of older stems after flowering stimulates new growth.

**Associates:** Douglas-fir, bigleaf maple, madrone, bitter cherry, vine maple, elderberry, mock orange, serviceberry, manzanita, salal, sword fern, kinnikinnick, and others.

**Benefits to wildlife:** Flowers provide nectar for bees, hummingbirds, and occasionally bushtits. Leaves provide food for zephyr and other butterfly larvae. Berries provide food for birds and many mammals. Cover is beneficial to many wild animals.

**Substitute for:** Butterfly bush (*Buddleja davidii*).

**How to propagate:** From seed planted in fall, semihardwood cuttings in summer, or hardwood cuttings in fall.

**Related species:** Wild gooseberry (*Ribes divaricatum*) has reddish flowers and dark, edible berries. It is thorny and an excellent shrub for wildlife in moist places.

*Rosa pisocarpa*
## Clustered wild rose

PLANT TYPE: Deciduous shrub

SIZE: 7 feet x 6 feet

LIGHT REQUIREMENTS: Full sun to partial shade

WATER REQUIREMENTS: Low to medium

HARDINESS ZONES: 7b to 9b

Also known as the pea or swamp rose, this is one of 20 rose species native to North America that spread slowly by rhizomes. Arching branches support delicate compound leaves and may have prickles. In late spring to midsummer, flowers bloom at the tips of young stems. As the fruits mature, they turn dark red and stay on the plant during winter and early spring. Grow it at the back of perennial borders, at the edge of woodland settings, or in large rain gardens.

**How big:** 7 feet tall × 6 feet wide; spreads slowly to form a thicket.

**Bloom traits:** Clusters of small 5-petaled flowers bloom at the tips of young stems in late spring to early summer. Fruits known as hips stay on the plant into winter.

**Sun and soil:** Full sun to partial shade. Can tolerate somewhat dry to very wet soil.

**Where it grows:** Generally open, moist areas at low to middle elevations.

**How to space it:** 6–8 feet apart. May not be suitable for very small gardens.

**Help it thrive:** Moderate summer water the first 2 years; occasional water thereafter when roots are established.

**Associates:** Cascara, red-twig dogwood, salal, Oregon grape, goatsbeard, and others.

**Benefits to wildlife:** Flowers provide forage for butterflies and bees. Hips provide winter food for juncos, grouse, grosbeaks, and other birds, as well as chipmunks, rabbits, deer, and other mammals. Host plant for mourning cloak butterfly larvae. Foliage is useful for leaf-cutter bees. Rose thickets provide cover or nesting sites for birds and small mammals.

**Substitute for:** Multiflora rose (*Rosa multiflora*).

**How to propagate:** From seed collected, cleaned of pulp, and planted outdoors in fall, or root cuttings in winter.

**Related species:** Nootka rose (*Rosa nutkana*), host species for western checkerspot butterfly larvae, does well in dryish to moist soil and colder conditions (4a to 9b), and has larger, solitary flowers and purplish, pear-shaped hips. **Baldhip rose** (*R. gymnocarpa*) is a smaller plant (to 5 feet tall) that blooms from late spring to late summer and tolerates dry to moist soil (5a to 9b) in partial shade.

*Rubus parviflorus*
# Thimbleberry

| PLANT TYPE: Deciduous shrub |
| SIZE: 4–6 feet |
| LIGHT REQUIREMENTS: Full sun to partial shade |
| WATER REQUIREMENTS: Low to medium |
| HARDINESS ZONES: 4a to 9b |

A deciduous, fast-growing, thornless shrub related to raspberries and blackberries. Upright, flexible branches have large, fuzzy, maplelike leaves. Showy 1- to 2-inch wide, gleaming-white flowers bloom in clusters and lead to raspberry-like fruits. Fruits, young shoots, and flowers are all edible. Useful for erosion control or as part of a hedgerow.

**How big:** 4–6 feet tall; spreads by rhizomes to form a thicket. Due to its spreading habit, this plant may not be suitable for very small gardens.

**Bloom traits:** Conspicuous, 5-petaled white flower clusters bloom at the tips of young stems in late spring to midsummer. Fruit is an aggregate composed of numerous drupelets around a central core. They ripen over the summer; taste varies, but they are usually delicious.

**Sun and soil:** Full sun to partial shade in well-drained, slightly acidic soil. Prefers moist soil but can tolerate dryish conditions. In full sun, more moisture is required.

**Where it grows:** Riparian sites or open or wooded areas in moist to dry conditions at low to high elevations.

**How to space it:** 6 feet apart.

**Help it thrive:** Moderate summer water until established; occasional water thereafter. Dead canes may be pruned to the ground to make space for new ones.

**Associates:** Sitka spruce, western hemlock, grand fir, Douglas-fir, western redcedar, elderberry, salal, salmonberry, sword fern, Hooker's fairy-bells, foamflower, vanilla leaf, and others.

**Benefits to wildlife:** Flowers provide food for butterflies and bees. Fruit and foliage attract birds and small and large mammals. Provides nesting material for native bees.

**Substitute for:** Himalayan blackberry (*Rubus discolor*).

**How to propagate:** From seed collected and planted in fall, semihardwood cuttings in summer, hardwood cuttings in winter, or rhizome division from fall to early spring.

**Related species:** Salmonberry (*Rubus spectabilis*) attracts hummingbirds and butterflies and needs similar conditions, but is not as cold hardy (6a to 9b). Magenta flowers are followed by orange, raspberrylike fruit. Forms thickets and may be assertive under moist conditions. **Black-cap raspberry** (*R. leucodermis* var. *leucodermis*) has 3- to 7-foot-tall arching stems and needs moisture; it produces delicious fruit that ripens in midsummer. Prune as you would conventional raspberries.

*Sambucus racemosa*
# Red elderberry

| | |
|---|---|
| PLANT TYPE: Deciduous shrub |
| SIZE: 8–18 feet x 10 feet |
| LIGHT REQUIREMENTS: Full sun to partial shade |
| WATER REQUIREMENTS: Low to medium |
| HARDINESS ZONES: 3b to 9b |

An attractive, medium-to-tall, upright deciduous shrub that may grow singly or form a clump or thicket. Leaves are compound, with 5 to 7 dark-green leaflets that may turn golden with an autumn chill. Showy, fragrant, conical inflorescences are made up of many small flowers. Berrylike fruits mature to a brilliant red and are especially valuable to wildlife. Roots, stems, and foliage are toxic to humans if eaten; fruit is edible but must be cooked.

**How big:** 8–18 feet tall × 8–10 feet wide.
**Bloom traits:** Conspicuous, lacy, cream-colored flowers bloom in midspring to early summer. Eye-catching pea-sized red fruits known as drupes ripen a few months later.
**Sun and soil:** Full sun to shade. Prefers moist, loamy, rich soil but is tolerant of dryer conditions and clay soils.
**Where it grows:** Moist habitats, including woodlands, grasslands, and along streams, from low to middle elevations.
**How to space it:** 10 feet apart.
**Help it thrive:** Drought tolerant, but does best with some summer water.
**Associates:** Douglas-fir, red alder, vine maple, red-twig dogwood, thimbleberry, sword fern, deer fern, woodland strawberry, and others.

**Benefits to wildlife:** Flowers provide nectar for butterflies and hummingbirds; pollen is important for various insects. Native bees use foliage for nesting material. Host plant for echo blue butterfly larvae. Fruits are eaten by many mammals and birds and are the main ingredient of band-tailed pigeons' summer diet. Foliage, bark, and buds are browsed by deer and other species.
**Substitute for:** European cranberry bush (*Viburnum opulus* var. *opulus*).
**How to propagate:** From seed, removed of pulp and planted soon after collection in late summer or fall.
**Related species:** Blue elderberry (*Sambucus nigra* ssp. *caerulea*) is a multistemmed large shrub or small tree that typically grows about twice as large. Fruit is dark blue and is used in making wine, jam, and pie.

## *Sedum spathulifolium*
## Broadleaf stonecrop

PLANT TYPE: Evergreen ground cover

SIZE: 1–4 inches

LIGHT REQUIREMENTS: Partial shade to sun

WATER REQUIREMENTS: Low to medium

HARDINESS ZONES: 5b to 9b

A succulent, mat-forming ground cover with rounded, flattened leaves that grow in rosettes. Leaf color is variable, from frosty gray to bluish-green and even various shades of red. Sparkling yellow, sweetly fragrant flowers burst forth in summer. Leaves will be tighter with sun, wider in shade. Grow this evergreen gem in rock gardens, along edges as ground cover, on green roofs, in nooks and crannies of rock walls, or in rather small pots—its roots like to be snug.

**How big:** 1–4 inches tall × 12 inches wide; spreads fairly slowly.

**Bloom traits:** Clusters of brilliant yellow, star-shaped flowers arise several inches above foliage in summer.

**Sun and soil:** Partial shade to sun with fast-draining, gritty, lean soil. Prefers some summer water but is drought tolerant.

**Where it grows:** Rocky outcrops and crevices, from coast to high elevations.

**How to space it:** 10–14 inches apart.

**Help it thrive:** Appreciates water during hot, dry periods.

**Associates:** Garry oak, ponderosa pine, madrone, oval-leaved viburnum, oceanspray, yarrow,

Related species *Sedum oreganum*

Menzies' delphinium, goldenrod, lupine, camas, nodding onion, mosses, liverworts, licorice fern, and others.

**Benefits to wildlife:** Popular with pollinators, including native bees, beetles, and flies. Host plant for mountain parnassian, brown elfin, and Moss' elfin butterfly larvae.

**Substitute for:** Nonnative sedum and sempervivem (hen and chicks).

**How to propagate:** From seed collected in late summer and planted in early spring, division of rooted clumps, or by shallowly planting stem pieces or rosettes in spring or early summer.

**Related species:** There are numerous cultivars available; 'Cape Blanco' is gorgeous. **Oregon stonecrop** (*Sedum oreganum*) has green, spoon-shaped leaves that turn reddish in full sun; it typically spreads faster than *S. spathulifolium* and grows from Alaska to California.

*Sorbus sitchensis*
# Mountain ash

| | |
|---|---|
| PLANT TYPE: | Deciduous shrub |
| SIZE: | 8–12 feet x 8–10 feet |
| LIGHT REQUIREMENTS: | Partial shade to sun |
| WATER REQUIREMENTS: | Low to medium |
| HARDINESS ZONES: | 3b to 8b |

A deciduous, upright, slow-growing multi-stemmed shrub with compound bluish-green leaves that turn yellow to bronze-red in autumn. Its smooth bark is reddish-brown and flowers are clusters of small white blossoms. Large bunches of berrylike fruits turn brilliant hues in late summer or fall and may persist until winter. Although this shrub grows mostly at middle to high elevations and produces less fruit at lower sites, it is included due to its tremendous wildlife appeal and resplendent beauty. Grow it at the edge of woodland gardens, in large rock gardens, or in other mostly sunny sites.

**How big:** 8–12 feet tall x 8–10 feet wide.

**Bloom traits:** Three-inch-wide dense, flat-topped clusters of small white flowers bloom in late spring to midsummer. Small fruits called pomes ripen to orangish-red in late summer to early fall.

**Sun and soil:** Partial shade to sun; not tolerant of deep shade. Moist to dry, well-drained soil.

**Where it grows:** Coniferous forests and forest openings, along streams, or on rocky hillsides, at middle to high elevations.

**How to space it:** 8–10 feet apart.

**Help it thrive:** Does best with some summer water, especially in hot areas.

**Associates:** Western hemlock, mountain hemlock, western white pine, Douglas-fir, subalpine fir, beargrass, woodland strawberry, and others.

**Benefits to wildlife:** Flowers provide for native bees and other pollinators. Fruit is eaten by birds such as waxwings, grosbeaks, thrushes, and finches, and many mammals. Twigs supply browse for deer and elk. Provides cover for birds and small mammals.

**Substitute for:** European mountain ash (*Sorbus aucuparia*).

**How to propagate:** From seed collected in fall and planted outdoors. Cleaned seeds may be stored.

**Related species:** Cascade mountain ash (*Sorbus scopulina*) is similar, but with slightly different leaf characteristics.

*Spiraea douglasii*
## Western spirea or Douglas' spirea

| | |
|---|---|
| PLANT TYPE: Deciduous shrub |
| SIZE: 4-6 feet x 4-6 feet |
| LIGHT REQUIREMENTS: Sun to partial shade |
| WATER REQUIREMENTS: Medium |
| HARDINESS ZONES: 4a to 9b |

A deciduous, fast-growing, spreading, multi-stemmed shrub for moist, sunny areas. Lustrous bluish-green leaves turn brilliant shades of yellow to red in the fall. Large, dazzling plumes of tiny pink flowers bloom throughout summer. Good hedgerow, bog, or rain garden plant. May be too assertive for small, moist gardens. Useful for erosion control and waterlogged soils.

**How big:** 4–6 feet tall × 4–6 feet wide; spreads into thickets by rhizomes.

**Bloom traits:** Showy pale- to deep-pink flowers bloom early to late summer. Fruits are small follicles.

**Sun and soil:** Sun to partial shade. Moist to wet conditions. Tolerates clay and gritty soils. Will not thrive in dry conditions, so if spread must be minimized, limit summer water after it's established.

**Where it grows:** Bogs, swamps, wet meadows, moist coniferous forests, and along streams and lakes, at low to middle elevations.

**How to space it:** 6 feet apart.

**Help it thrive:** Moderate summer water. Tolerates drought better if grown in some shade.

**Associates:** Western hemlock, Sitka spruce, quaking aspen, Oregon ash, Douglas maple, willows, twinberry, red-twig dogwood, salal, deer fern, blue-eyed grass, rushes, sedges, and others.

**Benefits to wildlife:** Flowers are important for native bees, butterflies, and other insects. Browse

species for deer. Provides nest sites for birds and cover for other small wildlife.

**Substitute for:** Tamarisk (*Tamarix ramosissima*), Japanese spirea (*Spiraea japonica*), butterfly bush (*Buddleja davidii*).

**How to propagate:** From seed collected in late summer or fall, hardwood or root cuttings in late fall, or division of plants with rhizomes.

**Related species: Shiny-leaved spirea** or **white spirea** (*Spiraea betulifolia* var. *lucida*), which grows 1–2 feet tall × 2–3 feet wide, has dense clusters of white to pale-pink flowers, can tolerate drier soil, and is useful as a foundation plant or low hedge. *S. douglasii* may hybridize with *S. betulifolia* to form **pyramid spirea** (S. × *pyramidata*).

*Symphoricarpos albus*

# Snowberry

| | |
|---|---|
| PLANT TYPE: Deciduous shrub | |
| SIZE: 4-7 feet x 5-7 feet | |
| LIGHT REQUIREMENTS: Sun to mostly shade | |
| WATER REQUIREMENTS: Low to medium | |
| HARDINESS ZONES: 3b to 9b | |

A twiggy, versatile, erect deciduous shrub that spreads by woody rhizomes. Stems support rounded, bluish-green leaves and small pairs of pink flowers very attractive to native bees. White berries hang on during winter. Use this ornamental shrub under large trees in woodland gardens, as part of a hedgerow, or on slopes to control erosion. Often used in restoration efforts.

**How big:** 4–7 feet tall × 5–7 feet wide; spreads by rhizomes.

**Bloom traits:** Tiny, paired, bell-shaped pink flowers bloom in summer. Half-inch white berries known as drupes grow in compact clusters and stand out in winter.

**Sun and soil:** Sun to mostly shade. Moist or dry soil; tolerates heavy soils.

**Where it grows:** Open forests and rocky slopes from low to middle elevations.

**How to space it:** 6 feet apart.

**Help it thrive:** Drought tolerant once established (2–5 years). May do best with some summer water in hot areas. Good air circulation will prevent powdery mildew.

**Associates:** Western hemlock, Douglas-fir, western redcedar, Garry oak, bitter cherry, bigleaf and vine maple, Indian plum, oceanspray, salal, sword fern, and others.

**Benefits to wildlife:** Flowers attract native pollinators. Fruit is eaten by grouse, pheasants, quail and other birds. Host plant for snowberry checkerspot butterfly larvae. May form dense thickets that provide shelter or nesting sites for many small birds and mammals

**Substitute for:** Japanese barberry (*Berberis thunbergii*).

**How to propagate:** From seed collected in winter and removed from pulp, with 2 months of warm stratification followed by 6 months of cold, or cuttings of woody runners while dormant, or hardwood cuttings in late fall or winter.

**Related species: Creeping snowberry** (*Symphoricarpos hesperius*), a California native, is shorter and also controls erosion.

## *Thuja plicata*
# Western redcedar

PLANT TYPE: Evergreen tree

SIZE: 75-150 feet x 25-50 feet

LIGHT REQUIREMENTS: Sun to shade

WATER REQUIREMENTS: Medium

HARDINESS ZONES: 3b to 9b

This majestic, evergreen conifer can live over 1,000 years. Branches droop elegantly and have lacy, fragrant foliage. Bark is a warm reddish-brown that peels in strips. Where space allows, it makes a wonderful natural screen and year-round wildlife magnet. Despite its common name, it is not a true cedar. The provincial tree of British Columbia.

**How big:** 75–150 feet tall × 25–50 feet wide, usually smaller in gardens.

**Bloom traits:** Small brown seed cones sit upright on branches when ripe. Pollen cones are smaller and shed yellow pollen in spring.

**Sun and soil:** Sun to shade, but thrives in partly shady conditions; seedlings need some shade. Moist, slightly acidic soil rich in organic matter, but is fairly drought tolerant once established.

**Where it grows:** Moist forests and along streams and swamps, at low to middle elevations.

**How to space it:** 20–30 feet apart.

**Help it thrive:** Summer water until established (2–5 years); will do best with some summer water afterward, especially in hot areas.

**Associates:** Douglas-fir, western hemlock, quaking aspen, Oregon ash, western flowering dogwood, willows, Nootka rose, oval-leaf viburnum, Indian plum, fairy bells, false solomon's seal, maidenhair fern, western bleeding heart, stream violet, vanilla leaf, trillium, and others.

**Benefits to wildlife:** Seeds are eaten by birds such as nuthatches, sparrows, and waxwings. Host plant for cedar hairstreak butterfly larvae and some moths. Browse species for deer and elk. Provides cover and nest sites for birds, including juncos and warblers, and many other wild animals. Cavity-nesting birds like woodpeckers may use cavities in mature trees and snags. Mammals such as squirrels may use the bark for nesting material.

**Substitute for:** English holly (*Ilex aquifolium*).

**How to propagate:** From seed collected in fall and sown outdoors soon afterward.

**Related species:** Some cultivars are available, such as 'Pendula,' with weeping branches, and 'Fastigiata,' with a narrow, columnar habit. Its only relative in North America is arborvitae (*Thuja occidentalis*), native to the northeastern United States and Canada.

*Tsuga heterophylla*
# Western hemlock

| | |
|---|---|
| PLANT TYPE: | Evergreen tree |
| SIZE: | 50-150 feet x 25-30 feet |
| LIGHT REQUIREMENTS: | Sun to shade |
| WATER REQUIREMENTS: | Medium |
| HARDINESS ZONES: | 4a to 9b |

The state tree of Washington, this tall, dark, and handsome conifer has feathery foliage and branches that gracefully droop downward. Fast growing and shade tolerant, it is at its best in spacious woodland settings where it can attain its full size and shape. It makes an impressive screen planted in drifts or as background trees where space allows, but this stately tree is not a good choice for small city lots or close to buildings, due to its shallow roots.

**How big:** 50–150 feet tall × 25–30 feet wide.

**Bloom traits:** Small cones that dangle at the tips of branches are produced in great number; they ripen in autumn and remain available through midwinter.

**Sun and soil:** Sun to shade; young trees naturally grow in the shade of other trees, so will need at least partial shade. Moist, acidic, well-drained soil rich in organic matter; often grows on rotting stumps and logs.

**Where it grows:** Moist forests, at low to middle elevations nearly throughout the region, except for the interior southwest of Oregon.

**How to space it:** 20–30 feet apart.

**Help it thrive:** Does best with some summer water, especially in hot areas, but can tolerate drought.

**Associates:** Western redcedar, Douglas-fir, grand fir, bigleaf and vine maple, Cascade Oregon grape, red huckleberry, tiger lily, bunchberry, and others.

**Benefits to wildlife:** Seeds are eaten by birds such as juncos, siskins, and crossbills, as well as mammals like squirrels and chipmunks. Host plant for pine white butterfly larvae. Woodpeckers eat ants on hemlock snags, and deer and elk browse the foliage. Provides hiding and thermal cover for many species, including northern flying squirrels. Wood is used by some mammals for nest building; woodpeckers nest in cavities that they make in mature or dead trees, while owls use natural cavities. Seedlings are eaten by rabbits and hares.

**Substitute for:** English holly (*Ilex aquifolium*).

**How to propagate:** From seed, collected in fall before cones open, and kept dry until seed is released, then sown outdoors out of full sunlight.

**Related species:** Mountain hemlock (*Tsuga mertensiana*) is a gem that also likes some shade, but grows much more slowly, and in gardens typically grows to about half the size of western hemlock. Wonderful grown in drifts, 10–15 feet apart, and it may also be cultivated in large containers.

*Vaccinium ovatum*
## Evergreen huckleberry

PLANT TYPE: Evergreen shrub

SIZE: 3–12 feet x 3–10 feet

LIGHT REQUIREMENTS: Partial shade to shade

WATER REQUIREMENTS: Low to medium

HARDINESS ZONES: 7a to 9b

This evergreen shrub has everything going for it: great looks year round, wildlife appeal, and delicious berries. Reddish stems have small, lustrous, leathery leaves that begin bronzy-red and turn dark green with age. Pink flowers bloom profusely from spring to summer and are followed by choice, small berries. Grow this very versatile, slow-growing shrub in a woodland garden, as part of a hedgerow, near a foundation, as a screen, or in a large container.

**How big:** 3–12 feet tall × 3–10 feet wide; smaller in sun, bigger in shade.

**Bloom traits:** Clusters of small, pink, urn-shaped flowers bloom from midspring to midsummer. Fruit is a deliciously sweet purple to black berry that ripens in late summer to fall.

**Sun and soil:** Partial shade to mostly shade. Fruits best with some sun. Moist, slightly acidic soil rich in organic matter; tolerates drought in shade or partial shade once established.

**Where it grows:** Coastal bluffs, conifer forests, edgings and openings, at low elevations.

**How to space it:** 6–10 feet apart.

**Help it thrive:** Does best with some summer water, especially in hot areas.

**Associates:** Sitka spruce, western hemlock, western redcedar, Douglas-fir, madrone, vine maple,

hazelnut, Pacific rhododendron, thimbleberry, salal, sword fern, deer fern, oxalis, and others.

**Benefits to wildlife:** Flowers provide forage for bees, butterflies, and hummingbirds. Berries are eaten by numerous bird species, including thrushes, towhees, flickers, chickadees, robins, waxwings, and band-tailed pigeons, and mammals such as foxes, chipmunks, and bears. Elk and deer may browse twigs and leaves. Provides year-round cover for birds and small mammals.

**Substitute for:** Spurge laurel (*Daphne laureola*), boxwood (*Buxus sempervirens*), Japanese holly (*Ilex crenata*).

**How to propagate:** From seed removed from berries in late summer or fall and sown outdoors, ground layering in spring, or by stem cuttings in spring; may self-sow. Established plants do not respond well to transplantation.

**Related species:** Though many other huckleberry species exist in the region, *V. ovatum* is the only evergreen one.

*Viburnum ellipticum*
## Oval-leaved viburnum or western viburnum

| | |
|---|---|
| PLANT TYPE: Deciduous shrub | |
| SIZE: 6–10 feet x 4–8 feet | |
| LIGHT REQUIREMENTS: Sun to partial shade | |
| WATER REQUIREMENTS: Low to medium | |
| HARDINESS ZONES: 5b to 9b | |

Although not common in cultivation, this upright, deciduous shrub has exceptional seasonal interest and wildlife appeal. Deep-green serrated leaves turn red in fall. White flat-topped flower clusters are replaced by red edible fruits that turn a glossy black in fall. Perfect in woodland garden edges and openings, cottage gardens, or as part of a hedgerow.

**How big:** 6–10 feet tall x 4–8 feet wide.

**Bloom traits:** Two-inch wide flower clusters known as cymes bloom at stem tips from late spring to early summer. Red fruits called drupes are about ½-inch-long and are edible.

**Sun and soil:** Sun to partial shade. Moist to dry, well-drained soil.

**Where it grows:** Open woodlands and moist to dry slopes, at low to middle elevations.

**How to space it:** 6–8 feet apart.

**Help it thrive:** Summer water until established (2–5 years). Drought tolerant afterward, but some summer water may be beneficial during extreme heat.

**Associates:** Garry oak, Douglas-fir, oceanspray, serviceberry, Indian plum, Oregon grape, baldhip rose, broad-leaved penstemon, fringecup, woodland strawberry, and others.

**Benefits to wildlife:** Flowers are visited by bees, butterflies such as the spring azure, and other insects. Fruit is eaten by bluebirds, thrushes, woodpeckers, finches, and waxwings. Provides cover for birds and other small wildlife species.

**Substitute for:** European cranberry bush (*Viburnum opulus* var. *opulus*), Russian olive (*Elaeagnus angustifolia*).

**How to propagate:** From seed collected and cleaned in fall and planted as soon as possible, or hardwood cuttings or rhizome division in late fall, or ground layering in fall.

**Related species:** Highbush cranberry (*Viburnum edule*) grows to a similar size but may need more summer water. It has smaller flat-topped flower clusters followed by conspicuous, edible, orangish-red fruits, and maplelike leaves that offer outstanding red fall color. **American cranberry bush** (*V. opulus* var. *americanum*) grows 8–12 feet tall and wide and has showy, 6-inch-wide white flower clusters, red fruits, and fall leaf color.

BOTTOM PHOTO Related species *Viola sempervirens*

## *Viola adunca*
# Early blue violet or hooked spur violet

| | |
|---|---|
| PLANT TYPE: | Deciduous perennial |
| SIZE: | 3–4 inches |
| LIGHT REQUIREMENTS: | Partial shade |
| WATER REQUIREMENTS: | Medium |
| HARDINESS ZONES: | 3b to 9b |

Demure yet lushly alluring, this little violet offers deep-green, heart-shaped leaves and deep-violet flowers that bloom for several months. Grow native violets along paths, where they may spread to form a lush carpet, and at the front of perennial borders or meadow gardens. Or even in pots—a garden is not complete without these important butterfly host plants. Tolerates salt spray. Flowers and leaves are edible.

**How big:** 3–4 inches tall; spreads slowly by small rhizomes.

**Bloom traits:** ½-inch-wide, deep-violet to blue flowers have 5 sepals and 5 petals, the lower of which often protrude outward; the upper 2 petals may have hooked spurs at their tips. Flowers bloom from midspring to midsummer (and sometimes fall) and are followed by small capsules with tiny brown seeds.

**Sun and soil:** Partial shade. Moist soil amended with organic matter. Tolerates sandy soil.

**Where it grows:** Open, moist woodlands, meadows, coastal headlands, and disturbed sites at low to middle elevations.

**How to space it:** 1–2 feet apart.

**Help it thrive:** Prefers summer water, but is somewhat drought tolerant.

**Associates:** Garry oak, bigleaf maple, black hawthorn, cascara, bitter cherry, serviceberry, snowberry, tall Oregon grape, Scouler's bellflower, western clematis, and others.

**Benefits to wildlife:** Primary larval host plant for the Oregon silverspot butterfly (a federally listed threatened species); also provides for hydaspe fritillary, callippe fritillary, zerene fritillary, western meadow fritillary, great spangled fritillary, and Mormon fritillary butterfly larvae. Nectar is used by the mardon skipper butterfly. Endangered in Washington and a candidate for federal endangered status.

**Substitute for:** English violet (*Viola odorata*), Labrador violet (*Viola labradorica*).

**How to propagate:** From seed collected in summer and sown outdoors in fall or early winter, or by division of rhizomes in summer.

**Related species:** Evergreen violet (*Viola sempervirens*) grows to 3 inches tall and has soft yellow flowers. **Yellow wood violet** or **stream violet** (*V. glabella*) has bright-yellow flowers and grows up to 12 inches tall. Both need at least partial shade and moist conditions.

*Xerophyllum tenax*

## Beargrass

| | |
|---|---|
| PLANT TYPE: | Evergreen perennial |
| SIZE: | 1–5 feet x 1–2 feet |
| LIGHT REQUIREMENTS: | Partial shade to sun |
| WATER REQUIREMENTS: | Low to medium |
| HARDINESS ZONES: | 3b to 9a |

Related to lilies, this slow-growing, evergreen perennial is a stunning plant when flowering and even when not. Journals of the Lewis and Clark expedition describe it as "luxouriant," in reference to its dense clumps of silvery green, lustrous—yet rough and tough—grasslike, gracefully arching leaves. Magnificent flower stalks can reach 5 feet tall but don't bloom every year. Grow it in somewhat open, moist, and cool woodland, meadow, or rock gardens. Useful for stabilizing soil. Unregulated and unsustainable commercial harvest of leaves for the floral industry, most of which is exported, poses a serious threat in parts of its range.

**How big:** 1–5 feet tall × 1–2 feet wide; will eventually form clumps.

**Bloom traits:** Sturdy green stalks topped with spectacular clusters of hundreds of small, scented flowers rise every few years from offshoots. Fruit is a small 3-lobed capsule that contains several seeds.

**Sun and soil:** Partial shade to mostly sun. Moist, well-drained soil; some supplemental summer water is beneficial.

**Where it grows:** Cool, moist meadows, roadsides, and forest openings, at low to high elevations.

**How to space it:** 1–2 feet apart.

**Help it thrive:** Moderate summer water.

**Associates:** Pacific silver fir, grand fir, mountain hemlock, western hemlock, Douglas-fir, western redcedar, mountain ash, huckleberries, fawn lilies, and others.

**Benefits to wildlife:** Bees, beetles, flies, and other insects consume its pollen and nectar. Migratory birds eat its seeds before fall flights. Flower stalks are a delicacy for elk, deer, and other mammals, while other species—from bears to mice—eat the fleshy leaf bases and use the leaves as nest material. Birds may nest in and under leaf clumps, as do small rodents like pocket gophers, which attract raptors.

**Substitute for:** Exotic ornamental grasses.

**How to propagate:** From seed collected after ripening in late summer or fall and planted outdoors in fall, or from young offsets.

**Related species:** None occur naturally in the Pacific Northwest.

# *plants for full shade or mostly shade*

**THE PLANTS IN THIS SECTION ARE SHADE LOVERS.** Some may thrive in the deep shade provided by evergreen trees and shrubs, or the north side of buildings. Others might need a touch of sun, thriving with perhaps just an hour or two of morning rays or the dappled light provided by tall, openly branched deciduous trees or shrubs. Keep in mind that many of these plants may be able to tolerate more sun in cool areas or with extra moisture, but they are placed in this section due to their primary need to be out of bright, hot sunlight. "Partial shade to full shade" means that the plant will do best with a little direct—especially morning—sun but will tolerate all-day shade. "Full shade to mostly shade" is reserved for those that do best with very little or no direct sunlight.

Star-flowered false solomon's seal (*Smilacina stellata*)

*Achlys triphylla*
# Vanilla leaf

| | |
|---|---|
| PLANT TYPE: Deciduous perennial | |
| SIZE: 1 foot tall | |
| LIGHT REQUIREMENTS: Shade to mostly shade | |
| WATER REQUIREMENTS: Medium | |
| HARDINESS ZONES: 6a to 9b | |

A graceful, gently spreading perennial that forms a lush, green, delicate carpet under forest trees. Large, stalked leaves divided into 3 horizontal leaflets arise at close intervals from creeping rhizomes. Dried leaves offer a vanilla-like fragrance. Small but showy spikes of tiny white flowers emerge above the leaves. Grow this lovely ground cover under shade trees and shrubs, or near shaded ponds or streams. With its demure demeanor, vanilla leaf may not compete well with more vigorous ground covers.

**How big:** 1 foot tall; spreads slowly.
**Bloom traits:** Blooms in late spring to early summer with little bottlebrush panicles composed of many small white flowers without petals. Fruits are small achenes that contain the seeds.
**Sun and soil:** Full shade to mostly shade. Moist soil rich in organic matter.
**Where it grows:** Shady, moist forests and along streams, at low to middle elevations.
**How to space it:** 2–3 feet apart.
**Help it thrive:** Moderate summer water.
**Associates:** Douglas-fir, western hemlock, western azalea, thimbleberry, western white anemone, western maidenhair fern, deer fern, false solomon's seal, bunchberry, oxalis, and others.
**Benefits to wildlife:** Flowers provide for bees and

other beneficial insects. Provides cover for small creatures.
**Substitute for:** Bishop's weed (*Aegopodium podagraria*), arum (*Arum italicum*).
**How to propagate:** From seed collected when ripe and planted outdoors soon afterward, or division of rhizomes in spring.
**Related species:** California vanilla leaf (*Achlys californica*) grows naturally near the coast and has more deeply lobed leaves.

*Adiantum aleuticum*
## Western maidenhair fern

| | |
|---|---|
| PLANT TYPE: Deciduous fern | |
| SIZE: 1–3 feet x 1–2 feet | |
| LIGHT REQUIREMENTS: Shade to mostly shade | |
| WATER REQUIREMENTS: Medium | |
| HARDINESS ZONES: 3b to 9b | |

An airy, perennial fern with delicate-looking structure and fine texture. Thin black stems support fan-shaped fronds with small, compound, bright-green leaflets. An unusual horizontally layered branching pattern creates a soft contrast to other woodland natives. Grow it in a moist understory, near a shaded pond, or in containers with ample moisture.

**How big:** 1–3 feet tall x 1–2 feet wide.
**Sun and soil:** Full shade to mostly shade. Moist soil rich in organic matter.
**Where it grows:** Shady, moist woods and ravines, along stream banks, and in rock crevices near waterfalls, at low to middle elevations.
**How to space it:** 2 feet apart.
**Help it thrive:** Moderate summer water, more in hot areas.
**Associates:** Douglas-fir, western hemlock, vine maple, thimbleberry, deer fern, sword fern, Scouler's corydalis, piggyback plant, goatsbeard, oxalis, and others.
**Benefits to wildlife:** Provides food and cover for birds and small mammals.
**Substitute for:** Yellow archangel (*Lamiastrum galeobdolon*).
**How to propagate:** Spores, or clump division in early spring.

**Related species:** Southern maidenhair fern (*Adiantum capillus-veneris*) is found only near hot mineral springs in British Columbia and south of our region. **Northern maidenhair fern** (*A. pedatum*), of which *A. aleuticum* was once considered a subspecies, has subtle differences and occurs mostly in the eastern United States.

*Anemone deltoidea*
# Western white anemone

| | |
|---|---|
| PLANT TYPE: Deciduous perennial | |
| SIZE: 1 foot x 1 foot | |
| LIGHT REQUIREMENTS: Shade to mostly shade | |
| WATER REQUIREMENTS: Medium | |
| HARDINESS ZONES: 6b to 9b | |

A charming little deciduous perennial with 1 conspicuous pure-white flower and 3 oval, toothed leaflets. Also known as Columbia windflower, this delicate woodlander is a spring bloomer that spreads politely by rhizomes to mingle with other understory plants. Grow it in the understory of woodland gardens with other ground covers, or in pots.

**How big:** 1 foot tall × 1 foot wide.
**Bloom traits:** Flowers have 5 white, petallike sepals and bloom from midspring to early summer. Fruits are clusters of spherical achenes.
**Sun and soil:** Full shade to mostly shade. Moist soil rich in organic matter.
**Where it grows:** Moist to dry, open to deep woodlands, at low to middle elevations.
**How to space it:** 1–2 feet apart.
**Help it thrive:** Low to moderate summer water.
**Associates:** Serviceberry, trillium, stream violet, star-flowered false solomon's seal, wild ginger, foamflower, bunchberry, and others.
**Benefits to wildlife:** Flowers provide nectar and pollen for native bees and other insects. Foliage creates cover for other species.
**Substitute for:** Nonnative anemones, arum (*Arum italicum*).
**How to propagate:** From seed collected in late summer or fall and sown outdoors soon after harvest, or by division in late fall or early spring.
**Related species:** Blue windflower (*Anemone oregana*) has larger bluish-purple, pink, or rarely, white flowers and needs similar conditions.

*Aruncus dioicus*
# Goatsbeard

| | |
|---|---|
| PLANT TYPE: Deciduous perennial |
| SIZE: 3–6 feet x 3–5 feet |
| LIGHT REQUIREMENTS: Partial shade to shade |
| WATER REQUIREMENTS: Medium |
| HARDINESS ZONES: 4a to 9b |

This elegant perennial is a graceful addition to woodland gardens and even sunnier spots. Eye-catching, misty plumes of tiny, delicate white flowers light up upright branches that support compound, ferny green leaves. Eventually forming a large clump, this is a plant with an outstanding presence for the back of a shady border, under tall trees, or as a beautiful screen or hedge.

**How big:** 3–6 feet tall × 3–5 feet wide.

**Bloom traits:** Large, feathery plumes of tiny, creamy white flowers bloom in early to midsummer. Seeds are produced in follicles on female plants, which tend to be slightly less showy.

**Sun and soil:** Partial shade to full shade, or even sunny spots in the cooler, northern reaches of the region. Not fussy, but thrives in slightly acidic soil rich in organic matter that is kept moist.

**Where it grows:** Moist forests, slopes, and along streams and shady roadsides, at low to middle elevations.

**How to space it:** 4–5 feet apart.

**Help it thrive:** Somewhat drought tolerant in cool, shady areas, but supplemental summer water is beneficial, especially in sunny or hot areas.

**Associates:** Douglas-fir, western hemlock, vine maple, Scouler's corydalis, deer fern, northern maidenhair fern, inside-out flower, stream violet, and others.

**Benefits to wildlife:** Attracts many insect species, including bees and mourning cloak butterflies, and hummingbirds. Seeds provide forage for small birds in winter. Provides cover for birds and other small animals. Leaves are browsed by deer and elk.

**Substitute for:** Knotweed (*Polygonum* spp).

**How to propagate:** From seed collected from follicles and planted outdoors in fall or spring. Seedlings will result naturally if both male and female plants are present.

**Related species:** No closely related species occur in the Northwest.

*Asarum caudatum*
# Wild ginger

| | |
|---|---|
| PLANT TYPE: | Semi-evergreen perennial |
| SIZE: | 3–6 inches |
| LIGHT REQUIREMENTS: | Shade to mostly shade |
| WATER REQUIREMENTS: | Medium |
| HARDINESS ZONES: | 4b to 9b |

A lush, evergreen perennial ground cover plant with lustrous, deep-green leaves and a wonderful ginger scent. Extraordinary 3-lobed burgundy flowers bloom secretively for several months beneath the foliage. Spreads fairly quickly by rhizomes to carpet the soil with its charming heart-shaped leaves. Makes a lovely edging along pathways in shady situations. Wild ginger is not closely related to tropical culinary ginger (*Zingiber officinale*).

**How big:** 3–6 inches tall; spreads slowly.

**Bloom traits:** Burgundy and brownish flowers have long, tapered lobes with twisted "tails," and bloom from midspring to midsummer. Fruit is a large capsule containing several angled seeds.

**Sun and soil:** Full shade to mostly shade. Consistently moist, slightly acidic soil, rich in organic matter.

**Where it grows:** Moist, shaded forest floors, at low to middle elevations.

**How to space it:** 1–2 feet apart.

**Help it thrive:** Moderate summer water, especially in warm areas.

**Associates:** Western hemlock, Douglas-fir, vine maple, hazelnut, trillium, western white anemone, ferns, bunchberry, and others.

**Benefits to wildlife:** Provides a protective cover for overwintering insects and other small creatures. Flowers probably self-pollinate. Seeds are

dispersed by ants. Garden slugs may be attracted to wild ginger, but any slug poison used will also kill native slugs that do not harm the plant.

**Substitute for:** Bishop's weed (*Aegopodium podagraria*).

**How to propagate:** From seed collected from ripe capsules in late summer, or by rooting sections of rhizome in spring or fall when plant is dormant.

**Related species:** Marbled wild ginger (*Asarum marmoratum*), with mottled leaves, is native to southwestern Oregon and northwestern California.

*Blechnum spicant*

# Deer fern

| | |
|---|---|
| PLANT TYPE: | Evergreen fern |
| SIZE: | 2 feet x 2 feet |
| LIGHT REQUIREMENTS: | Shade to mostly shade |
| WATER REQUIREMENTS: | Medium to high |
| HARDINESS ZONES: | 5b to 9b |

A strongly textured, mostly evergreen, medium-sized fern that adds lushness to the woodland garden, as well as color—new fronds are often a coppery red in springtime. Somewhat unusual in that it produces 2 types of fronds: evergreen, sterile fronds that arch horizontally, and spore-bearing (fertile), upright fronds with more narrow leaflets. Grow this beauty next to rotting logs, stumps, and where it can be admired—at the front of shaded beds, tucked into moist rock walls, or along paths.

**How big:** 2 feet tall × 2 feet wide.
**Sun and soil:** Full shade to mostly shade. Soil needs to be rich in organic matter and kept moist.
**Where it grows:** Moist conifer forests, at low to middle elevations.
**How to space it:** 2 feet apart.
**Help it thrive:** Moderate summer water. Transplanting appears to cause little stress to the plant.
**Associates:** Sitka spruce, western hemlock, western redcedar, red alder, noble fir, red huckleberry, thimbleberry, salal, bunchberry, foamflower, sword fern, oak fern, wild ginger, trillium, stream violet, and others.
**Benefits to wildlife:** Provides year-round cover for small animals and soil-dwelling creatures.

Birds may use leaves as nesting material. Rabbits, deer, and elk browse the leaves, especially during winter.
**Substitute for:** English ivy (*Hedera helix*), bittersweet nightshade (*Solanum dulcamara*).
**How to propagate:** Spores, cultivated on moist soil.
**Related species:** Most other *Blechnum* species are native to tropical regions of the southern hemisphere.

*Cimicifuga elata* syn. *Actaea elata*
# Tall bugbane

| | |
|---|---|
| PLANT TYPE: | Deciduous perennial |
| SIZE: | 3–6 feet x 3 feet |
| LIGHT REQUIREMENTS: | Partial shade to shade |
| WATER REQUIREMENTS: | Medium |
| HARDINESS ZONES: | 5b to 8b |

A rare, deciduous, flowering perennial with a woody rhizome. Blooms in a narrow, bottle-brush-like panicle of flowers. Leaves are dark green, compound, and coarsely lobed. Fruit is a small, poisonous follicle. Grow this woodland plant under large trees or next to tall shrubs in rich, moist soil. An uncommon species with unstable wild populations due to disturbances such as logging, fire suppression, recreation, invasive species, wild collection, and pollinator decline, it is red-listed in British Columbia and a species of concern in Washington and Oregon.

**How big:** 3–6 feet tall x 3 feet wide.
**Bloom traits:** Inflorescences composed of many white to pale-pink flowers are several inches long and bloom from early to late summer. Fruit is a flattened follicle containing many seeds.
**Sun and soil:** Partial shade to full shade; flowers better with dappled sunlight during spring. Best in slightly acidic, well-drained, moist soil rich in organic matter.
**Where it grows:** Moist, shady, mature woodlands, north-facing slopes, and old-growth forest at mainly low elevations.
**How to space it:** 3–4 feet apart.
**Help it thrive:** Moderate summer water.
**Associates:** Douglas-fir, bigleaf and vine maple, western redcedar, red alder, hazelnut, western sword fern, inside-out flower, oxalis, and others.

**Benefits to wildlife:** Flowers provide for bumblebees and other bees, syrphid flies, and beetles. Provides cover for many small forest animals.
**Substitute for:** Black bugbane (*Cimicifuga racemosa*).
**How to propagate:** From seed collected in late summer or fall. May self-sow but is not assertive.
**Related species:** Red baneberry (*Actaea rubra*) needs the same conditions and grows to 3 feet tall. Flower clusters are round and are followed by glossy red (or sometimes white) berries.

*Cornus unalaschkensis*
## Bunchberry

| | |
|---|---|
| PLANT TYPE: Deciduous ground cover | |
| SIZE: 4–8 inches | |
| LIGHT REQUIREMENTS: Shade to partial shade | |
| WATER REQUIREMENTS: Medium to high | |
| HARDINESS ZONES: 3b to 9b | |

One of the most beautiful plants to grace the forest floor, this little dogwood is a perfect addition to a moist woodland garden. Bright-green, conspicuously veined leaves are some-times evergreen and always lovely, and may turn bright shades in autumn when subjected to cold temperatures. Pincushionlike early summer flowers brighten shady areas and later offer fruits for wildlife. Grow this treasure that spreads politely to form a luxurious green carpet, with other moisture-loving plants where it can be appreciated close-up—along pathways, next to sitting areas, or near ponds or water features.

**How big:** 4–8 inches tall; spreads slowly by rhizomes in moist conditions.

**Bloom traits:** Tiny greenish-white flowers with a purple tinge grow in clusters and are surrounded by 4 much larger, creamy white, petallike bracts that fall as the fruits develop; they bloom in early to midsummer and sometimes autumn. Bunches of glossy, berrylike red fruits called drupes, each with a single seed, ripen in late summer or autumn.

**Sun and soil:** Full shade to partial shade in cool areas, with ample moisture throughout the year. Requires acidic soil (pH 4–5) rich in organic matter. Not very easy to establish; try growing it on or near moist stumps or dead wood, as found in nature.

**Where it grows:** Moist forests, bogs or meadows, at low to high elevations.

**How to space it:** 2 feet apart.

**Help it thrive:** Supplemental summer water will be necessary, unless grown in a naturally moist area.

**Associates:** Douglas-fir, western hemlock, vine maple, red huckleberry, maidenhair fern, deer fern, woodland strawberry, false solomon's seal, fairy bells, oxalis, and others.

**Benefits to wildlife:** Flowers attract bees and other insects. Fruit is eaten by birds such as thrushes, sparrows, vireos, and grouse.

**Substitute for:** English ivy (*Hedera helix*).

**How to propagate:** From seed collected in fall, cleaned of pulp, and planted outdoors.

**Related species:** *Cornus canadensis* is one of the parents of *C. unalaschkensis* but has a smaller range in the Northwest. Its extremely slight differences make cultivation the same.

*Corydalis scouleri*
## Scouler's corydalis

PLANT TYPE: Deciduous perennial

SIZE: 3–4 feet x 3–4 feet

LIGHT REQUIREMENTS: Shade to mostly shade

WATER REQUIREMENTS: Medium

HARDINESS ZONES: 7b to 9b

The darling of the moist woodland set, this deciduous perennial is delicate in texture and lush in form. Lacy foliage of the freshest green adorns hollow stems. Tall inflorescences of enchanting pink flowers bloom in spring and early summer. An exquisite choice for the understory in cool, moist, shaded woodland gardens. If conditions are adequate, will spread slowly by rhizomes to form large colonies. This plant is Blue-listed (at risk) in British Columbia.

**How big:** 3–4 feet tall × 3–4 feet wide.

**Bloom traits:** Spurred, deep-pink to lavender pink flowers bloom in late spring to early summer. Fruit is a pear-shaped capsule that encloses small black seeds.

**Sun and soil:** Full shade to mostly shade. Moist soil rich in organic matter.

**Where it grows:** Cool, moist woodlands near streams and shaded roadside ditches, at low to middle elevations.

**How to space it:** 3–4 feet apart.

**Help it thrive:** Moderate summer water.

**Associates:** Sitka spruce, western hemlock, western redcedar, bigleaf maple, red alder, red elderberry, salmonberry, western maidenhair fern, deer fern, and others.

**Benefits to wildlife:** Flowers attract bees and butterflies. Seeds are eaten by birds such as song sparrows and finches.

**Substitute for:** Bittersweet nightshade (*Solanum dulcamara*), nonnative, garden-variety corydalis.

**How to propagate:** From seed collected when capsules are dry (but before they explode!), and planted outdoors.

**Related species:** Golden corydalis (*Corydalis aurea*) is a biennial that needs similar conditions.

*Delphinium trolliifolium*
## Columbian larkspur

PLANT TYPE: Deciduous perennial

SIZE: 2–5 feet x 1–2 feet

LIGHT REQUIREMENTS: Shade to partial shade

WATER REQUIREMENTS: Medium

HARDINESS ZONES: 6b to 9b

An old-fashioned charmer, this deciduous perennial is upright and has large, deeply dissected leaves. Showy, deep-blue flowers bloom along tall spikes, creating a colorful show in late spring. Perfect in moist, shady, cottage gardens, perennial borders, or woodland gardens, or near ponds or streams. All larkspurs are toxic if ingested.

**How big:** 2–5 feet tall x 1–2 feet wide.

**Bloom traits:** Deep-blue and white, spurred flowers bloom in late spring to early summer. Fruit is a follicle that encloses winged, dark brown seeds.

**Sun and soil:** Full shade to partial shade. Moist soil rich in organic matter.

**Where it grows:** Moist forests and along streams, at low to middle elevations in southern Washington and Oregon.

**How to space it:** 1–2 feet apart.

**Help it thrive:** Moderate summer water.

**Associates:** Indian plum, snowberry, red baneberry, fairy bells, foamflower, fringecup, woodland strawberry, and others.

**Benefits to wildlife:** Flowers are very attractive to native bees, hummingbirds, and butterflies. Seed-eating birds may consume the seeds.

**Substitute for:** Bittersweet nightshade (*Solanum dulcamara*).

**How to propagate:** From seed collected when follicles dry and planted outdoors in fall; protect from slugs. Stems are fragile, so use extreme care when transplanting. May hybridize with other delphiniums.

**Related species:** Sierra larkspur (*Delphinium glaucum*) grows at middle to high elevations. Nuttall's larkspur (*D. nuttallii*) is on the watch list in Washington.

*Dicentra formosa*

## Western bleeding heart or Pacific bleeding heart

| | |
|---|---|
| PLANT TYPE: Deciduous perennial | |
| SIZE: 8–16 inches | |
| LIGHT REQUIREMENTS: Partial shade to shade | |
| WATER REQUIREMENTS: Medium | |
| HARDINESS ZONES: 7a to 9b | |

With delicate, finely divided foliage and puffy little flowers, this succulent perennial ground cover will steal your heart. Be careful in small gardens, though: With rich soil and enough moisture, this assertive little charmer tends to take all the space it can get and may shade out perennials that don't appear until later in spring. Makes an enchanting carpet under trees, shrubs, and taller perennials.

**How big:** 8–16 inches tall; spreads by rhizomes.

**Bloom traits:** Heart-shaped pink flowers with little spurs bloom on leafless stems from early spring to midsummer. Fruits are slender capsules that contain a few black seeds.

**Sun and soil:** Partial shade to full shade. Moist, light soil rich in organic matter.

**Where it grows:** Moist forests, ravines, and along streams, at low to middle elevations.

**How to space it:** 2 feet apart.

**Help it thrive:** Moderate summer water.

**Associates:** Western hemlock, Douglas-fir, bigleaf and vine maples, Indian plum, red-twig dogwood, salmonberry, false solomon's seal, fairy bells, Scouler's corydalis, sword fern, western maidenhair fern, and others.

**Benefits to wildlife:** Flowers attract insects like bees and bee flies. Host plant for clodius parnassian butterfly larvae. Ants are lured to seeds with

a fatty substance to assist seed dispersal.

**Substitute for:** Herb Robert (*Geranium robertianum*), yellow archangel (*Lamiastrum galeobdolon*).

**How to propagate:** From seed collected when capsules are ripe and planted outdoors in fall, or by division of rhizomes in early spring.

**Related species:** Dutchman's breeches (*Dicentra cucullaria*) has spring-blooming white to pale-pink flowers with yellow tips; it occurs in northwest Oregon and southern Washington near the Columbia River.

*Gymnocarpium dryopteris*
# Oak fern

PLANT TYPE: Deciduous fern

SIZE: 1 foot tall

LIGHT REQUIREMENTS: Shade

WATER REQUIREMENTS: Low to medium

HARDINESS ZONES: 3b to 9b

Delicate in appearance, this low, deciduous fern forms a lush carpet in mostly shady conditions. Soft green fronds unfurl in the cool of early spring. Grow this lovely ground cover under shade trees, at the edge of woodland gardens, or near streams and other moist places.

**How big:** 1 foot tall; spreads slowly.

**Sun and soil:** Mostly shade to full shade. Moist to somewhat dry soil, acidic (pH 5–6.5) and rich in organic matter.

**Where it grows:** Cool, shady forests and along streams at low to middle elevations.

**How to space it:** 2–4 feet apart.

**Help it thrive:** Moderate summer water until established. Will do best with occasional water afterward, but can take some drought once established.

**Associates:** Alder, vine maple, red-twig dogwood, twinberry, devil's club, highbush cranberry, thimbleberry, star-flowered false solomon's seal, bunchberry, stream violet, and others.

**Benefits to wildlife:** Provides food and cover for small birds, mammals, and other wild animals.

**Substitute for:** Yellow archangel (*Lamiastrum galeobdolon*).

**How to propagate:** Spores scattered on moist soil.

**Related species:** Western oak fern (*Gymnocarpium disjunctum*) has larger leaves and needs similar conditions.

*Mahonia nervosa*

## Cascade Oregon grape or longleaf mahonia

| | |
|---|---|
| PLANT TYPE: Evergreen low shrub | |
| SIZE: 2 feet x 2 feet | |
| LIGHT REQUIREMENTS: Shade to mostly shade | |
| WATER REQUIREMENTS: Low | |
| HARDINESS ZONES: 5a to 9b | |

A low, handsome evergreen shrub with thick leaves on foot-long branches that grow in a rosette. Flower stalks rise above foliage and put on a showy display from early to late spring, followed by berries that ripen to a deep, dusty blue. Older foliage may turn burgundy during the cold months. A popular horticulture plant for nearly 200 years, it makes a wonderful addition to dry woodland settings, especially when grown en masse or among ferns in shaded borders. Though slow to establish, it will eventually form a colorful, dense ground cover over many years.

**How big:** 2 feet tall × 2 feet wide; spreads very slowly by rhizomes.

**Bloom traits:** 8-inch-long panicles of fragrant, yellow flowers begin blooming in early spring. Fruits are deep blue, tart, edible berries that ripen in late summer to fall.

**Sun and soil:** Full shade to mostly shade. Moist to dry soil rich in organic matter.

**Where it grows:** Moist to dry forests, at low to middle elevations.

**How to space it:** 2–3 feet apart.

**Help it thrive:** Supplemental summer water may be beneficial in hot areas. Spreading is easily controlled by root pruning if necessary.

**Associates:** Douglas-fir, western hemlock, redwood, Garry oak, madrone, oceanspray, Pacific

rhododendron, Indian plum, vine maple, salal, Oregon boxwood, sword fern, vanilla leaf, oxalis, and many more.

**Benefits to wildlife:** Flowers attract Anna's hummingbirds, bees, and painted lady butterflies. Host species for brown elfin butterfly larvae. Berries are eaten by birds such as towhees, robins, sparrows, and waxwings. Browse species for deer and elk. Provides cover for small birds, mammals, and other wildlife.

**Substitute for:** English ivy (*Hedera helix*), lesser celandine (*Ranunculus ficaria*).

**How to propagate:** From seed collected from fruit in late summer, cleaned of pulp, and planted outdoors.

**Related species:** Low Oregon grape (*Mahonia repens*) is another evergreen spreader that grows to about 3 feet tall. It is perfect for dry, shady conditions and can take some sun.

*Oxalis oregana*
## Wood sorrel or Oregon oxalis

| | |
|---|---|
| PLANT TYPE: Deciduous perennial |
| SIZE: 3–5 inches |
| LIGHT REQUIREMENTS: Shade to mostly shade |
| WATER REQUIREMENTS: Low to medium |
| HARDINESS ZONES: 7a to 9b |

This low understory plant forms lush carpets in moist to dry woodlands with cloverlike leaves. White to pink flowers peek out from soft, dark foliage that may fold inward at night and in sunlight. Plant this charming woodlander and pollinator plant if you want fairly quick ground cover that will keep weeds at bay in shady places where it won't be walked on. May be most suitable in large gardens, or where it can be contained due to its enthusiastic growth. This plant is a species of concern in British Columbia.

**How big:** 3–5 inches tall; spreads readily by rhizomes.

**Bloom traits:** 5-petaled pink or white flowers bloom on short stems from midspring to midsummer. Fruit is a capsule.

**Sun and soil:** Full shade to mostly shade. Moist, acidic (pH 5–6.5) soil rich in organic matter preferred; can tolerate drought in full shade.

**Where it grows:** Moist shady forests and drier open or shrubby areas, at low to middle elevations.

**How to space it:** 1–3 feet apart for quick coverage.

**Help it thrive:** Moderate summer water preferred. Spread may be controlled by less than optimal conditions.

**Associates:** Douglas-fir, redwood, huckleberries, goatsbeard, false solomon's seal, Cascade Oregon grape, sword fern, western maidenhair fern, Scouler's corydalis, fairy lantern, trillium, and others.

**Benefits to wildlife:** Flowers attract many native bees, syrphid flies, and butterflies. Seeds may be eaten by seed-eating birds like sparrows and juncos, as well as small rodents. Rabbits may browse on foliage. Plants provide shelter for insects and other small creatures.

**Substitute for:** Yellow archangel (*Lamiastrum galeobdolon*), periwinkle (*Vinca minor*).

**How to propagate:** From seed collected in summer or fall, or by division of rhizomes in early spring or fall.

**Related species:** Western yellow oxalis (*Oxalis suksdorfii*) has bright-yellow flowers, occurs in southwestern Washington and south into Oregon at low elevations, and spreads much more slowly. It is listed as a sensitive species in Washington. **Trillium-leaved sorrel** (*O. trilliifolia*) has clusters of white or pale pink flowers.

*Polemonium carneum*
## Royal Jacob's ladder

| | |
|---|---|
| PLANT TYPE: | Deciduous perennial |
| SIZE: | 1–2 feet x 2 feet |
| LIGHT REQUIREMENTS: | Partial shade |
| WATER REQUIREMENTS: | Medium |
| HARDINESS ZONES: | 7a to 9b |

A charming, uncommon, deciduous, woodland perennial with lush, finely divided compound leaves in ladderlike arrangements. Lovely 5-petaled flowers bloom from late spring through mid- or late summer. Grow this plant with other partly shaded perennials in borders, cottage or woodland gardens, moist rock gardens, or near a stream or pond. Listed as a threatened species in Washington. Wild populations are threatened by grazing, logging, and pesticide use.

**How big:** 1–2 feet tall × 2 feet wide.

**Bloom traits:** Pale-peach, yellow, or lavender cup-shaped flowers bloom in loose clusters at the tips of stems in late spring to midsummer. Fruit is a small 3-celled capsule with several seeds.

**Sun and soil:** Mostly shade to partial shade. Thrives in moist, well-drained soil, rich in organic matter.

**Where it grows:** Moist, open forests and woodlands, prairie edges, roadsides, and along streams, at low to middle elevations in Oregon and Washington.

**How to space it:** 2 feet apart.

**Help it thrive:** Moderate summer water. May be somewhat drought tolerant in cool areas.

**Associates:** Serviceberry, western white anemone, false solomon's seal, tall bugbane, fairy bells, woodland strawberry, and others.

**Benefits to wildlife:** Flowers attract bees, butterflies, and bee flies, and birds may eat the seeds.

**Substitute for:** Bachelor's button (*Centaurea cyanus*).

**How to propagate:** From seed collected in late summer and planted outdoors soon afterward; may self-sow.

**Related species:** Showy Jacob's-ladder (*Polemonium pulcherrimum*) grows to about 1 foot tall, with fragrant blue flowers; it tolerates more sun and is hardier (zones 3b to 9b).

*Polypodium glycyrrhiza*
# Licorice fern

PLANT TYPE: Summer deciduous fern

SIZE: 10–16 inches

LIGHT REQUIREMENTS: Shade to partial shade

WATER REQUIREMENTS: Low to medium

HARDINESS ZONES: 7a to 9b

This attractive, versatile fern stays green during the fall and winter months and dies back in spring. Spreading by rhizomes that taste like licorice, it has fronds that usually reach about 1 foot long. Often found growing on the bark of mature maples, it is also appropriate around mossy rocks and logs, where it is quite drought tolerant. Tuck it into shaded rock gardens and next to moist dead wood for a winter splash of greenery.

**How big:** 10–16 inches tall; spreads slowly by rhizomes.

**Sun and soil:** Full shade to partial shade. Moist, rich soil is best, but can tolerate drought in full shade once established.

**Where it grows:** Moist shady forests and drier, rocky, open areas at low to middle elevations.

**How to space it:** 2–3 feet apart.

**Help it thrive:** Keep slightly moist year round, especially in hot areas.

**Associates:** Bigleaf maple, Douglas-fir, Garry oak, madrone, red-twig dogwood, red-flowering currant, salal, Indian plum, false solomon's seal, fairy bells, Cascade Oregon grape, sword fern, vanilla leaf, wild ginger, foamflower, inside-out flower, trillium, and others.

**Benefits to wildlife:** Flowers attract many native bees, syrphid flies, and butterflies. Seeds may be eaten by birds like sparrows and juncos, as well as small rodents. Rabbits may browse on foliage. Plants provide shelter for insects and other small creatures.

**Substitute for:** Herb Robert (*Geranium robertianum*).

**How to propagate:** By spores, or rhizome division in spring or fall of nonwild specimens.

**Related species: Western polypody** (*Polypodium hesperium*) begins its growth in the spring, has shorter fronds, and is perfect for rock gardens and nooks and crannies of stone walls.

*Prosartes smithii*
## Smith's fairy lantern

| | |
|---|---|
| PLANT TYPE: | Deciduous perennial |
| SIZE: | 2–3 feet x 2–3 feet |
| LIGHT REQUIREMENTS: | Partial shade to shade |
| WATER REQUIREMENTS: | Medium |
| HARDINESS ZONES: | 3b to 9b |

This graceful deciduous woodland perennial, related to lilies, has soft green leaves and stems. Dainty, white bell-shaped flowers dangle from stem tips for many weeks, under leaves that protect them from rain. Also known as *Disporum smithii,* this is an excellent choice for moist woodland gardens or shaded perennial beds.

**How big:** 2–3 feet tall x 2–3 feet wide.

**Bloom traits:** Flowers are pendant, soft-white bells with 6 petallike tepals that often bloom in pairs. Fruits are brilliant orange to red oval berries that ripen in late summer.

**Sun and soil:** Partial shade to full shade. Moist soil rich in organic matter.

**Where it grows:** Shady, moist woodlands, at low to middle elevations.

**How to space it:** 3 feet apart.

**Help it thrive:** Although somewhat tolerant of drought once established, it does best with some summer water.

**Associates:** Douglas-fir, western redcedar, Pacific rhododendron, evergreen huckleberry, sword fern, deer fern, vanilla leaf, Columbian larkspur, oxalis, small-flowered alumroot, evergreen violet, and others.

**Benefits to wildlife:** Flowers attract bees and other pollinators. Fruit is eaten by squirrels, chipmunks, and birds like robins and towhees. Plants provide shelter for insects and other small creatures.

**Substitute for:** Bittersweet nightshade (*Solanum dulcamara*).

**How to propagate:** From seed collected from berries in late summer or fall, cleaned of pulp and planted outdoors soon afterward, or by rhizome division in early spring; may self-sow.

**Related species:** Equally enchanting, **Hooker's fairy bells** (*Prosartes hookeri*) has fuzzy leaves and stems, and white bell-shaped flowers that nod at stem tips.

*Rhododendron macrophyllum*

# Pacific rhododendron or western rhododendron

| | |
|---|---|
| PLANT TYPE: | Evergreen shrub |
| SIZE: | 10–20 feet x 10 feet |
| LIGHT REQUIREMENTS: | Partial shade to shade |
| WATER REQUIREMENTS: | Medium |
| HARDINESS ZONES: | 7a to 9b |

A large, evergreen shrub with an upright, open, spreading habit. Leaves are deep green, oblong, and leathery. The state flower of Washington, it offers a spectacular floral display for several months that rivals that of hybridized rhododendrons. Grows well in acidic soils in dappled shade under tall trees. May be toxic if ingested.

**How big:** 10–20 feet tall x 10 feet wide; may form a thicket.

**Bloom traits:** Showy, pale-pink to deep-magenta flower clusters occur at branch tips from late spring to midsummer.

**Sun and soil:** Partial shade to full shade; will produce more blossoms with some sun. Prefers moist, well-drained, moderately to slightly acidic soil (pH 4.5–6.5) high in organic matter, but may tolerate nutrient-poor soils.

**Where it grows:** Moist to dry forest margins, from sea level to middle elevations.

**How to space it:** 10–15 feet apart. Useful for erosion control.

**Help it thrive:** Summer water until established (2–5 years); will do best with some summer water afterward, especially in hot areas. Prune only to remove dead or broken branches; do not shear.

**Associates:** Douglas-fir, hemlock, redwood, salal, red elderberry, evergreen huckleberry, beargrass, sword ferns, inside-out flower, and other woodland plants.

**Benefits to wildlife:** Flowers provide for hummingbirds, bumblebees, and other insects. Seeds are eaten by birds. Plants offer nest sites for birds and cover for many animals.

**Substitute for:** English laurel (*Prunus laurocerasus*), Portugal laurel (*Prunus lusitanica*), English hawthorn (*Crataegus monogyna*).

**How to propagate:** From seed harvested in fall or cuttings in summer or fall.

**Related species:** The stunning **western azalea** (*Rhododendron occidentale*) grows to 10 feet tall and has very fragrant white to pink-and-yellow flowers that bloom from late spring to midsummer; it needs some sun and occurs in southwestern Oregon. **Cascade rhododendron** (*R. albiflorum*) grows to 6 feet tall, with creamy white flowers from early to late summer, at middle to high elevations. Both species may be difficult to establish.

*Smilacina racemosa*

# False solomon's seal

| | |
|---|---|
| PLANT TYPE: Deciduous perennial | |
| SIZE: 1–3 feet x 1–3 feet | |
| LIGHT REQUIREMENTS: Full shade to partial shade | |
| WATER REQUIREMENTS: Medium | |
| HARDINESS ZONES: 6b to 9b | |

The large, showy, fragrant plumelike flower clusters of this deciduous perennial brighten up shady woodlands. Arching 1- to 3-foot stems are graceful and slightly zigzagged. Grow this jewel in shaded woodland settings or under large trees. Also known as *Maianthemum racemosum.*

**How big:** 1–3 feet tall x 1–3 feet wide; spreads slowly by rhizomes.

**Bloom traits:** Large, branched panicles of fragrant, small white flowers bloom in spring to early summer. Fruit is a translucent berry with multiple seeds that turn from green to red in late summer to early fall. Edible, but with a bitter aftertaste.

**Sun and soil:** Full shade to partial shade; plants will be stunted with too much sun. Prefers moderately acidic soil (pH 5–6.5) with abundant organic matter. Does best with summer moisture, but will tolerate slightly dry conditions in cool areas.

**Where it grows:** Moist forests, ravines, and near streams at low to middle elevations.

**How to space it:** 2 feet apart.

**Help it thrive:** Summer water, especially in hot areas.

**Associates:** Western hemlock, Douglas-fir, western redcedar, vine maple, goatsbeard, corydalis, maidenhair fern, sword fern, piggyback plant, bleeding heart, oxalis, trillium, vanilla leaf, and others.

**Benefits to wildlife:** Flowers are pollinated by a variety of small bees, flies, and beetles that collect or feed on pollen. Berries may be eaten by woodland birds and small rodents. Foliage is browsed occasionally by deer.

**Substitute for:** Bittersweet nightshade (*Solanum dulcamara*), arum (*arum italicum*).

**How to propagate:** From seed collected in late summer or fall and planted in shady conditions outdoors before they dry out; may take 2 years to germinate. Or by rhizome division in fall or early spring.

**Related species:** Star-flowered false solomon's seal (*Smilacina stellata*) is a more diminutive, slowly spreading ground cover to 1 foot tall, with clusters of small, white starlike flowers in spring and early summer.

RIGHT Related species *Smilacina stellata*

*Tiarella trifoliata* var. *trifoliata*

## Threeleaf foamflower

| | |
|---|---|
| PLANT TYPE: Deciduous perennial | |
| SIZE: 8–14 inches x 10–14 inches | |
| LIGHT REQUIREMENTS: Shade to mostly shade | |
| WATER REQUIREMENTS: Medium | |
| HARDINESS ZONES: 5a to 9b | |

A delightful little woodland perennial with hairy, prominently veined green leaves divided into 3 leaflets. Sprays of delicate, tiny white to pale-pink flowers bloom for a very long period on leafy stems. Grow this charming plant en masse throughout a woodland garden, along shaded steps and pathways, or near ponds or streams.

**How big:** 8–14 inches tall × 10–14 inches wide; spreads very slowly by rhizomes.

**Bloom traits:** Panicles of white to very pale pink flowers bloom from late spring through late summer. Fruit is a capsule containing several seeds.

**Sun and soil:** Full shade to mostly shade. Moist, well-draining soil high in organic matter. Can handle drought only in cool areas.

**Where it grows:** Moist coniferous forests and along shaded streams, at low to middle elevations.

**How to space it:** 1 foot apart.

**Help it thrive:** Does best with some summer water, especially in hot areas.

**Associates:** Douglas-fir, western hemlock, western redcedar, Sitka spruce, Pacific silver fir, vine maple, red elderberry, oceanspray, Pacific rhododendron, baldhip rose, sword fern, Cascade Oregon grape, salal, beargrass, and others.

**Benefits to wildlife:** Flowers provide nectar and pollen for bees and other insects. Seeds are eaten by birds. Plants provide shelter for insects and other small creatures.

**Substitute for:** Yellow archangel (*Lamiastrum galeobdolon*).

**How to propagate:** From seed collected in summer or fall when ripe and planted in fall or early spring, or by division of rhizomes in fall or spring.

**Related species:** Cutleaf foamflower (*Tiarella trifoliata* var. *laciniata*) has finely divided leaves and a smaller natural range. **One-leaf foamflower** (*Tiarella t.* var. *unifoliata*) has undivided palmate leaves and is native to middle to high elevations. Both species' ranges overlap somewhat with that of *Tiarella t.* var. *trifoliata*.

*Tolmiea menziesii*
## Piggyback plant

| | |
|---|---|
| PLANT TYPE: Semi-evergreen perennial | |
| SIZE: 1 foot x 1 foot | |
| LIGHT REQUIREMENTS: Partial shade to shade | |
| WATER REQUIREMENTS: Medium | |
| HARDINESS ZONES: 5b to 9b | |

This attractive, semi-evergreen woodland plant has fuzzy, scalloped leaves. Flowering stems with intriguing, graceful little flowers rise above the whorl of basal leaves and bloom throughout summer. Little plantlets may form on top of older leaves near their base; hence the common name. As falling autumn leaves and gravity press them to the soil, they take root. Grow it in a woodland setting for a wonderful ground cover, or tuck it into mostly shaded rock gardens or rock walls. May be grown in pots or even as houseplants.

**How big:** 1 foot tall × 1 feet wide; spreads very slowly by rhizomes.

**Bloom traits:** Flower stalks produce burgundy-chocolate colored blossoms from late spring into summer. Fruit is a capsule containing spiny seeds.

**Sun and soil:** Full to partial shade. Moist, well-drained soil rich in organic matter.

**Where it grows:** Moist forests, cliffs, and near streams, at low to middle elevations.

**How to space it:** 1–2 feet apart.

**Help it thrive:** Does best with some summer water, especially in hot areas.

**Associates:** Douglas-fir, western hemlock, western redcedar, bigleaf and vine maple, red alder, salal, thimbleberry, trillium, false solomon's seal, lady fern, maidenhair fern, oxalis, and others.

**Benefits to wildlife:** Flowers provide pollen and nectar for bees and other insects. Plants provide shelter for insects and other small creatures.

**Substitute for:** Periwinkle (*Vinca minor* or *V. major*), lesser celandine (*Ranunculus ficaria*).

**How to propagate:** From seed collected in autumn and planted outdoors, or perhaps more enjoyably by leaf propagules: detach a mature leaf with a little plantlet growing on top and press it into moist soil. Rhizomes may also be divided in spring.

**Related species:** This plant has no close relatives.

*Trillium ovatum*

## Western trillium or wake robin

| | |
|---|---|
| PLANT TYPE: Perennial bulb | |
| SIZE: 1–2 feet x 1–2 feet | |
| LIGHT REQUIREMENTS: Shade to mostly shade | |
| WATER REQUIREMENTS: Medium | |
| HARDINESS ZONES: 4a to 9b | |

Nothing says spring quite like trillium, and of the 5 species that grow in the region, this one is the most widespread and unmistakeable. Large white flowers—which should not be picked—bloom throughout spring above a whorl of 3 broad green leaves. Dormancy begins as summer approaches. Grow this lovely perennial in a shady or woodland setting, where it hopefully will self-sow to create a drift of indescribable elegance.

**How big:** 1–2 feet tall × 1–2 feet wide.

**Bloom traits:** Large white flowers bloom on short stems (called peduncles) from early to late spring, depending on elevation. Petals age to pink or burgundy. Fruit is a fleshy yellow capsule.

**Sun and soil:** Full shade to mostly shade. Moist, well-drained soil rich in organic matter, slightly acidic (pH 5–6.5).

**Where it grows:** In cool, moist forests and near shaded streams, at low to middle elevations.

**How to space it:** 1–2 feet apart.

**Help it thrive:** Can withstand minor droughts during summer dormancy but occasional supplemental summer water will sustain it. Don't transplant mature trilliums unless the need is dire.

**Associates:** Grand fir, Sitka spruce, Douglas-fir, western redcedar, western hemlock, coast redwood, bigleaf maple, red alder, Pacific rhododendron, sword fern, salal, vanilla leaf, oxalis, and more.

**Benefits to wildlife:** Seeds are dispersed by ants. Birds and mammals eat the fruit.

**Substitute for:** Lesser celandine (*Ranunculus ficaria*).

**How to propagate:** From seed collected when capsules begin to open in summer and sown in deep containers that are kept moist and left outdoors.

**Related species:** Giant white trillium (*Trillium albidum*) has fragrant flowers and often has mottled leaves. The delicate **brook trillium** (*T. rivale*) has white petals spotted with purple and occurs only in southwestern Oregon and northwestern California, along with the uncommon **giant purple trillium** (*T. kurabayashii*), an exciting and colorful addition. **Small-flowered trillium** (*T. parviflorum*), native in southwestern Washington and northwestern Oregon, isn't quite as showy but is unusual and fragrant.

RIGHT Related species *Trillium kurabyashii*

*Vaccinium parviflorum*
# Red huckleberry

PLANT TYPE: Deciduous shrub

SIZE: 5–10 feet x 5–10 feet

LIGHT REQUIREMENTS: Partial shade to shade

WATER REQUIREMENTS: Medium

HARDINESS ZONES: 4a to 9b

An open, upright, deciduous shrub with oval, light-green leaves growing on angular, twiggy stems. Spring-blooming greenish-pink flowers are followed by brilliant red berries in mid- to late summer. Grow this lovely, graceful shrub in a woodland garden, preferably in close contact with decaying logs or stumps, which is how it is nearly always found in nature.

**How big:** 5–10 feet tall × 5–10 feet wide.

**Bloom traits:** Single, small, inconspicuous greenish-pink flowers bloom from midspring to early summer. Late-summer-ripening berries are bright red and delicious when fully ripe.

**Sun and soil:** Partial shade to full shade. Moist, acidic soil rich in organic matter and decaying wood.

**Where it grows:** Moist, coniferous coastal forests and mixed evergreen forests, at low to middle elevations.

**How to space it:** 5–10 feet apart.

**Help it thrive:** Moderate summer water, especially during hot periods. Established plants do not respond well to transplantation.

**Associates:** Incense cedar, Pacific madrone, Douglas-fir, western redcedar, western hemlock, red alder, salal, thimbleberry, bunchberry, oak fern, wild ginger, and others.

**Benefits to wildlife:** Flowers provide nectar for hummingbirds, bees, and other insects. Berries are consumed by many birds, including flickers, jays, thrushes, chickadees, towhees, and bluebirds. Many mammals, including deer mice, white-footed mice, raccoons, pikas, ground squirrels, chipmunks, foxes, and squirrels, also eat the berries. Important browse species for mountain beavers, deer, and elk. May form dense thickets that provide shelter or nesting sites for many small birds and mammals.

**Substitute for:** Himalayan blackberry (*Rubus discolor*).

**How to propagate:** From seed removed from berries in late summer or fall and sown outdoors, ground layering in spring, or by stem cuttings in spring; may self-sow.

**Related species:** Black huckleberry (*Vaccinium membranaceum*) has berries with spectacular taste, needs the same conditions, and typically grows to 6 feet tall and wide at higher elevations.

*Vancouveria hexandra*
## Inside-out flower

PLANT TYPE: Deciduous perennial

SIZE: 12–16 inches

LIGHT REQUIREMENTS: Shade to partial shade

WATER REQUIREMENTS: Low to medium

HARDINESS ZONES: 7a to 9b

This deciduous perennial has airy leaflets, shaped like a duck's footprint, that are a refreshing bright green in springtime. Nodding, delicate white flowers that appear to be turned inside-out arise from leafless stems and bloom for several months. Makes a lovely ground cover beneath tall trees or shrubs or other shaded areas.

**How big:** 12–16 inches tall; spreads slowly by rhizomes.

**Bloom traits:** White blossoms that resemble shooting stars grow on smooth stalks from leafless stems in late spring to early summer. Fruit is a follicle containing small black seeds.

**Sun and soil:** Full shade to partial shade. Moist to occasionally dry soil, rich in organic matter.

**Where it grows:** Moist, shady wooded sites and forest edges, at low to middle elevations.

**How to space it:** 2–3 feet apart.

**Help it thrive:** Drought tolerant once established, but does best with some summer water, especially in hot areas.

**Associates:** Douglas-fir, red elderberry, vine maple, evergreen huckleberry, red huckleberry, tall bugbane, goatsbeard, ferns, trillium, and others.

**Benefits to wildlife:** Provides cover and seeds for birds and other small animals. May be pollinated by bees, ants, or wasps.

**Substitute for:** English ivy (*Hedera helix*).

**How to propagate:** From seed collected in summer and kept warm and dry until fall, when they are planted outdoors, or by division of rhizomes in early spring.

**Related species:** Two other species occur naturally in southwestern Oregon but may be difficult to find and grow: **Redwood inside-out flower** (*Vancouveria planipetala*), is shorter; **yellow inside-out flower** (*V. chrysantha*), a species of concern in Josephine and Curry Counties in Oregon, has yellow flowers.

*Woodwardia fimbriata*
## Giant chain fern

| | |
|---|---|
| PLANT TYPE: Evergreen fern | |
| SIZE: 4–6 feet x 6–8 feet | |
| LIGHT REQUIREMENTS: Shade to mostly shade | |
| WATER REQUIREMENTS: Medium | |
| HARDINESS ZONES: 6a to 9b | |

The North American version of a tree fern, this exquisitely textured, very large fern usually stays evergreen. Growing up to 10 feet tall in the wild, it typically grows to about half that in garden settings. Under favorable conditions it forms large clumps that make a stunning and vividly green addition to moist, mostly shady places. Tolerates salt spray. Classified as a species of concern in British Columbia and a sensitive species in Washington, it is threatened by invasive species, logging, and wild collection.

**How big:** 4–6 feet tall x 6–8 feet wide.
**Bloom traits:** Spore-bearing sori are oval and located end to end, parallel to the underside of the midrib of the leaflets, resembling a chain.

**Sun and soil:** Full shade to mostly shade. Moist soil rich in organic matter. Can handle some sun with adequate moisture.
**Where it grows:** In moist forests, shaded coastal bluffs, and along streams and springs, at low to middle elevations.
**How to space it:** 4–6 feet apart.
**Help it thrive:** Moderate summer water. Easily overcome by invasive species and even some native species such as western sword ferns, so provide some protection.
**Associates:** Redwood, vine maple, huckleberries, baneberry, oak fern, wild ginger, trillium, oxalis, and others.
**Benefits to wildlife:** Provides year-round cover, food, and nesting material to birds and other animals.
**Substitute for:** Japanese aralia (*Fatsia japonica*).
**How to propagate:** Spores, or *very careful* clump division of cultivated plants in early spring. May self-sow under optimal conditions.
**Related species:** Two other *Woodwardia* species occur in North America, but neither is found in the Pacific Northwest.

# APPENDIX A: *quick plant guide for specific situations*

## Plants for acidic soil

*Arbutus menziesii*, 170–71
*Arctostaphylos columbiana*, 172
*Arctostaphylos uva-ursi*, 173
*Asarum caudatum*, 274
*Calocedrus decurrens*, 177
*Cimicifuga elata*, 276
*Cornus unalaschkensis*, 277
*Erythronium* spp., 228
*Gaultheria shallon*, 232–33
*Lewisia* spp., 190
*Mahonia* spp., 238, 282–83
*Oxalis* spp., 284–85
*Pinus contorta*, 196–97
*Polystichum* spp., 243
*Rhododendron* spp., 288
*Smilacina* spp., 290–91
*Thuja plicata*, 259
*Trillium* spp., 294–95
*Vaccinium* spp., 262–63, 296

## Plants for erosion control

*Acer circinatum*, 214
*Arbutus menziesii*, 170–71
*Arctostaphylos columbiana*, 172
*Arctostaphylos uva-ursi*, 173
*Ceanothus prostrates*, 180

LEFT Male catkins of coast silk tassel bush (*Garrya elliptica*) in winter. *G. elliptica*—and *G. fremontii*, which occurs over a wider range—can be used in large hedgerows.

*Cornus sericea*, 222
*Festuca idahoensis*, 185
*Holodiscus discolor*, 188
*Lupinus polyphyllus*, 192
*Polystichum munitum*, 243
*Ribes aureum*, 204–05
*Symphoricarpos* spp., 258

## Plants for heavy soil

*Arctostaphylos uva-ursi*, 173
*Camassia* spp., 178
*Cornus sericea*, 222
*Corylus cornuta* var. *californica*, 223
*Delphinium nudicaule*, 224
*Holodiscus discolor*, 188
*Oemleria cerasiformis*, 239
*Pseudotsuga menziesii*, 201
*Symphoricarpos* spp., 258

## Plants for hedgerows

*Acer circinatum*, 214
*Amelanchier alnifolia*, 215
*Ceanothus* spp., 180
*Clematis ligusticifolia*, 219
*Cornus sericea*, 222
*Corylus cornuta* var. *californica*, 223
*Crataegus douglasii*, 183
*Garrya* spp., 231
*Holodiscus discolor*, 188
*Lonicera ciliosa*, 236
*Lonicera involucrata*, 237
*Mahonia aquifolium*, 238
*Oemleria cerasiformis*, 239

*Paxistima myrsinites*, 240
*Philadelphus lewisi*, 241
*Rhamnus purshiana*, 245
*Rhododendron* spp., 288
*Ribes* spp., 204, 246–47
*Rosa* spp., 248–49
*Salix* spp., 206–07
*Sambucus* spp., 252–53
*Spiraea douglasii*, 257
*Symphoricarpos albus*, 258
*Vaccinium ovatum*, 262–63
*Viburnum* spp., 264

## Plants with high drought tolerance

*Achillea millefolium* var. *occidentalis*, 168
*Allium* spp., 169
*Amelanchier alnifolia*, 215
*Arbutus menziesii*, 170–71
*Arctostaphylos* spp., 172–73
*Calocedrus decurrens*, 177
*Camassia* spp., 178
*Ceanothus* spp., 180
*Crataegus douglasii*, 183
*Dodecatheon hendersonii*, 225
*Festuca idahoensis*, 185
*Garrya fremontii*, 231
*Gaultheria shallon*, 232–33
*Holodiscus discolor*, 188
*Lewisia* spp., 190
*Lilium washingtonianum*, 235
*Lonicera ciliosa*, 236
*Mahonia aquifolium*, 238
*Paxistima myrsinites*, 240

Nodding onion (*Allium cernuum*) is drought tolerant, unattractive to deer, and thrives in rock gardens.

# APPENDIX B: *references*

Art, Henry Warren. *The Wildflower Gardener's Guide: Pacific Northwest, Rocky Mountain, and Western Canada Edition.* Pownal, VT: Storey Communications, 1990.

Benachour, Nora and Gilles-Eric Séralini. "Glyphosate Formulations Induce Apoptosis and Necrosis in Human Umbilical, Embryonic, and Placental Cells." December, 2008. http://pubs.acs.org/doi/abs/10.1021/tx800218n.

Boersma, P. Dee, S. H. Reichard, and A. N. Van Buren, eds. *Invasive Species in the Pacific Northwest.* Seattle, WA: University of Washington Press, 2006.

Brosi, Berry J., and Heather M. Biggs. "Single Pollinator Species Losses Reduce Floral Fidelity and Plant Reproductive Function." *Proceedings of the National Academy of Sciences,* no. 32 (2013): 13044-13048.

Brown, E. R., tech. ed. *Management of Wildlife and Fish Habitats in Forests of Western Washington and Oregon.* Publication No. R-6-F&WL-192-1985. Portland, OR: USDA Forest Service, Pacific Northwest Region, 1985.

California Environmental Protection Agency Air Resources Board, "A Report to the California Legislature on the Potential Health and Environmental Impacts of Leaf Blowers." 2000. www.nonoise.org/resource/leafblowers/carbleafblower2000.pdf

Callaway, R. M., D. Cipollini, and K. Barto. "Novel weapons: Invasive plant suppresses fungal mutualists in America but not in its native Europe." *Ecology,* no. 4 (2008): 1043-1055.

Carris, L. M., C. R. Little, and C. M. Stiles. APSnet, "Introduction to Fungi." 2012. http://www.apsnet.org/edcenter/intropp/PathogenGroups/Pages/IntroFungi.aspx.

Carson, Rachel. *Silent Spring.* New York: Houghton Mifflin, 2002.

Charnley, Susan, and Susan Hummel. USDA Forest Service, PNW Research Station, "People, Plants, and Pollinators: The Conservation of Beargrass Ecosystem Diversity in the Western United States." 2011. http://cdn.intechopen.com/pdfs/20141/InTech-People_plants_and_pollinators_the_conservation_of_beargrass_ecosystem_diversity_in_the_western_united_states.pdf.

Chivian, Eric, and Aaron Bernstein. "How Our Health Depends on Biodiversity." 2010. http://chge.med.harvard.edu/sites/default/files/resources/182945%20HMS%20Biodiversity%20booklet.pdf

Commoner, Barry. *The Closing Circle: Nature, Man, and Technology.* New York: Alfred A. Knopf, 1971.

Conard, Susan G., Annabelle E. Jaramillo, et al. USDA Forest Service, "The Role of the Genus Ceanothus in Western Forest Ecosystems." USDA Forest Service General Technical Report, PNW-182. 1995. www.californiachaparral.com/images/Cenanothus_nitrogen_pnw_gtr182.pdf.

Edge, W. D. "Wildlife of Agriculture, Pastures, and Mixed Environs." In D. H. Johnson and T. A. O'Neill (eds.), *Wildlife-Habitat Relationships in Oregon and Washington.* Corvallis, OR: Oregon State University Press, 2001. 342–360.

Ferguson, Howard L, Kevin Robinette, and Kate Stenberg. "Wildlife of Urban Habitats." In D. H. Johnson and T. A. O'Neill (eds.), *Wildlife-Habitat Relationships in Oregon and Washington.* Corvallis, OR: Oregon State University Press, 2001. 342–360.

Flora of North America Editorial Committee, eds. *Flora of North America North of Mexico.* 16+ vols. New York and Oxford: Flora of North America Association, 1993.

Forestpathology.org, "White Pine Blister Rust." USDA Natural Resources Conservation Service. Last modified December 13, 2009. www.forestpathology.org/dis_wpbr.html.

Franklin, Jerry F., and C. T. Dyrness. *Natural Vegetation of Oregon and Washington.* Corvallis, OR: Oregon State University Press, 1988.

Fremstad, Eli. NOBANIS, "Invasive Alien Species Fact Sheet—*Lupinus polyphyllus.*" 2010. www.nobanis.org/files/factsheets/Lupinus polyphyllus.pdf.

Gisler, Steven D. US Fish and Wildlife Service, "Developing biogeographically based population introduction protocols for at-risk Willamette Valley plant species." 2004. www.fws.gov/oregonfwo/species/data/KincaidsLupine/Documents/ODA2004ReportLupinusSulphureus.pdf.

Goulson, Dave. "An overview of the environmental risks posed by neonicotinoid insecticides." *Journal of Applied Ecology*, no. 4 (2013): 977–987.

———. *Bumblebees: Behaviour, Ecology, and Conservation.* New York: Oxford University Press. 2010.

Gray, Andrew. "Distribution and Abundance of Invasive Plants in Pacific Northwest Forests." In Timothy B. Harrington and Sarah H. Reichard (eds.), United States Department of Agriculture, "Meeting the Challenge: Invasive Plants in Pacific Northwest Ecosystems." 2007. www.fs.fed.us/pnw/pubs/pnw _gtr694.pdf.

Harder, L. D., and R. M. R. Barclay. "The functional significance of poricidal anthers and buzz pollination: Controlled pollen removal from Dodecatheon." *Functional Ecology*, no. 4 (1994): 509–517.

Herring, Peg. Oregon State University Extension Service, "English ivy listed as a noxious weed." 2003. http://extension.oregonstate.edu/gardening/english -ivy-listed-noxious-weed.

Hippocrates. The Internet Classics Archive, "On Airs, Waters, and Places." http://classics.mit.edu /Hippocrates/airwatpl.html.

Hitchcock, Leo H., and Arthur Cronquist. *Flora of the Pacific Northwest: An Illustrated Manual.* Seattle, WA: University of Washington Press, 1973.

Hopwood, Jennifer, Mace Vaughan, et al. The Xerces Society, "Are Neonicotinoids Killing Bees? A Review of Research into the Effects of Neonicotinoid Insecticides on Bees, with Recommendations for Action." www.xerces.org/wp-content /uploads/2012/03/Are-Neonicotinoids-Killing-Bees _Xerces-Society1.pdf.

Jackson, Philip L., and A. Jon Kimerling, eds. *Atlas of the Pacific Northwest.* Corvallis, OR: Oregon State University Press, 2003.

James, David G., and David Nunnallee. *Life Histories of Cascadia Butterflies.* Corvallis, OR: Oregon State University Press, 2011.

Jarvis, Robert L., and Michael F. Passmore. US Fish and Wildlife Service, "Ecology of band-tailed pigeons in Oregon. Biological Report 6." 1992. www.dtic.mil/cgi-bin/GetTRDoc?AD=ADA323047.

Johnson, David H., and T. A. O'Neil, eds. *Wildlife-Habitat Relationships in Oregon and Washington.* Corvallis, OR: Oregon State University, 2001.

Kaye, Thomas N., and Beth Lawrence. "Fitness effects of inbreeding and outbreeding on golden paintbrush (*Castilleja levisecta*): Implications for recovery and reintroduction." 2003. http://appliedeco.org/reports /Castilleja%20levisecta%20breeding%20system.pdf.

Kolbert, Elizabeth. "Turf War." *The New Yorker*, July 21, 2008.

Kruckeberg, Arthur R. *Gardening with Native Plants of the Pacific Northwest.* Seattle, WA: University of Washington Press, 1996.

Link, Russell. *Landscaping for Wildlife in the Pacific Northwest.* Seattle, WA: University of Washington Press, 1999.

Lunau, Klaus, and Sarah H. Papiorek, et al. "Avoidance of achromatic colours by bees provides a private niche for hummingbirds." *The Journal of Experimental Biology,* no. 214 (2011): 1607-1612. http://jeb.biologists.org/content/214/9/1607.full.pdf html.

Mäntylä, Elina, Tero Klemola, et al. "Low light reflectance may explain the attraction of birds to defoliated trees." *Behavioral Ecology*, no. 2 (2008): 325–330.

Martin, Justin. *Genius of Place: The Life of Frederick Law Olmsted.* Cambridge, MA: Da Capo Press, 2012.

Mineau, Pierre, and Mélanie Whiteside. "Pesticide Acute Toxicity Is a Better Correlate of US Grassland Bird Declines than Agricultural Intensification." *PLOS One*, February 20, 2013. www.plosone.org/article /info:doi/10.1371/journal.pone.0057457.

Morlan, J. C., E. F. Blok, et al. *Wetland and Land Use Change in the Willamette Valley, Oregon: 1994 to 2005.* Portland, OR: US Fish and Wildlife Service, and Salem, OR: Oregon Department of State Lands, 2010.

Neill, William. *Butterflies of the Pacific Northwest.* Missoula, MT: Mountain Press Publishing Company, 2007.

Olson, Deanna H., Joan C. Hagar, Andrew B. Carey, John H. Cissel, and Frederick J. Swanson. "Wildlife of Westside and High Montane Forests." In D. H. Johnson and T. A. O'Neill (eds.), *Wildlife-Habitat Relationships in Oregon and Washington.* Corvallis, OR: Oregon State University Press, 2001. 187–212.

Opler, Paul, Michael Clady, Catherine Macdonald, Paul Hammond, and Dennis Murphy. US Fish and Wildlife Service, "Revised Recovery Plan for the Oregon Silverspot Butterfly (*Speyeria zerene hyppolyta*)." www.fws.gov/arcata/es/inverts/orss /documents/2001 Revised Recovery Plan for the Oregon Silverspot Butterfly-optimized.pdf.

Pojar, Jim, and Andy MacKinnon. *Plants of the Pacific Northwest Coast: Washington, Oregon, British Columbia & Alaska.* Vancouver, BC: Lone Pine Publishing, 2004.

Pollan, Michael. "Why Mow? The Case Against Lawns." *The New York Times Magazine.* May 28, 1989. http://michaelpollan.com/articles-archive /why-mow-the-case-against-lawns/.

Primack, Richard B. *Essentials of Conservation Biology.* 5th ed. Sunderland, MA: Sinauer Associates, 2010.

Randall, John M. "Weed control for the preservation of biological diversity." *Weed Technology*, no. 2 (1996): 370–383.

Robson, Kathleen, and Alice Richter. *Encyclopedia of Northwest Native Plants for Gardens and Landscapes.* Portland, OR: Timber Press, 2008.

Rose, Robin, Caryn E. C. Chachulski, and Diane L. Haase. *Propagation of Pacific Northwest Native Plants*. Corvallis, OR: Oregon State University Press, 1998.

Rypstra, Ann L., and Christopher M. Buddle. "Spider silk reduces insect herbivory." *Biology Letters*. no. 1 (2013). http://rsbl.royalsocietypublishing.org /content/9/1/20120948.full.

Science Daily, "Researchers Discover Birds Protect Trees In Neotropics By Eating Insects." June 24, 2003. www.sciencedaily.com/releases/2003 /06/030624090714.htm.

Schultz, Jan. USDA Forest Service, Eastern Region, "Conservation Assessment for Douglas Hawthorn (*Crataegus douglasii*) Lindley." 2003. www.fs.usda .gov/Internet/FSE_DOCUMENTS/fsm91_054142.pdf.

Smithsonian Tropical Research Institute, "The allometry of CNS size and consequences of miniaturization in orb-weaving and cleptoparasitic spiders." November, 2011. www.sciencedirect.com /science/article/pii/S1467803911000727

Spivak, Marla, Eric Mader, Mace Vaughan, and Ned H. Euliss Jr. "The Plight of the Bees." *Environmental Science and Technology,* no. 45 (2011): 34–38.

The State of the Birds 2013: Report on Private Lands. www.stateofthebirds.org.

Stinson, Kristina A., Stuart A. Campbell, Jeff R. Powell, Benjamin E. Wolfe, et al. PLOS Biology, "Invasive Plant Suppresses the Growth of Native Tree Seedlings by Disrupting Belowground Mutualisms." April, 2006. www.plosbiology.org/article /info:doi/10.1371/journal.pbio.0040140.

Tallamy, Douglas W. *Bringing Nature Home: How You Can Sustain Wildlife with Native Plants.* Portland, OR: Timber Press, 2009.

US Fish and Wildlife Service. *Oregon silverspot butterfly (Speyeria zerene hippolyta) revised recovery plan.* Portland, OR: 2001.

——."Pesticides and Wildlife." Last modified February 13, 2013. www.fws.gov/contaminants/Issues /Pesticides.cfm.

US Geological Survey, National Wildlife Health Center. "Salmonellosis." Last modified May 21, 2013. http ://www.nwhc.usgs.gov/disease_information/other _diseases/salmonellosis.jsp.

University of Oxford, "Plants Use Latex to Harm and Heal." www.ox.ac.uk/media/news_stories /2013/131030.html.

Veseley, David G., and Daniel K. Rosenberg. Oregon Wildlife Institute, "Wildlife Conservation in the Willamette Valley's Remnant Prairie and Oak Habitats: A Research Synthesis." 2010. www .oregonwildlife.org/publication/view/wildlife -conservation-in-the-willamette-valleys-remnant -prairies-and-oak-habitats-a-research-synthesis.

Washington Department of Fish and Wildlife, "Status of the Oregon Silverspot Butterfly (*Speyeria zerene hippolyta*) in Washington." July, 1993. http://wdfw .wa.gov/publications/01522/.

Weisman, Alan. *The World Without Us.* New York: St. Martin's, 2007.

Wilson, E. O. *Letters to a Young Scientist.* New York: W. W. Norton, 2013.

The Xerces Society. *Attracting Native Pollinators.* North Adams, MA: Storey Publishing, 2011.

# APPENDIX C: *resources*

## Books

Evans, Elaine, Ian Burns, and Maria Spivak. *Befriending Bumble Bees: A Practical Guide to Raising Local Bumble Bees.* University of Minnesota Extension Service Publication P-8484. St. Paul, MN: University of Minnesota Extension Service, 2007.

Haggard, Peter, and Judy Haggard. *Insects of the Pacific Northwest.* Portland, OR: Timber Press, 2006.

Kimmerer, Robin Wall. *Gathering Moss: A Natural and Cultural History of Mosses.* Corvalis, OR: Oregon State University Press, 2003.

Kruckeberg, Arthur. *Gardening with Native Plants of the Pacific Northwest.* 2nd ed. Seattle, WA: University of Washington Press, 1996.

Link, Russell. *Landscaping for Wildlife in the Pacific Northwest.* Seattle, WA: University of Washington Press, 2002.

———. *Living with Wildlife in the Pacific Northwest.* Seattle, WA: University of Washington Press, 2004.

Moskowitz, David. *Wildlife of the Pacific Northwest: Tracking and Identifying Mammals, Birds, Reptiles, Amphibians, and Invertebrates.* Portland, OR: Timber Press, 2010.

Neill, William. *Butterflies of the Pacific Northwest.* Missoula, MT: Mountain Press Publishing Co., 2007.

Pojar, Jim, and Andy MacKinnon. *Plants of the Pacific Northwest.* Vancouver, BC: Lone Pine, 2004.

Robson, Kathleen, and Alice Richter. *Encyclopedia of Northwest Native Plants for Gardens and Landscapes.* Portland, OR: Timber Press, 2008.

Rose, Robin, Caryn E. C. Chachulski, and Diane L. Haase. *Propagation of Pacific Northwest Native Plants.* Corvallis, OR: Oregon State University Press, 1998.

Stein, Sara. *Noah's Garden: Restoring the Ecology of Our Own Back Yards.* New York: Houghton Mifflin Co., 1993.

Tallamy, Douglas W. *Bringing Nature Home: How You Can Sustain Wildlife with Native Plants.* Portland, OR: Timber Press, 2009.

Turner, Mark, and Phyllis Gustafson. *Wildflowers of the Pacific Northwest.* Portland, OR: Timber Press, 2006.

The Xerces Society. *Attracting Native Pollinators.* North Adams, MA: Storey Publishing, 2011.

## Websites

A & L Western Laboratories, Inc. (soil analysis). www.al-labs-west.com.

British Columbia Ministry of Environment, *Ecoregions of British Columbia.* www.env.gov.bc.ca/ecology /ecoregions/.

BugGuide (Identification, images, and information). www.bugguide.net.

The Cornell Lab of Ornithology, *All About Birds.* www.allaboutbirds.org/guide/search.

*Dictionary of Botanical Epithets* www.winternet.com/~chuckg /dictionary.html.

E-Flora BC. *Electronic Atlas of the Flora of British Columbia.* www.geog.ubc.ca/biodiversity /eflora/.

Garry Oak Ecosystems Recovery Team, *Ethical Guidelines for the Collection and Use of Native Plants* www.goert.ca/gardeners_restoration /guidelines_native.php.

Garry Oak Meadow Preservation Society, *Garry Oak Ecosystems: What are they? Why are they important?* www.garryoak.info/page0/page0 .html.

King County, WA, *2013 King County Noxious Weed List.* www.kingcounty.gov/environment /animalsAndPlants/noxious-weeds /laws/list.aspx.

Native Plant Society of British Columbia, *Salvaging Native Plants.* www.npsbc.ca/pdf/NPSBC_Native _Plant_Salvaging.pdf.

Oregon Department of Agriculture, *ODA Plant Programs, Noxious Weed Control.* www.oregon.gov/ODA/PLANT /WEEDS/Pages/index.aspx.

The Oregon Rain Garden Guide: A Step-by-Step Guide to Landscaping for Clean Water and Healthy Streams. http://seagrant.oregonstate.edu /sgpubs/onlinepubs/h10001.pdf.

Oregon State University Dept. of Botany & Plant Pathology, *Oregon Flora Project.* www.oregonflora.org.

Oregon State University Extension Service, *Attract Reptiles and Amphibians to Your Yard.* http://ir.library.oregonstate.edu/xmlui /bitstream/handle/1957/19615 /ec1542.pdf.

Portland (OR) Department of Planning and Sustainability, *Portland Plant List.* www.portlandoregon.gov /auditor/34460?a=322280.

Portland State University, *Oregon Biodiversity Information Center.* www.orbic.pdx.edu/index.html.

Rain Garden Handbook for Western Washington. https://fortress.wa.gov/ecy /publications/publications/1310027.pdf.

USDA Natural Resources Conservation Service, *Plants Database.* www.plants.usda.gov/java/.

Washington Department of Fish and Wildlife, *Butterflies and How to Attract Them.* http://www.wdfw.wa.gov/living /butterflies/.

Washington Department of
Natural Resources, *Field Guide to
Washington's Ecological Systems.*
www1.dnr.wa.gov/nhp/refdesk/pubs
/wa_ecological_systems.pdf.

Washington State Noxious Weed
Control Board.
www.nwcb.wa.gov.

## Nonprofit Organizations

Depave
P.O. Box 12503
Portland, OR 97212
www.depave.org

Garry Oak Ecosystems Recovery Team
841 Ralph Street
Victoria, BC V8X 3E1
Canada
T: 250-383-3427
www.goert.ca/index.php

Institute for Applied Ecology
and Native Seed Network
P.O. Box 2855
Corvallis, OR 97333
T: 541-753-3099
www.appliedeco.org
www.nativeseednetwork.org

National Audubon Society
www.audubon.org

Native Plant Society
of British Columbia
1917 West 4th Avenue, Suite 195
Vancouver, BC V6J 1M7
Canada
T: 604-255-5719
www.npsbc.ca

Native Plant Society of Oregon
P.O. Box 902
Eugene, OR 97440
www.npsoregon.org

Northwest Coalition for
Alternatives to Pesticides
P.O. Box 1393
Eugene, OR 97440
T: 541-344-5044

Plant Amnesty
P.O. Box 15377
Seattle, WA 98115
T: 206-783-9813
www.plantamnesty.org

South Sound Prairie Landscape
Working Group
www.southsoundprairies.org

Stewardship Partners
1411 4th Avenue, Suite 1425
Seattle, WA 98101
T: 206-292-9875
www.stewardshippartners.org

Washington Native Plant Society
6310 Northeast 74th Street, Suite 215E
Seattle, WA 98115
T: 206-527-3210
www.wnps.org

The Xerces Society
628 Northeast Broadway, Suite 200
Portland, OR 97232
T: 503-232-6639
F: 503-233-6794
www.xerces.org

## Retail Sources for Plant Material

Many nurseries have limited hours
or are open only by appointment,
so check websites or call for
hours and events. This list is not
exhaustive and not an endorse-
ment of any business.

### OREGON

Birds & Bees Nursery
3709 Southeast Gladstone Street
Portland, OR 97202
T: 503-788-6088
www.birdsandbeespdx.com

Bosky Dell Natives
23311 Southwest Bosky Dell Lane
West Linn, OR 97068
T: 503-638-5945
www.boskydellnatives.com

Champoeg Nursery Inc.
9661 Yergen Road Northeast
Aurora, OR 97002
T: 503-678-6348
www.champoegnursery.com

Doak Creek Native Plant Nursery
83331 Jackson Marlow Road
Eugene, OR 97405
T: 541-484-9206
www.doakcreeknursery.com

Echo Valley Natives
18883 South Ferguson Road
Oregon City, OR 97045
T: 503-631-2451
www.echovalleynatives.com

Forest Farm
14643 Watergap Road
Williams, OR 97554
T: 541-846-7269
www.forestfarm.com

Garden Fever
3433 Northeast 24th Avenue
Portland, OR 97212
T: 503-287-3200
www.gardenfever.com

Humble Roots Farm and Nursery LLC
Mosier, OR 97040
T: 503-449-3694
www.humblerootsnursery.com

Karma's Forest
Cheshire, OR
T: 541-998-2436
www.karmasforest.com

Livingscape Nursery
3926 North Vancouver Avenue
Portland, OR 97227
T: 503-248-0104
www.livingscape.com

Oregon Native Plant Nursery
P.O. Box 886
Woodburn, OR 97071
T: 503-981-2353
www.wildflower.org/suppliers
/show.php?id=4522

Pacific Northwest Natives
1525 Laurel Heights Drive Northwest
Albany, OR 97321
T: 541-928-8239
www.pacificnwnatives.com

Plant Oregon
8677 Wagner Creek Road
Talent, OR 97540
T: 541-535-3531
www.plantoregon.com

Portland Nursery
5050 Southeast Stark Street
Portland, OR 97215
T: 503-231-5050
9000 Southeast Division Street
Portland, OR 97216
T: 503-788-9000
www.portlandnursery.com

Willamette Gardens
3290 Southwest Willamette Avenue
Corvallis, OR 97333
T: 541-990-0948
www.willamettegardens.com

## WASHINGTON

Aldrich Berry Farm & Nursery
190 Aldrich Road
Mossyrock, WA 98564
T: 360-983-3138

Burnt Ridge Nursery
432 Burnt Ridge Road
Onalaska, WA 98570
T: 360-985-2873
www.burntridgenursery.com

Clark's Native Trees and Shrubs
3130 State Route 530 Northeast
Arlington, WA 98223
T: 360-435-9473

Fancy Fronds
P.O. Box 1090
Gold Bar, WA 98251
T: 360-793-1472
www.fancyfrondsnursery.com

Friendly Natives Plants and Design
466 Piper Road
Quilcene, WA 98376
T: 206-387-5943
www.friendlynatives.net

Go Natives!
2112 Northwest 199th
Shoreline, WA 98177
T: 206-799-1749
www.gonativesnursery.com

Inside Passage Seeds
P.O. Box 639
Port Townsend, WA 98368
T: 800-361-9657
www.insidepassageseeds.com

Judd Creek Nursery
20929 111th Avenue Southwest
Vashon, WA 98070
T: 206-463-9641

Keeping It Green Nursery
19401 96th Avenue Northwest
Stanwood, WA 98292
T: 360-652-1779
www.keepingitgreennursery.com

Madronamai Northwest
  Native Garry Oaks
3923 Mount Baker Highway
Everson, WA 98247
T: 360-592-2200
www.madronamai.com

MsK Rare and Native Plant Nursery
  at the Kruckeberg Botanic Garden
20312 15th Avenue Northwest
Shoreline, WA 98177
T: 206-546-1281
www.kruckeberg.org/msk

Plantas Nativa LLC
210 East Laurel Street
Bellingham, WA 98225
T: 360-715-9655
www.plantasnativa.com

Sound Native Plants Inc.
P.O. Box 7505
Olympia, WA 98507
T: 360-352-4122
www.soundnativeplants.com

Tadpole Haven Native Plants
20322 197th Avenue Northeast
Woodinville, WA 98077
T: 425-788-6100
www.tadpolehaven.com

Watershed Garden Works
2039 44th Avenue
Longview, WA 98632
T: 360-423-6456
www.watershedgardenworks.com

Woodbrook Native Plant Nursery
5919 78th Avenue Northwest
Gig Harbor, WA 98335
T: 253-857-6808
www.woodbrooknativeplantnursery
  .com

## BRITISH COLUMBIA

BC's Wild Heritage Plants
47330 Extrom Road
Sardis, BC V2R 4V1
T: 604-858-5141
www.bcwildheritage.com

Fraser's Thimble Farms
175 Arbutus Road
Salt Spring Island, BC V8K 1A3
T: 250-537-5788
www.thimblefarms.com

Galiano Conservancy Native
  Plant Nursery
13680 Porlier Pass Road
Galiano Island, BC V0N 1P0
T: 250-539-2424
www.galianoconservancy.ca
  /native-plant-nursery

Natural Abundance
  Native Plant Nursery
3145 Frost Road
Nanaimo, BC V9R 5B1
T: 250-714-1990
www.nalt.bc.ca

The Natural Gardener
Garden Store Ltd.
4376 West 10th Avenue
Vancouver, BC V6R 2H7
T: 604-224-2207
www.thenatural-gardener.com

Nature's Garden Seed Co.
Duncan, BC
T: 250-715-0715; 1-877-302-7333
www.naturesgardenseed.com

Pacific Rim Native Plant Nursery
43359 Hillkeep Place
Chilliwack, BC V2R 4A4
T: 604-792-9279
www.hillkeep.ca

Saanich Native Plants
741 Haliburton Road
Saanich, BC V8Y 1H7
T: 778-679-3459
www.saanichnativeplants.com

Streamside Native Plants
7455 Island Highway West
Bowser, BC V0R 1G0
T: 250-757-9999
www.streamsidenativeplants.com

UBC Shop in the Garden
6804 Southwest Marine Drive
Vancouver, BC V6T 1Z4
T: 604-822-4529
www.botanicalgarden.ubc.ca/shop
  -in-the-garden

# Index

# Acknowledgments

I give heartfelt thanks to the people who helped make this book a reality. It's difficult to adequately thank my husband, Rick Weber, but I'll try. Besides acting as my technical advisor, equipping me with fantastic camera gear, and spending countless hours assisting me on photo shoots, he provided the love and encouragement that kept me sane and pressing forward. Rick also spent many weekends producing the maps in this book and is responsible for nearly all of the wonderful bird photographs.

My sisters, Barbara Stark and Carol Stark, gave helpful advice and long-distance support. Kate Rogers, Kirsten Colton, and others at Skipstone offered their expertise, enthusiasm, and patience when I needed it most. Members of Portland Hikers, the staff at East Multnomah Soil and Water Conservation District, members of the Native Plant Society of Oregon, and Andrew Merritt (Humble Roots) were helpful in locating some of the plants to photograph. Candace Fallon, Suzanne Granahan, Rich Hatfield, and Eric Mader, of the Xerces Society, assisted in pollinator identification. Terry Glase, Rosemary Taylor, and Paul Slichter graciously donated photographs. Lory Duralia (Bosky Dell Natives) welcomed a photo shoot of her ponds and antique architectural salvage creations. Audubon Society of Portland's Steve Engel shared avian knowledge, and Connie and Dennis Clemmens, Roberta Dyer, Lisa Graebner, Angela Gusa, Barbara Spears, Zue Stevenson, and Karen Summers shared their insightful opinions or ideas.

In writing the text I drew from a variety of published sources in addition to my own experience, so gratitude goes to all the ecologists, entomologists, botanists, naturalists, and other writers who smoothed the path before me. And special thanks go to all of the people who have been responsibly propagating native plants and educating others about them for many years.

## About the Xerces Society
## for Invertebrate Conservation

Named after the first butterfly known to become extinct, the Xerces Society is a nonprofit organization that protects wildlife through the conservation of invertebrates and their habitat. For over forty years, the society has been at the forefront of invertebrate protection worldwide, harnessing the knowledge of scientists and the enthusiasm of citizens to implement conservation programs. For information on their programs and work, visit www.xerces.org.

## About the Author

Eileen M. Stark is a landscape designer and consultant specializing in wildlife habitat gardens. An advocate for animals from an early age, she holds a bachelor's degree in biology and has a broad background in ecology and wildlife conservation. Her work and volunteer stints have revolved around animal protection, including political campaigns to protect wildlife, wildlife rehabilitation, and various research projects. Eileen completed Master Gardener training and has gardened in the Pacific Northwest since 1990. Her writing and photographs have appeared in regional and national publications.

She lives in Portland with her husband, Richard Weber (who contributed bird photographs to this book), and rescued cats. When not gardening, she hikes whenever she can, searching for the right light or polishing her naturalist skills.

Find her online at www.realgardensgrownatives.com.

## About Skipstone

Skipstone is an imprint of Seattle-based nonprofit publisher Mountaineers Books. It features thematically related titles that promote a deeper connection to our natural world through sustainable practice and backyard activism. Our readers live smart, play well, and typically engage with the community around them. Skipstone guides explore healthy lifestyles and how an outdoor life relates to the well-being of our planet, as well as of our own neighborhoods. Sustainable foods and gardens; healthful living; realistic and doable conservation at home; modern aspirations for community—Skipstone tries to address such topics in ways that emphasize active living, local and grassroots practices, and a small footprint.

Our hope is that Skipstone books will inspire you to effect change without losing your sense of humor, to celebrate the freedom and generosity of a life outdoors, and to move forward with gentle leaps or breathtaking bounds.

All of our publications, as part of our 501(c)(3) nonprofit program, are made possible through the generosity of donors and through sales of more than 600 titles on outdoor recreation, sustainable lifestyle, and conservation. To donate, purchase books, or learn more, visit us online:

SKIPSTONE

LIVE LIFE

MAKE RIPPLES

www.skipstonebooks.org
www.mountaineersbooks.org

 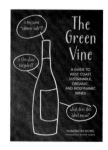 

Other Skipstone titles you might enjoy!